First edition: December 2019

Publishing by ASK Publishing Co., Ltd.
2-6, Shimomiyabi-cho, Shinjuku-ku, Tokyo 162-8558, Japan
Phone: 03-3267-6864
www.ask-books.com/

ISBN978-4-86639-322-3

Printed in Japan

つなぐ
にほんご

初級 Basic

文法解説書

Translation of Main Text and Grammar Notes

 Human

執筆 辻 和子 小座間 亜依

英語版 English Edition

ask PUBLISHING

はじめに

　この本は、『つなぐにほんご 初級1』『つなぐにほんご 初級2』で勉強している方々に、各課で扱われている文型の使い方を確認していただくために作りました。

　日常生活に必要なコミュニケーションができるようになるために、『つなぐにほんご』を使って、日常生活のいろいろな場面の話し方を練習します。始めに場面会話の練習をして、その場面の会話ができるようになったら、会話で使った文型を使う練習をします。まず場面会話で、イラストを見て言いたいことがわかった後でモデル会話を聞いて言ってみる、場面会話ができるようになったら、そこで使った文型の使い方を確認して応用練習をする、という流れです。もちろん文型を使う練習をする中で文型の使い方がわかりますが、本書を読んでいただければ、文型の使い方が明確に理解できて、確信をもって応用することができるでしょう。

　このように、練習をする中で「こういう使い方をするのか」と気づくことで学習が自分のものになり、解説を読んでさらに確信になると考えていることから、本書はパートの学習後に読んでいただきたいと考えています。もちろん、「文型の使い方がわかってから使う練習をしたい」という方は、パートの学習の前にこの本を読んでいただければ、文型の使い方を理解した上で、場面会話の練習、文型練習をすることもできます。

　また、本書は、学習したパートの文型の使い方を、確認し、理解するという目的から、そのパートで使われている文型の使い方に絞って解説をしています。ひとつの文型を取り上げて、そのさまざまな使い方を詳しく解説する「文法書」とは異なることをご承知くださいますよう、お願いします。

2019年12月

辻 和子・小座間 亜依

（ヒューマンアカデミー日本語学校）

Introduction

This book was created to allow people who are studying with *Tsunagu Nihongo* Basic 1 and *Tsunagu Nihongo* Basic 2 to confirm how to use sentence patterns found in each lesson.

Use *Tsunagu Nihongo* to learn how to speak in various commonly encountered situations in order to be able to better communicate in everyday life in Japan. Start by practicing situation-based conversation, and when you are able to converse in that situation, you will then practice using the sentence pattern used in the conversation. Once you know what you want to say after looking at the illustration of a given situation, listen to the model conversation and read it out loud. Then, after you are able to have a conversation in the given situation, practice applying the sentence patterns used in the conversation. You will of course learn how to use the sentence patterns while practicing them, but by reading this book, you will come to more clearly understand the sentence patterns and be able to readily apply them with confidence.

We believe that through repeated practice, you will be able to see how the sentence patterns are used and make them your own, and the added explanations will also help to boost your confidence in using them, so you should read this book after studying each corresponding part in the *Tsunagu Nihongo* textbooks. Of course, for learners who would like to practice using sentence patterns after they have first learned and understood them, reading this book before practicing the parts will allow you to practice the situational conversations and sentence patterns after you have understood the sentence patterns.

In addition, this book only explains how to use the sentence patterns used in the parts of the *Tsunagu Nihongo* textbooks to help you confirm and understand the use of the sentence patterns. Please understand that this book is not a grammar book that explains how to use each sentence pattern in depth. Rather, this book solely focuses on explaining how to use each sentence pattern in certain circumstances and contexts.

December 2019
Kazuko Tsuji and Ai Ozama
(Human Academy Japanese Language School)

この本の構成　ほん こうせい　Layout of this Book

各パートは、以下のような構成になっています。
かく　いか　こうせい

Each part is structured as showed below.

Can-do Check ➡ Grammar Notes ➡ Vocabulary and Expression ➡ Conversation Scenario

Can-do Check ✔

そのパートの目標の翻訳です。
もくひょう　ほんやく

This is a translation of the goal of each part.

Grammar Notes ✎

❶ 各パートで扱っている文型を提出順に解説しています。
かく　あつか　ぶんけい　ていしゅつじゅん　かいせつ

The sentence patterns for each part are listed and explained in order of appearance.

❷ 文型の接続は、表で示されています。
ぶんけい　せつぞく　ひょう　しめ

Conjunction forms of sentence patterns are shown in a chart.

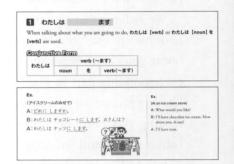

| 1 | わたしは | 　　　　　 | ます |

When talking about what you are going to do, わたしは [verb] or わたしは [noun] を [verb] are used.

Conjunctive Form

わたしは	verb (～ます)	
	noun を	verb (～ます)

❸ 文型の使い方の例は、できるだけ会話で示しました。
ぶんけい　つか　かた　れい　かいわ　しめ
会話には翻訳を入れています。
かいわ　ほんやく　い

The example conversations show how to use the sentence patterns. Translations of the conversations are also included.

Ex.
(アイスクリームのみせで)
A: どれに しますか。
B: わたしは チョコレートに します。Aさんは？
A: わたしは ナッツに します。

Ex.
(At an ice cream store)
A: What would you like?
B: I'll have chocolate ice cream. How about you, A-san!
A: I'll have nuts.

❹ 同一文型の異なる使い方は、提出されているパートでそ
どういつぶんけい　こと　つか　かた　ていしゅつ
れぞれ解説しています。
かいせつ
そのパートよりも前のパートで扱われているものは、「他の使い方」として再度紹介しています。
まえ　あつか　ほか　つか　かた　さいどしょうかい

Different ways of using of the same sentence patterns are covered in the presented parts. Previously introduced ways of using sentence patterns that were already covered in previous parts are introduced as other ways of using this sentence pattern.

❺ 必要に応じてイラストで解説のポイントを示しています。
ひつよう　おう　かいせつ　しめ

Explanation points are shown with illustrations when needed.

~まで

[time] まで is used to show the continuation of an action until a given time.

Ex.1
まいにち がっこうで 15時まで べんきょうします。

Ex.1
I study at school until 15:00.

Ex.2
来年の 5月まで 日本に います。

Ex.2
I will be in Japan until May of next year.

までに by
15時までに 電話を してください。
Please call by 15:00.

まで until
15時まで がっこうに います。
I will be at school until 15:00.

❻ 文型の解説の補足説明を □ で示しています。
ぶんけい　かいせつ　ほそくせつめい　しめ

Additional notes for sentence patterns are shown in the □.

Vocabulary and Expression 🗯

そのパートで学習する語彙と表現です。
がくしゅう　ごい　ひょうげん

The vocabulary and expressions learned in each part is shown here.

Conversation Scenario 💬

そのパートの場面会話の翻訳です。
ばめんかいわ　ほんやく

The conversation scenario for each part is here.

凡例　Explanatory Notes
<ruby>凡例<rt>はんれい</rt></ruby>

この<ruby>本<rt>ほん</rt></ruby>では、<ruby>以下<rt>いか</rt></ruby>のような<ruby>記号<rt>きごう</rt></ruby>を<ruby>使<rt>つか</rt></ruby>っています。
This book uses the following notations.

Conjunctive Form

<ruby>接続<rt>せつぞく</rt></ruby>を<ruby>表<rt>ひょう</rt></ruby>で<ruby>表<rt>あらわ</rt></ruby>しています。
Conjunction forms are shown in charts.

Ex.

・verb ます form 〈～ます〉

<ruby>動詞<rt>どうし</rt></ruby>ます<ruby>形<rt>けい</rt></ruby>の「ます」をとる、という<ruby>意味<rt>いみ</rt></ruby>です。
This means to drop the **ます** from the **ます** form of the verb.

・い adjective 〈～い く〉

い<ruby>形容詞<rt>けいようし</rt></ruby>の「い」をとって「く」をつける、という<ruby>意味<rt>いみ</rt></ruby>です。
This means to drop the **い** from the **い** adjective and replace it with **く**.

・な adjective plain form 〈～だ〉

な<ruby>形容詞<rt>けいようし</rt></ruby><ruby>普通形<rt>ふつうけい</rt></ruby>の「だ」をとる、という<ruby>意味<rt>いみ</rt></ruby>です。
This means to drop **だ** from the plain form of the **な** adjective.

・noun plain form 〈～だ な〉

<ruby>名詞<rt>めいし</rt></ruby><ruby>普通形<rt>ふつうけい</rt></ruby>の「だ」をとって「な」をつける、という<ruby>意味<rt>いみ</rt></ruby>です。
This means to drop **だ** from the plain form of the noun and replace it with **な**.

・sentence とは、ここでは「まとまった<ruby>内容<rt>ないよう</rt></ruby>を<ruby>表<rt>あらわ</rt></ruby>すことば」の<ruby>意味<rt>いみ</rt></ruby>で<ruby>使<rt>つか</rt></ruby>っています。
The word "sentence" is used here to mean words that express complete and coherent content.

Careful !

<ruby>間違<rt>まちが</rt></ruby>えやすいところや、<ruby>特<rt>とく</rt></ruby>に<ruby>注意<rt>ちゅうい</rt></ruby>してほしいことが<ruby>書<rt>か</rt></ruby>いてあります。
Things that are easy to mistake or things to be particularly careful of are written here.

◆

<ruby>取<rt>と</rt></ruby>り<ruby>上<rt>あ</rt></ruby>げた<ruby>文型<rt>ぶんけい</rt></ruby>に<ruby>含<rt>ふく</rt></ruby>まれるその<ruby>他<rt>ほか</rt></ruby>の<ruby>文法項目<rt>ぶんぽうこうもく</rt></ruby>や<ruby>表現<rt>ひょうげん</rt></ruby>などが<ruby>書<rt>か</rt></ruby>いてあります。
Additional grammar notes and expressions relating to each sentence pattern are written here.

＊

<ruby>同一文型<rt>どういつぶんけい</rt></ruby>の<ruby>異<rt>こと</rt></ruby>なる<ruby>使<rt>つか</rt></ruby>い<ruby>方<rt>かた</rt></ruby>が<ruby>書<rt>か</rt></ruby>いてあります。
Different ways of using the same sentence pattern are written here.

<ruby>参照<rt>さんしょう</rt></ruby>する<ruby>課<rt>か</rt></ruby>や、<ruby>教科書<rt>きょうかしょ</rt></ruby>のページ<ruby>番号<rt>ばんごう</rt></ruby>を<ruby>示<rt>しめ</rt></ruby>しています。
The lesson and page number in the textbook being referenced are shown here.

もくじ

Lesson 1　あいさつする Giving greetings

Lesson 2　かいものする Going shopping

Lesson 3　でんしゃや バスに のる Taking the train or bus

Lesson 4　まいにち することを はなす Talking about daily life

Lesson 5　しょくじする Having a meal

Lesson 6　よていや した ことを はなす Talking about plans and what you did

10

1 ①はじめまして ②おしごとは？

Can-do Check ✓

☐ You can introduce yourself to people you meet for the first time.

☐ You can ask and tell people you meet for the first time about work and where you're from.

Grammar Notes 🖉

1 わたしは [　　　　　] です

When talking about yourself, **わたしは ～です** is used. Add information like your name, nationality and age in place of ～ .

Ex.1 わたしは たなかです。	**Ex.1** I'm Tanaka.
Ex.2 わたしは だいがくせいです。	**Ex.2** I'm a college student.
Ex.3 わたしは 21さいです。	**Ex.3** I'm 21 years old.

When the subject **わたしは** is already understood, it can be omitted.

Ex. わたしは きむらです。 かいしゃいんです。 24さいです。	**Ex.** I'm Kimura. I'm an office worker. I'm 24 years old.

◆ When saying where you belong to, such as school or company, **XのY** is used, as in **にほんごがっこうの がくせい**.

Ex.1 Ａ：Ｂさんは だいがくせい ですか。 Ｂ：いいえ。わたしは にほんごがっこうの がくせいです。	**Ex.1** A: Are you a university student, B-san? B: No. I'm a student at a Japanese language school.
Ex.2 たなか：はじめまして。Ｘしゃの たなかです。 やまだ：はじめまして。Ｙしゃの やまだです。	**Ex.2** Tanaka: Nice to meet you. I'm Tanaka from X Company. Yamada: Nice to meet you, too. I'm Yamada from Y Company.

❷ [____] さん は [____] です

When talking about someone else's nationality, occupation, or age, **～さんは ～です** is used. Generally, **さん** is added to the end of people's names, but it is not added when talking to others about your own family members.

Ex.1

トムさんは カナダじんです。25さいです。

Ex.1

Tom-san is Canadian. He's 25 years old.

Ex.2

いもうとの まりこは かいしゃいんです。25さいです。

Ex.2

My younger sister Mariko is an office worker. She is 25 years old.

When describing people, things or matters, **～は ～です** is used.

【noun X】は【noun Y】です

Ex.1

あしたは にちようびです。

Ex.1

Tomorrow is Sunday.

Ex.2

わたしは がくせいです。がっこうは HAだいがくです。

Ex.2

I'm a student. My school is HA University.

Ex.3

としょかんは やすみです。

Ex.3

The library is closed.

---

❸ X は Y です。Z も Y です。

When talking about two or more people (X, Z), if the second person's nationality, occupation, age, etc. (Y) is the same as the first person's, the particle **も** is used when talking about the second person. If they are not the same, the particle **は** is used for both people.

Ex.1

たなかさんは にほんじんです。きむらさんも にほんじんです。

Ex.1

Tanaka-san is Japanese. Kimura-san is also Japanese.

Ex.2

たなかさんは にほんじんです。チンさんは ちゅうごくじんです。

Ex.2

Tanaka-san is Japanese. Chen-san is Chinese.

4

_____ は ___ X ___ ですか。

┌ はい、___ X ___ です。

└ いいえ、___ X ___ じゃ ありません。___ Y ___ です。

When asking a question, **〜は Xですか** is used. When forming a question, the particle **か** is added. **はい** is used when answering a question in the affirmative, and **いいえ** is used when answering in the negative. **〜じゃ ありません** is the negative form of **〜です**.

Ex.1

A：サラさん<u>は</u> かいしゃいんですか。

サラ：<u>はい</u>、かいしゃいん<u>です</u>。

Ex.2

A：キムさん<u>は</u> かいしゃいんですか。

キム：<u>いいえ</u>、かいしゃいん<u>じゃ ありません</u>。
　　　<u>がくせい</u>です。

Ex.1

A: Sarah-san, are you an office worker?

Sarah: Yes, I'm an office worker.

Ex.2

A: Kim-san, are you an office worker?

Kim: No, I'm not an office worker.
　　I'm a student.

わたし is used to refer to oneself. **あなた** is used to refer to others, but using **あなた** in conversations can be impolite, so it is often either omitted or the other person's name or job title (such as **せんせい** or **かちょう**) are used instead.

Ex.1

A：○ キムさんは かいしゃいんですか。

　　△ あなたは かいしゃいんですか。

キム：いいえ、がくせいです。

Ex.2

A：おくには どちらですか。

B：アメリカです。

Ex.3

A：トムさんの おくには どちらですか。

トム：カナダです。

Ex.1

A: Kim-san, are you an office worker?

Kim: No, I'm a student.

Ex.2

A: What country are you from?

B: America.

Ex.3

A: Tom-san, what country are you from?

Tom: Canada.

[noun X] の [noun Y] is used to express possession of something.

Ex.

わたしの くに   my country

タンさんの とけい   Tang-san's watch

にほんの かいしゃ   Japanese company

The **だれ** in **だれですか** is used to express a question. Some other words that express questions are **なに** (what), **どこ** (where), **いつ** (when), **いくつ** (how many), **いくら** (how much), **どうして** (why), **どう** (how) and **どちら** (which).

Ex.1 A：あの ひとは <u>だれ</u>ですか。 B：シンさんです。	**Ex.1** A: Who is that person? B: Shin-san.
Ex.2 A：Bさんの くには <u>どこ</u>ですか。 B：ベトナムです。	**Ex.2** A: B-san, where are you from? B: Vietnam.
Ex.3 A：Bさんの たんじょうびは <u>いつ</u>ですか。 B：6がつ 15にちです。	**Ex.3** A: B-san, when is your birthday? B: It's June 15.

Vocabulary and Expression 🐾

はじめまして Nice to meet you. ／こんにちは Hello.

あ ah ／どうぞ よろしく おねがいします Pleased to meet you.

～さん Mr. / Ms. ／（お）くに country ／どちら which ／わたし I ／そうですか I see.

（お）しごと work, job ／～ご：にほんご language: Japanese ／がっこう school

がくせい student ／いいえ no ／かいしゃいん company employee, office worker

きょうし teacher ／こちら this ／～じん：にほんじん people: Japanese

すみません Excuse me. ／にほん Japan ／かた person ／はい Yes

だいがくせい university student ／あの ひと that person

だれですか Who are you?, Who are they? ／せんせい teacher

Conversation Scenario 💬

⟨Speaking at a cultural exchange party⟩

Sarah: Hello. I'm Sarah. Nice to meet you.

Tang: Oh, I'm Tang. Nice to meet you, too.

Sarah: Tang-san, where are you from?

Tang: Vietnam. How about you?

Sarah: I'm from France.

Tang: I see.

Sarah: Tang-san, what do you do?

Tang: I'm a student at a Japanese language school.

Sarah: Oh, I see.

Tang: Are you a student, too, Sarah-san?

Sarah: No, I'm not a student. I'm an office worker.

Tang: I see.

2 いい てんきですね

Can-do Check ✓

☐ You can give greetings to neighbors.
☐ You can hold simple conversations like talking about the weather.

Grammar Notes ✎

1-1 How To Greet People

Try greeting the people you meet in your daily life with **おはようございます**, **こんにちは** and **こんばんは**. By adding comments about the weather like **あついですね** or **あめですね** to your greetings, you can make the conversation more personal and also make it easier to move into to your next topic. Talking about the weather is something you can do with anybody, whether you know them or not, or if they are your seniors or work colleagues. If you don't have time for a casual conversation, just saying something brief like **あついですね** or **そうですね** and bowing a bit is a perfectly natural greeting, as well.

1-2 Types of Greetings

おはようございます: This is a greeting used in the morning. **おはよう** is used when greeting friends, family and people who are your juniors.
こんにちは: This is a greeting used in the afternoon.
こんばんは: This is a greeting used in the evening.

さようなら, しつれいします: This is a greeting used when leaving. **しつれいします** is used in formal settings or when at work.
しつれいします, おつかれさまでした: **しつれいします** or **おさきに しつれいします** are said when leaving one's workplace to the people who are still there working. They respond by saying **おつかれさまでした**. **しつれいします** can also be used when leaving a room.

おやすみなさい: This is a greeting said before going to bed.
どうぞ: This expression is used when giving someone a gift, offering something like tea or a seat or when giving someone permission to do something.

ありがとうございます: This expression is used to convey gratitude. **ありがとう** is used with friends, family and people who are close to you.

いってきます, いってらっしゃい: **いってきます** is said when going out, and **いってらっしゃい** is said as a response. **いってきます** is said when you are leaving but will return later. If you will not be returning, **さようなら** or **しつれいします** are used.

すみません: This expression is used to get someone's attention or to apologize or show appreciation.

ごめんなさい: This expression is used to apologize to family and close friends.

2 ⬜⬜⬜⬜⬜ **ね。**

The particle **ね** is added to the end of sentences to express a desire from the speaker for understanding and a response from the listener or to express mutual understanding. The intent may change depending on the intonation.

Ex.1

A：あついですね。

B：そうですね。

Ex.1

A: It's hot, isn't it? (seeking understanding)

B: Yes, it is. (agreement)

Ex.2

A：とうきょうの なつは あついです。

B：あついですね。

Ex.2

A: Summer in Tokyo is hot.

B: Yes, it sure is hot. (expressing sympathy)

Ex.3

A：あついですね。

B：う～ん。そうですね。

Ex.3

A: It's hot, isn't it? (seeking understanding)

B: Umm, I guess. (not agreement, currently thinking)

3 **すみません。** ⬜⬜⬜⬜⬜ **おねがいします。**

When asking someone to do a favor, **すみません** is used to get their attention, followed by asking for your favor and then ending with **おねがいします**.

17

Ex.1

すみません。でんわばんごうを おねがいします。

Ex.2

すみません。おおきい こえで おねがいします。

Ex.3

すみません。これ、おねがいします。

Ex.4

すみません。(お) しずかに おねがいします。

Ex.1

Excuse me. Please tell me your phone number.

Ex.2

Excuse me. Please say it a little louder.

Ex.3

Excuse me. This one, please.

Ex.4

Excuse me. Please be quiet.

Vocabulary and Expression

いい てんきですね The weather is nice, isn't it? ／てんき weather

おはようございます Good morning. ／そうですね That's right., Yes it is. ／え？ Sorry?, Huh?

すみません Sorry. ／もう いちど one more time ／おねがいします please ／そうです That's right.

いってらっしゃい Off you go., See you later. ／いってきます I'm off., I'm going.

あさ morning ／ひる daytime ／よる night ／こんばんは Good evening.

さようなら Good bye. ／しつれいします Sorry to be leaving before you.

おつかれさまでした Good job., Good work., Thanks for your hard work.

おやすみなさい Good night. ／どうぞ Here you are. ／ありがとうございます Thank you.

すみません Excuse me, Sorry, Thank you ／ごめんなさい I'm sorry. ／あめ rain

あつい hot (weather) ／さむい cold ／ゆっくり slowly ／えいご English

Conversation Scenario

〈Speaking with people in the neighborhood〉

Tang: Good morning.

Yamada: Good morning.

Tang: The weather is nice, isn't it?

Yamada: Yes, it is. Are you going to school?

Tang: Huh? I'm sorry. Could you say that again?

Yamada: School?

Tang: Oh, yes. That's right.

Yamada: I see. See you.

Tang: I'll be going then.

Can-do Check ✓

☐ You can properly greet those that you will come to rely on in the neighborhood.

☐ You can ask and respond to questions about moving.

Grammar Notes ✎

1 -1   は   から きました

When explaining where someone came from **～は ～から きました** is used. **きました** is the past form of **きます**. The particle **から** express the starting point from which an action occurred. **わたしは** or **～さんは** can be omitted if they are already understood by the listener.

Ex.1
わたしは がくせいです。
（わたしは）インドから きました。

Ex.2
トムさんは アメリカから きました。
（トムさんは）えいごの せんせいです。

Ex.3
たなかさんは かいしゃいんです。
（たなかさんは）おおさかから きました。

Ex.1
I'm a student.
I came from India.

Ex.2
Tom-san came from America.
He is an English language teacher.

Ex.3
Tanaka-san is an office worker.
He is from Osaka.

「～から」「～まで」

～から denotes a starting point and **～まで** denotes an end point.

Ex.1
とうきょうから しんじゅくまで
でんしゃに のります。

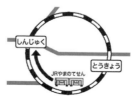

Ex.2
いえから かいしゃまで 1じかん かかります。

Ex.1
I will take a train from Tokyo to Shinjuku.

Ex.2
It takes an hour to get from my home to my office.

1-2　おくには どちらですか ― ＿＿＿＿＿です

おくに is a polite form of くに. どちら is a polite form of どこ. おくには どちらですか is used to avoid offending someone you are meeting for the first time.

1-3　＿place X＿ の どちらですか ― ＿place Y＿ です

When you want to ask for more specific information about a place, 【place X】 の どちらですか is used. When answering, 【place X】 の 【place Y】 です or 【place Y】 です is used. 【place Y】 is an area located within 【place X】.

Ex.1
A：ちゅうごくの どちらですか。
B：ペキンです。

Ex.2
A：とうきょうの どちらですか。
B：しんじゅくです。

Ex.1
A: Where in China?
B: Beijing.

Ex.2
A: Where in Tokyo?
B: Shinjuku.

1-4　いつ ＿＿＿＿へ きましたか ― ＿＿＿＿（に）きました

いつ is an interrogative term concerning time. When you express the direction of movement 【place】へ is used.

Ex.1
いつ にほんへ きましたか。

Ex.2
いつ がっこうへ きましたか。

Ex.1
When did you come to Japan?

Ex.2
When did you come to school?

When answering about when you came somewhere, 【time】（に）きました is used. The particle に is used to express time. However, words for less specific units of time such as きのう (yesterday), きょう (today), あした (tomorrow), せんしゅう (last week), こんしゅう (this week), らいしゅう (next week), きょねん (last year), ことし (this year), らいねん (next year), あさ (morning), ひる (day time) and よる (night) do not use the particle に.

Ex.

A：いつ にほんへ きましたか。

B：4がつ 15にちに きました。

　4がつに きました。

　20XXねんに きました。

　きのう きました。

　せんしゅうの どようび きました。

　せんげつ きました。

　きょねん きました。

Ex.

A: When did you come to Japan?

B: I came on April 15.

I came in April.

I came in 20XX.

I came yesterday.

I came last Saturday.

I came last month.

I came last year.

2　＿＿＿＿＿ は ＿＿＿＿＿ を ｛ のみます・のみません・のみますか
たべます・たべません・たべますか

The negative form of the verb **〜ます** is **〜ません**. The interrogative form of the verb can be made by adding **か** to the end of this, making **〜ますか**. The negative forms of the verbs **のみます** (drink) and **たべます** (eat) are **のみません** and **たべません**, and the interrogative forms are **のみますか** and **たべますか**.

When talking about who drinks what or who eats what, 【person】は 【thing】を のみます／たべます is used.

Ex.1

わたしは さかなを たべます。

Ex.1

I eat fish.

Ex.2

キムさんは さかなを たべません。

Ex.2

Kim-san does not eat fish.

Ex.3

A：トムさんは さかなを たべますか。

トム：はい、たべます。

Ex.3

A: Tom-san, do you eat fish?

Tom: Yes, I do.

あなたは is not used when who you are talking to is already understood.

Ex.1

A：コーヒーを のみますか。

B：はい、のみます。

Ex.1

A: Do you drink coffee?

B: Yes, I do.

Ex.2

A：おさけを のみますか。

B：いいえ、のみません。

Ex.2

A: Do you drink alcohol?

B: No, I don't.

「～ます」「～ません」

This can be used to describe what you are doing now as well as things you do habitually.

Ex.1

わたしは あまい ものを <u>たべません</u>。

Ex.2

（レストランで）

A：なにを たべますか。

B：わたしは ケーキを <u>たべます</u>。

Ex.1

I don't eat sweets. (habitual)

Ex.2

(At a restaurant)

A: What are you going to eat?

B: I'm going to have some cake. (now)

Vocabulary and Expression

きます・きました come from / came from ／せんしゅう last week

ああ ah ／あのう Um., Excuse me.

コーヒー coffee ／のみます drink ／すきです like ／これ this ／わあ wow

───

～がつ：1がつ month: January ／きょねん last year ／あまい もの sweets

たべます eat ／ケーキ cake ／クッキー cookie ／チョコレート chocolate

（お）さけ alcohol ／ビール beer ／ワイン wine ／にほんしゅ sake, Japanese rice wine

しょうちゅう shochu (Japanese white distilled liquor)

Conversation Scenario

〈Giving greetings when moving house〉

Tanaka: Yes.

Tang: Hello. I'm Tang from room 101. Nice to meet you.

Tanaka: Oh, I'm Tanaka. Nice to meet you, too.

Tang: I came here last week from Vietnam.

Tanaka: Where in Vietnam?

Tang: Ho Chi Minh.

Tanaka: Oh, I see.

Tang: Excuse me, Tanaka-san. Do you drink coffee?

Tanaka: Yes, I do. I like coffee.

Tang: This is Vietnamese coffee. Please have some.

Tanaka: Wow! Thank you very much.

1 これ ください

Can-do Check ✓

☐ You can tell the clerk what you want to buy.

☐ You can tell the clerk how many you want.

☐ You can ask the clerk how much something is.

Grammar Notes 🖊

1 いくらですか ― ⬚⬚⬚⬚ えんです。

When asking about the price of something **いくらですか** is used. **えん** is added after the price.

Ex.

A：<u>いくらですか</u>。

B：1,000<u>えんです</u>。

Ex.

A: How much is this?

B: It's 1,000 yen.

◆When saying the total amount of a price for two or more things, **ぜんぶで ～えんです** is used.

Ex.

A：コーヒー ひとつと ケーキ ひとつ ください。

B：ありがとうございます。<u>ぜんぶで</u> 700<u>えんです</u>。

Ex.

A: One coffee and one slice of cake, please.

B: Thank you. That'll be 700 yen in total.

Careful !

4えん is read as **よえん**.　×よんえん、しえん

14えん：○ じゅうよえん　×じゅうよんえん、じゅうしえん

44えん：○ よんじゅうよえん　×よんじゅうよんえん、よんじゅうしえん

This is how various prices in 〜えん are read.

1円 えん	いちえん ichi en	100円 えん	ひゃくえん hyaku en
2円 えん	にえん ni en	200円 えん	にひゃくえん ni hyaku en
3円 えん	さんえん san en	300円 えん	さんびゃくえん san byaku en
4円 えん	**よえん yo en**	400円 えん	よんひゃくえん yon hyaku en
5円 えん	ごえん go en	500円 えん	ごひゃくえん go hyaku en
6円 えん	ろくえん roku en	600円 えん	ろっぴゃくえん roppyaku en
7円 えん	ななえん nana en	700円 えん	ななひゃくえん nana hyaku en
8円 えん	はちえん hachi en	800円 えん	はっぴゃくえん happyaku en
9円 えん	きゅうえん kyuu en	900円 えん	きゅうひゃくえん kyuu hyaku en
10円 えん	じゅうえん juu en	1,000円 えん	せんえん sen en
40円 えん	よんじゅうえん yon juu en		
？	なんえん nan en		

2　これ・それ・あれ・どれ

これ is used when talking about something near yourself.

それ is used when talking about something near the person you are speaking to.

あれ is used when talking about something far away from both yourself and the person you are speaking to that you are both aware of.

どれ is used when talking about something unspecified or unknown.

Ex.1

A：<u>これ</u>は いくらですか。

B：<u>それ</u>は 1,000円です。

Ex.2

A：<u>それ</u>は いくらですか。

B：<u>これ</u>は 1,000円です。

Ex.3

A：<u>あれ</u>は いくらですか。

B：<u>あれ</u>は 1,000円です。

Ex.4

A：1,000円の かばんは <u>どれ</u>ですか。

B：わかりません。

Ex.5

A：いくらですか。

B：<u>どれ</u>ですか？

A：<u>これ</u>です。

B：<u>それ</u>は 1,000円です。

Ex.1

A: How much is this?

B: That's 1,000 yen.

Ex.2

A: How much is that?

B: This is 1,000 yen.

Ex.3

A: How much is that?

B: That's 1,000 yen.

Ex.4

A: Which one is the 1,000 yen bag?

B: I don't know.

Ex.5

A: How much?

B: Which one?

A: This one.

B: That's 1,000 yen.

---

3 いくつですか。― number です。

~つ is a counter used for things like balls, eggs, cake, chairs and other similar things.

~つ can also be used to count numbers from 1 to 9. For numbers larger than 9, **~こ** is used.

~つ can also be used when ordering food.

Ex.1

A：コーヒーを <u>ふたつ</u> ください。

てんいん：はい。 コーヒーを <u>ふたつ</u>ですね。

Ex.2

A：りんごを ください。

てんいん：<u>いくつ</u>ですか。

A：<u>ふたつ</u>です。

Ex.1

A: Two cups of coffee, please.

Clerk: Okay. Two coffees.

Ex.2

A: I'd like some apples, please.

Clerk: How many?

A: Two, please.

The counter used to count something varies depending on what is being counted
(☞ See p. 139 in the textbook).

	Counter	Interrogative form
Used for round things or small masses of things Ex. balls, cakes, apples, eggs, bags, sandwiches, chairs, etc.	〜つ、〜こ	いくつ、なんこ
Used for thin flat things Ex. paper, shirts, etc.	〜まい	なんまい
Used for long objects Ex. pencils, pens, umbrellas, etc.	〜ほん	なんぼん

〜ほん is used when counting long objects. Depending on the number, **〜ほん** may change to **〜ぽん** or **〜ぼん**.

・〜ほん：2（にほん）、4（よんほん）、5（ごほん）、7（ななほん）、9（きゅうほん）

・〜ぽん：1（いっぽん）、6（ろっぽん）、8（はっぽん）、10（じゅっぽん）

・〜ぼん：3（さんぼん）

4

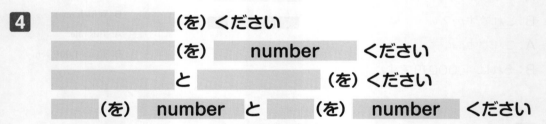

When buying something, 【thing】（を）ください is used. The particle を is often omitted. 【thing】（を）【number】ください is used when saying the number of things you would like to buy.

Ex.1
A：りんごを ください。
てんいん：いくつですか。
A：いつつ／5こ ください。

Ex.2
A：この シャツを 2まい ください。
てんいん：はい。

Ex.1
A: I'd like some apples, please.
Clerk: How many?
A: Five, please.

Ex.2
A: Two of these shirts, please.
Clerk: Okay.

When buying two different kinds of things 【thing X】と【thing Y】と【thing Z】（を）く ださい is used. When you say the number of each thing 【thing X】（を）【number】と 【thing Y】（を）【number】と【thing Z】（を）【number】ください is used.

Ex.1

A：あかい ペンと あおい ペンを ください。

てんいん：はい。

Ex.1

A: A red pen and a blue pen, please.

Clerk: Okay.

Ex.2

A：あかい ペンを 3ぼんと あおい ペンを
　2ほん ください。

てんいん：はい。

Ex.2

A: Three red pens and two blue pens, please.

Clerk: Okay.

Ex.3

（ケーキやで）

A：チョコレートケーキ みっつと
　レモンケーキ ふたつ ください。

てんいん：はい。チョコレートケーキ みっつと
　レモンケーキ ふたつですね。

Ex.3

(At a cake store)

A: Three chocolate cakes and two lemon cakes, please.

Clerk: Okay. Three chocolate cakes and two lemon cakes.

おねがいします can be used instead of ください when you are ordering something.

Ex.

（レストランで）

A：コーヒー みっつ おねがいします。

てんいん：はい。コーヒー みっつですね。

Ex.

(At a restaurant)

A: Three cups of coffee, please.

Clerk: Okay. Three coffees.

てんいん clerk, staff ／いらっしゃいませ Welcome.

チーズバーガー cheeseburger ／オレンジ orange ／ジュース juice

ぜんぶで altogether, in total ／〜えん：100 えん 〜 yen: 100 yen ／え Pardon?

りんご apple ／はな flower ／ハンバーガー hamburger ／シャツ shirt ／いす chair

テレビ television, TV ／みず water ／ほん book ／くるま car ／かばん bag ／じゃあ okay, well

〜に します have[take] this (one) ／ボール ball ／コップ cup

つくえ desk ／みかん mandarin orange ／レモン lemon ／パイナップル pineapple

メロン melon ／ポテト french fries ／サンドイッチ sandwich ／おにぎり rice ball

プリン pudding ／アイスクリーム ice cream ／こうちゃ black tea ／コーラ coke, coca cola

ポップコーン popcorn ／コロッケ croquette ／ドーナッツ donut

Conversation Scenario 💬

〈Buying a hamburger〉

Clerk: Welcome.

Kim: This, please.

Clerk: Okay. A cheeseburger. How many?

Kim: Two please.

Clerk: Okay.

Kim: And two orange juices, please.

Clerk: Okay. That's 560 yen.

Kim: Excuse me, how much?

Clerk: It's 560 yen.

Kim: Okay.

2 くつうりばは どこですか

2-2

Can-do Check ✓

☐ You can ask the clerk where a department is.

☐ You can ask the clerk where certain items are.

Grammar Notes 🖊

1 ＿＿＿＿＿＿ は どこですか

— ＿＿＿＿＿＿ は ＿＿＿＿＿＿ です

When asking where something is, **どこですか** is used.

Ex.

A：ネクタイうりばは どこですか。

てんいん：1かいです。

Ex.

A: Where is the necktie department?

Clerk: On the first floor.

◆ **〜かい** readings

1	いっかい
2	にかい
3	さんかい・さんがい
4	よんかい
5	ごかい
6	ろっかい
7	ななかい
8	はちかい・はっかい
9	きゅうかい
10	じゅっかい
？	なんがい

2 ＿＿＿＿＿＿ は どこに ありますか

— ＿＿＿＿＿＿ は ＿＿＿＿＿＿ です

When asking where something is, **〜は どこに ありますか** is used. When answering,

【thing】は 【place】です is used.

◆【place】：【thing that serves as a reference point】 の 【location】 is used when explaining where something is.

◆ Words that express the location of something

となり next to　　　まえ in front　うしろ behind

Ex.1

A：たまごは どこに ありますか。

てんいん：たまごは ぎゅうにゅうの となりです。

Ex.1

A: Where are the eggs?

Clerk: The eggs are next to the milk.

Ex.2

A：さかなは どこに ありますか。

てんいん：たまごの まえです。

Ex.2

A: Where is the fish?

Clerk: They're in front of the eggs.

Ex.3

A：にくは どこに ありますか。

てんいん：さかなの となりです。

Ex.3

A: Where is the meat?

Clerk: It's next to the fish.

Ex.4

A：パンは どこですか。

てんいん：にくの うしろです。

Ex.4

A: Where is the bread?

Clerk: It's behind the meat.

◆ The particle **に** is used when conveying a place where something is.

Ex.1

A：すみません。かさうりばは どこに ありますか。

てんいん：2かいに あります。

Ex.1

A: Excuse me. Where is the umbrella department?

Clerk: It's on the second floor.

Ex.2

A：めがねは どこに ありますか。

B：テレビの ひだりに あります。

Ex.2

A: Where are my glasses?

B: They're to the left of the TV.

(☞ See p.95 in the textbook)

◆**こちら**, **そちら**, **あちら** and **どちら** are used when describing the direction of something.

こちら is used to refer to something in your direction.

そちら is used to refer to something in the direction of the other person.

あちら is used to refer to something in a direction different from both your own and the other person's.

どちら is used when you do not know what direction something is in.

こちら

そちら

あちら

どちら

Ex.

A：すみません。 でぐちは <u>どちら</u>ですか。

B：<u>そちら</u>です。

Ex.

A: Excuse me.
   Where is the exit?

B: It's over there.

Vocabulary and Expression 🐛

くつ shoes ／うりば department, floor ／〜かい：４かい 〜 floor: fourth floor

ビジネスシューズ business shoes ／あちら over there ／スニーカー sneakers ／となり next to

___

とけい watch ／めがね glasses ／くつした socks ／セーター sweater ／かさ umbrella

ぼうし hat ／ネクタイ necktie ／ちか basement ／しょくひん food product ／パン bread

ちゅうしゃじょう parking lot ／なんがい which floor

たまご egg ／まえ in front, before ／うしろ behind ／やさい vegetable ／にく meat

ぎゅうにゅう milk ／さかな fish ／くだもの fruit ／ぶどう grapes ／バナナ banana

わかりました Okay., I see., Got it. ／どうも Thanks. ／トイレ toilet, bathroom ／かいだん stairs

Conversation Scenario 💬

⟨Asking where a department is at a department store⟩

Lee: Excuse me.

Clerk A: Yes. Welcome.

Lee: Where is the shoe department?

Clerk A: The shoe department is on the fourth floor.

Lee: Thank you very much.

Lee: Excuse me. Where are the business shoes?

Clerk B: Business shoes are over there. They are next to the sneakers.

Lee: Thank you very much.

3 くろいの、ありますか

Can-do Check ✓

☐ You can ask if there are any other items.
☐ You can leave the shop without buying anything.

Grammar Notes ✏️

1 この・その・あの・どの

When talking about one thing out of many, **この**【noun】, **その**【noun】and **あの**
【noun】are used.

この【noun】is used for things that are close to or nearby you.

その【noun】is used for things that are close to or nearby the other person.

あの【noun】is used for things that are far away from both you and the other person.

どの【noun】is used when you do not know which one something is.

Ex.1
A：この かばんは いくらですか。
てんいん：その かばんは 5,000円です。

Ex.2
A：あの ぼうしは いくらですか。
てんいん：どの ぼうしですか。
A：あの くろい ぼうしです。
てんいん：あの ぼうしは 10,000円です。

Ex.1
A: How much is this bag?
Clerk: That bag is 5,000 yen.

Ex.2
A: How much is that hat?
Clerk: Which hat?
A: That black hat.
Clerk: That hat is 10,000 yen.

2 い ＝ いの

◆Nouns describing colors

あか (red), あお (blue), くろ (black), しろ (white), きいろ (yellow), ちゃいろ (brown), みどり (green) and むらさき (purple) are some of the nouns used to describe colors. When using adjective forms to describe colors, they can either be formed using 【color noun】いです or 【color noun】い 【noun】(as in あかいです, あかい かばん, しろいです, しろい くつ), or using 【color noun】です or 【color noun】の 【noun】(as in みどりです, みどりの かばん, むらさきです, むらさきの くつ).

Ex.1
わたしの くつは <u>あか／あかい</u>です。

Ex.1
My shoes are red.

Ex.2
<u>あかい</u> くつを かいました。

Ex.2
I bought red shoes.

Ex.3
トムさんの ぼうしは <u>みどり</u>です。

Ex.3
Tom-san's hat is green.

Ex.4
<u>みどり</u>の ぼうしを かいました。

Ex.4
He bought a green hat.

◆Using の in place of a noun

When repeatedly using nouns with 【い adjective】＋【noun】, の may be used as a pronoun in place of the noun.

Ex.1
A：この シャツ、おおき<u>い</u>のは ありますか。
てんいん：はい、あります。
「おおきいの」＝「おおきい シャツ」

Ex.1
A: Do you have this shirt in a large?
Clerk: Yes, we do.

Ex.2
A：しろい くつは ありますか。
てんいん：すみません。しろ<u>い</u>のは ありません。
「しろいの」＝「しろい くつ」

Ex.2
A: Do you have any white shoes?
Clerk: I'm sorry. We don't have any in white.

3 [　　　] い です

Words like **おおきい** and **くろい** that are used to describe a bag like **おおきい かばん** or **くろい かばん** are called **けいようし** (adjectives). Adjectives that end in **〜い** are called **い adjectives** (**いけいようし**).

い adjectives can be used as **【い adjective】です** as in **これは ちいさいです** or as **【い adjective】＋【noun】** as in **ちいさい かばんです**.

Ex.1
この シャツは <u>おおきいです</u>。

Ex.2
<u>おおきい</u> シャツは ありませんか。

Ex.3
<u>あおい</u> ボールペンを ください。

Ex.1
This shirt is big.

Ex.2
Do you have any big shirts?

Ex.3
A blue ballpoint pen, please.

4 [　　　] くないです

The negative form of an **い** adjective is **〜い くない**.

おおきい big → おおきくない not big

ながい long → ながくない not long

あかい red → あかくない not red

Ex.1
A：その シャツは おおきいですか。
B：いいえ、<u>おおきくない</u>です。

Ex.2
A：その かばんは おもいですか。
B：いいえ、<u>おもくない</u>です。

Ex.1
A: Is that shirt big?
B: No, it's not big.

Ex.2
A: Is that bag heavy?
B: No, it's not heavy.

Vocabulary and Expression 😊

くろい black ／みせて ください Please show me. ／しろい white

ちょっと a little ／おもい heavy ／かるい light ／ちいさい small ／また again

いいですね That's good., It's good. ／くろ・くろい black ／しろ・しろい white

あか・あかい red ／ちゃいろ・ちゃいろい brown ／きいろ・きいろい yellow

あお・あおい blue ／うみ sea ／ちょっと… not quite right, don't really like ／タオル towel

おおきい big ／ながい long ／みじかい short

たかい expensive ／やすい cheap, not expensive ／パソコン computer ／じてんしゃ bike, bicycle

もう すこし a little more ／おいしい delicious, good ／おもしろい interesting, funny

ゲーム game ／ジャケット jacket ／どうですか How about...?

ちょうど いいです It's just right. ／びょういん hair salon ／ひと person ／いろ color

Conversation Scenario 💬

〈Buying a bag〉

Sarah: Excuse me. Please show me that bag.

Clerk: The white bag?

Sarah: No, the black one.

Clerk: Okay. Here you are.

Sarah: It's a little heavy. Do you have any lighter ones?

Clerk: Yes, we do. Here.

Sarah: Oh, this is a little small. Sorry. I'll come again some other time.

Clerk: Thank you very much.

1 なんで いきますか

Can-do Check ✓

☐ You can ask and give directions to destinations.

☐ You can explain what you want to do.

Grammar Notes ✏

1-1 ⬚⬚⬚⬚ は ⬚⬚⬚⬚ で ⬚⬚⬚⬚ へ ⎰ いきます
　　　　　　　　　　　　　　　　　　　　　⎱ きます

When explaining where you go and how you go there, **いきます**, **きます** can be used. The negative form of **いきます** is **いきません**, the passive form is **いきました** and the negative passive form is **いきませんでした**. Similarly, **きます** becomes **きません**, **きました** and **きませんでした**.

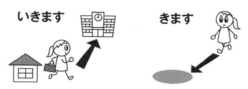

	いきます go	**きます** come
Negative form	いきません	きません
Passive form	いきました	きました
Negative passive form	いきませんでした	きませんでした

◆ 【place】 へ is used when stating a destination. へ denotes a direction. どこへ is used when forming a question.

Ex.1

A：わたしは かいしゃへ いきます。

B：わたしは がっこうへ いきます。

Ex.1

A: I'm going to my office.

B: I'm going to school.

Ex.2

A：Bさんは どこへ いきますか。

B：わたしは きょうとへ いきます。

Ex.2

A: B-san, where are you going?

B: I'm going to Kyoto.

Ex.3

A：Bさんは せんしゅう きょうとへ いきましたか。

B：いいえ、いきませんでした。

Ex.3

A: B-san, did you go to Kyoto last week?

B: No, I didn't.

3-1

Ex.4

A：Ｂさんは きのう かいしゃ<u>へ</u> きましたか。

B：はい、きました。

◆ 【means of transportation】で

【means】で is used to convey a means of transportation. で denotes the means.

Ex.1

A：わたしは でんしゃ<u>で</u> かいしゃへ いきます。

B：わたしは ちかてつ<u>で</u> いきます。

Ex.2

A：わたしは しんかんせん<u>で</u> きょうとへ きました。

B：わたしは ひこうき<u>で</u> きました。

Ex.3

A：わたしは バス<u>で</u> いきます。

B：わたしは じてんしゃ<u>で</u> いきます。

Ex.4

A: B-san, did you come to the office yesterday?

B: Yes, I did.

Ex.1

A: I'll go to my office by train.

B: I'll go by metro.

Ex.2

A: I came to Kyoto by shinkansen.

B: I came by plane.

Ex.3

A: I'll go by bus.

B: I'll go by bike.

Careful！

あるいて is used to describe going somewhere on foot.

Ex.

A：たなかさんは でんしゃで ここへ きましたか。

たなか：いいえ。わたしは <u>あるいて</u> きました。

Ex.

A: Tanaka-san, did you come here by train?

Tanaka: No. I walked here.

１-2 ＿＿＿＿＿＿＿は ＿＿＿＿＿＿＿へ なんで ｛ いきますか / きますか
― ＿＿＿＿＿＿＿で ｛ いきます / きます

When asking about someone's means of transportation, なんで is used.

Ex.1

A：Ｂさんは <u>なんで</u> がっこうへ きますか。

B：わたしは <u>バスで</u> きます。

Ex.1

A: B-san, how do you come to school?

B: I come by bus.

Ex.2

A：Ｂさんは <u>なんで</u> ここへ きましたか。

B：わたしは <u>あるいて</u> きました。

Ex.2

A: B-san, how did you get here?

B: I walked here.

2 わたし は 〜たい です／〜たくない です

When talking about something you want to do, **わたしは 〜たいです** is used. When talking about something you do not want to do, **わたしは 〜たくないです** is used. **〜たくない** is the negative form of **〜たい**, and it is conjugated as **〜たい くない**. **わたしは** can be omitted when it is already understood to be the subject.

Conjunctive Form

わたし	は	verb 〈〜ます〉	たい	です
			たい くない	

Ex.1

A：わたしは ほっかいどうへ いきたいです。

B：わたしは いきたくないです。

Ex.2

A：なつやすみに くにへ かえりたいです。

B：そうですか。

Ex.1

A: I want to go to Hokkaido.

B: I don't want to go.

Ex.2

A: I want to go back to my country during summer vacation.

B: I see.

When using 【noun】を【verb】 to talk about something you want to do, 【noun】を 〜たいです or 【noun】が 〜たいです can be used. 【noun】が 〜たいです is used when you want to emphasize the noun or when answering the question **なにが 〜たいですか**. **〜が たべたいです** or **〜が のみたいです** are often used when using **たべたいです** or **のみたい です**.

Ex.1

A：きょうは なにを したいですか。

B：そうですね。えいがを みたいです。

Ex.2

A：どの えいがが みたいですか。

B：この えいがが みたいです。

Ex.3

A：あついですね。ビールが のみたいです。

B：わたしは つめたい みずが のみたいです。

Ex.4

（スポーツジムで）

A：なにを／が したいですか。

B：ヨガを／が したいです。

Ex.1

A: What do you want to do today?

B: Hmm. I want to see a movie.

Ex.2

A: What movie do you want to see?

B: I want to see this movie.

Ex.3

A: It's hot, isn't it? I want to drink a beer.

B: I want to drink cold water.

Ex.4

(At a sports gym)

A: What do you want to do?

B: I want to do yoga.

Aさんは ～たいと おもって います or **Aさんは ～たいと いって います** can be used to talk about what other people want to do.

Ex.

A：たなかさんが やまださんに あいたいと いって いました。

B：そうですか。わたしも やまださんにさんに あいたいです。

Ex.

A: Tanaka-san said he wants to see Yamada-san.

B: Oh, really? I want to see Yamada-san, too.

Vocabulary and Expression 🐾

いきます go ／にちようび Sunday ／でんしゃ train ／あるいて walk

うち house ／～ふん、ぷん：5ふん、10ぷん ～ minute(s): five minutes, ten minutes

ぐらい about ／～じ：9じ ～ o'clock: nine o'clock ／えき station

- -

バス bus ／ちかてつ subway ／バイク motorbike, motorcycle ／タクシー taxi

らいしゅう next week ／しんかんせん shinkansen, bullet train ／まいにち everyday

かいしゃ company ／ここ here ／えいが movie ／みます see, watch ／きょう today

ゆき snow ／どようび Saturday

Conversation Scenario 💬

〈Going to Ebisu〉

Marie: Wow! Where is this place?

Kim: Ebisu. Why don't we go there on Sunday?

Marie: Yeah, I want to go!

Kim: Then let's go! How will we get there?

Marie: I'll go by train. How about you, Kim-san?

Kim: I'm going to walk there.

Marie: What?! Walk?

Kim: Yeah. Ebisu is about a 10 -minute walk away from my home.

Marie: Really? Then see you on Sunday.

Kim: Six o'clock at Ebisu Station.

Marie: Okay!

Can-do Check ✓

☐ You can ask where the bus stop or train station are.

☐ You can ask about the bus times.

☐ You can confirm where the bus is going.

Grammar Notes ✎

1 ここ・そこ・あそこ・どこ

ここ is used for places that are close to you.

そこ is used for places that are close to the other person.

あそこ is used for places that are not close to you or the other person that you are both aware of.

どこ is used when you do not know where something is.

Ex.1

A：ペンは ありますか。

B：はい。<u>ここ</u>に あります。

Ex.1

A: Do you have a pen?

B: Yes. It's right here.

Ex.2

A：<u>ここ</u>は いま 7じです。<u>そこ</u>は いま なんじですか。

B：<u>ここ</u>は いま 9じです。

Ex.2

A: It's 7:00 here now. What time is it there?

B: It's 9:00 here now.

Ex.3

A：かぎは <u>どこ</u>ですか。

B：<u>あそこ</u>です。あの つくえの ひきだしの なかです。

Ex.3

A: Where is the key?

B: It's over there. It's in the drawer in that desk.

2 ［place］に ［facility, thing］が あります

When describing where something is, **【place】に 【facility, thing】が あります** is used.

Ex.
あそこに コンビニが あります。

Ex.
There is a convenience store over there.

When asking where a facility is located, **【facility】は どこですか** is used.

Ex.
A：すみません。ちかてつの えきは どこですか。
B：あそこです。ぎんこうの となりです。

Ex.
A: Excuse me. Where is the metro station?
B: It's over there. It's next to the bank.

When asking whether a facility is nearby or not, **この ちかくに 【facility】は ありますか** is used.

Ex.
A：この ちかくに ゆうびんきょくは ありますか。
B：はい。あの コンビニの まえに あります。

Ex.
A: Is there a post office nearby?
B: Yes. It's in front of that convenience store.

＊This can also be used in stores when asking or explaining where a department or product is (☞ Lesson 2-2).

3 -1 なんじですか。― ［　　　　　］です。

When asking what time it is, **なんじですか** is used.

じゅうにじ
じゅういちじ　いちじ
じゅうじ
くじ kuji　にじ
はちじ　さんじ
しちじ shichiji　よじ yoji
ろくじ　ごじ

ごじゅうごふん　ごふん
ごじゅっぷん　じゅっぷん
よんじゅうごふん　じゅうごふん
よんじゅっぷん　にじゅっぷん
さんじゅうごふん　にじゅうごふん
さんじゅっぷん
はん

01	**いっぷん ip pun**	11	**じゅういっぷん juuippun**
02	にふん nifun	12	じゅうにふん juunifun
03	**さんぷん san pun**	13	じゅうさんぷん juusan**pun**
04	**よんぷん yon pun**	14	じゅうよんぷん juuyon**pun**
05	ごふん gofun	15	じゅうごふん juugofun
06	**ろっぷん rop pun**	16	**じゅうろっぷん juuroppun**
07	ななふん nanafun	17	じゅうななふん juunanafun
08	はちふん・**はっぷん** hachifun・**happun**	18	じゅうはちふん・**じゅうはっぷん** juuhachifun・**juuhappun**
09	きゅうふん kyuufun	19	じゅうきゅうふん juukyuufun
10	**じゅっぷん juppun**	20	**にじゅっぷん nijuppun**

3 - 2

Ex.

A：すみません。いま なんじ<u>ですか</u>。

B：<u>9じ 20ぷん</u>です。

Ex.

A: Excuse me. What time is it now?

B: It's 9:20.

3 -2 ＿＿＿＿＿ は なんじに きますか
― ＿＿＿＿＿ に きます／＿＿＿＿＿ です

When asking when a bus or train will be coming, **【vehicle】は なんじに きますか／なんじですか** is used. It can also be used to ask when a person will be coming. **【time】に きます** or **【time】です** will be used when answering.

Ex.1

A：Cさんは きょう <u>なんじに きますか</u>。

B：<u>2じに きます</u>。

Ex.1

A: What time is C-san coming today?

B: She's coming at 2:00.

Ex.2

A：つぎの でんしゃは <u>なんじですか</u>。

B：<u>11じ 45ふんです</u>。

Ex.2

A: What time does the next train come?

B: At 11:45.

4 なんばんの ＿＿＿＿＿ ですか ― ＿＿＿＿＿ ばん です

When asking what number a bus or train is, **なんばんの 【vehicle】ですか** is used. **【number】ばんです** is used when answering.

Ex.

A：すみません。さくらまちへ いきたいです。

　　<u>なんばんの</u> バス<u>ですか</u>。

B：3<u>ばんです</u>。

It can also be used to ask room or reception numbers.

Ex.

A：つぎの じゅぎょうは <u>なんばんの</u> きょうしつですか。

B：４０３です。

Ex.

A: Excuse me. I want to go to Sakuramachi. What number bus goes there?

B: The number 3.

Ex.

A: What room is the next class in?

B: Room number 403.

Vocabulary and Expression 🎴

この ちかく nearby ／バスてい bus stop ／おんなの ひと woman

ゆうびんきょく post office ／いいえ No problem. ／つぎの next

えっと um ／うんてんしゅ driver

ぼうえき trade ／〜や：ほんや 〜 shop: bookstore ／スーパー supermarket

コンビニ convenience store ／ぎんこう bank ／はなや flower shop ／カフェ cafe, coffee shop

こうえん park ／びょういん hospital ／むかい across ／ええ yes, yeah

デパート department store ／いま now

〜はん：11じはん half past 〜 , 〜 thirty: half past eleven, eleven thirty

〜ばん：5ばん number 〜 : number five

Conversation Scenario 💬

〈Taking the bus〉

Shin: Excuse me. Is there a bus stop near here?

Woman A: Yes. There's a post office right there. It's right in front of that.

Shin: Oh, thank you.

Woman A: No problem.

Shin: Umm, what time does the next bus come?

Woman B: Let's see. At 3：15.

Shin: So, 3：15. Thank you.

Woman B: No problem.

Shin: Excuse me. Does this bus go to Roppongi?

Driver: Yes, it does.

3 なんばんせんですか

Can-do Check ✓

☐ You can ask about the price, travel time and platform.

☐ You can say where you are.

Grammar Notes 🖊

1

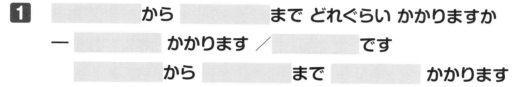

When asking about how long it will take to get from one place to another, 【**point of departure**】から【**point of arrival**】まで どれぐらい かかりますか is used.

Ex.

A：ここから えきまで どれぐらい かかりますか。

B：バスで 10ぷん かかります。

Ex.

A: How long will it take to get from here to the station?

B: It'll take 10 minutes on the bus.

When asking about the price of getting from one place to another, **いくらです か** or **いくら かかりますか** are used.

Ex.

A：ここから えきまで いくらですか／いくら かかりま すか。

B：210円です／210円 かかります。
　　 えん　　　　　えん

Ex.

A: How much is it from here to the station? / How much does it cost to get from here to the station?

B: It's 210 yen. / It costs 210 yen.

◆ Describing how long something takes

When talking about hours, **～かん** is used.

・**～じかん** hour

Ex.

いえから かいしゃまで <u>1じかん</u> かかります。

Ex.

It takes an hour to get from my home to my office.

・**～ふん／ぷん（かん）** minute

Ex.

いえから えきまで あるいて <u>20ぷん</u> かかります。

Ex.

It takes 20 minutes to walk from my home to the station.

◆ **～ぐらい**

When talking about approximate times or costs, **【time, cost】ぐらい** is used.

Ex.

A：とうきょうから おおさかまで <u>どれぐらい</u> かかりますか。

B：しんかんせんで <u>2じかんはんぐらい</u>です。

Ex.

A: How long does it take to get from Tokyo to Osaka?

B: It takes about two and a half hours by shinkansen.

2 　　　　　　　**は どこに いますか ―** 　　　　　　　**に います**

When describing where a person is, **【place】に【person】が います** is used.

Ex.

あそこに キムさんが います。

Ex.

Kim-san is over there.

When asking where a person is, **【person】は どこに いますか** is used. **【place】に います** is used when answering. **【place】です** can also be used to answer **どこですか**.

Ex.1

A：Bさん、いま <u>どこに いますか</u>。

B：<u>えきに います</u>。

Ex.1

A: B-san, where are you right now?

B: At the station.

Ex.2

A：トムさんは いま <u>どこですか</u>。

B：<u>かいぎしつです</u>。

Ex.2

A: Where is Tom-san right now?

B: In the meeting room.

Vocabulary and Expression 😊

～ばんせん：6ばんせん platform number ～ : platform number six
えきいん station staff ／かかります take ／もしもし Hello.
これから from now ／のります ride

～かん：2じかん for: two hours ／ひこうき airplane ／いえ house
コピーき photocopier, copy machine ／ロビー lobby

Conversation Scenario 💬

〈Taking the train〉

Marie: Excuse me. How much is it to Ebisu?

Station staff: It's 170 yen.

Marie: I see. How long will it take to get to Ebisu from here?

Station staff: About 20 minutes.

Marie: What platform is it?

Station staff: It's platform number 6.

Marie: I see. Thank you.

Marie: Hello?

Kim: Hello. Marie-san, where are you now?

Marie: I'm in Ikebukuro. I'm about to get on the train.

3-3

47

1 あさ がっこうで べんきょうします

Can-do Check ✓

☐ You can talk about your daily life.

☐ You can talk about what time and for how long you do things.

Grammar Notes ✏

1 -1 ＿＿＿＿＿＿ます

The **ます** form of verbs is used to describe something you are going to do from now or something you do regularly.

Ex.1

わたしは あさ 6じに おきます。よる 12じに ねます。

Ex.1

I wake up at 6:00 in the morning. I go to sleep at 12:00 at night.

Ex.2

リンさんは まいにち ジョギングします。

Ex.2

Lin-san goes jogging every day.

1 -2 ＿＿＿＿を＿＿＿＿ます

Some verbs are constructed as 〜 を 〜 . なにを しますか is used when asking a question. The particle **を** is used to denote the object of the verb.

Conjunctive Form

noun	を	verb〈〜ます〉

Ex.1

A：コーヒーを のみます。

B：わたしは こうちゃを のみます。

Ex.1

A: I drink coffee.

B: I drink black tea.

Ex.2

A：どようび なにを しますか。

B：テニスを します。

Ex.2

A: What will you do on Saturday?

B: I'm going to play tennis.

Various Particles

Particles come before verbs and denote the place, time or objective of an action.

Ex.

	Ex.
Destination : がっこう**へ**／**に** いきます。	I go to school.
Point of departure : いえ**を** でます。	I leave my house.
Point of arrival : がっこう**に** つきます。	I arrive at school.
Means of transportation : バス**で** いきます。	I go by bus.
Time : 9じ**に** いきます。	I go at 9:00.
Person doing the action : たなかさん**が** きます。	Tanaka-san comes.
Same : やまださん**も** きます。	Yamada-san comes, too.
Multiple subjects : たなかさん**と** やまださんが います。	Tanaka-san and Yamada-san are here.
Place : ロビー**に** います。／としょかん**で** べんきょうします。	I'm in the lobby. / I study in the library.
Object of the action : にほんご**を** べんきょうします。	I study Japanese.

4-1

---

2 _____ **から** _____ **まで** _____ **ます**

When stating when something begins, 【time】**から** is used. When stating when something will end, 【time】**まで** is used.

Ex.1

わたしは 9じ<u>から</u> 6じ<u>まで</u> しごとを します。

Ex.1

I work from 9:00 to 6:00.

Ex.2

なつやすみは 7がつ 21にち<u>から</u> 8がつ 31にち<u>まで</u> です。

Ex.2

Summer vacation is from July 21 to August 31.

3 ［place］で ［verb］ます

~ で ~ is used to state a place where an action is being done. When you ask a question, **どこで ~ますか** is used.

Conjunctive Form

place	で	verb〈~ます〉

Ex.

A：ごご えいがを みます。

B：どこで みますか。

A：しんじゅくで みます。

Ex.

A: I'm going to see a movie in the afternoon.

B: Where are you going to see it?

A: I'm going to see it in Shinjuku.

When repeating the same noun, as in 【noun】＋**します**, it is normally shortened to just **します**.

Ex.

A：ごご べんきょうします。

B：どこで しますか。

A：としょかんで します。

Ex.

A: I'm going to study in the afternoon.

B: Where?

A: In the library.

Vocabulary and Expression 🐾

べんきょうします study ／いつも always ／はやい early ／おきます wake up ／へえ wow
まいあさ every morning ／ジョギングします jog ／その あと after that
シャワーを あびます take a shower ／きもちが いいです feel good
また あとで See you later. ／がんばって ください Please do your best.

かきます write ／ききます listen ／よみます read ／かいます buy ／きます wear
はなします talk, speak ／（りょうりを）つくります cook ／（しゃしんを）とります take a picture
かいものします go shopping ／さんぽします go for a walk ／サッカー soccer
します do, play ／カード card ／おんがく music ／しゃしん photo
かえります go home, go back ／ねます sleep ／ばんごはん dinner ／あした tomorrow
ごぜん morning ／アルバイト part-time job ／ごご afternoon ／じゅぎょう lesson, class
あれ？ Hmm?, What? ／やすみ day off, closed ／みせ shop ／まいしゅう every week
およぎます swim ／ジム gym ／プール pool ／ショッピング shopping ／ダンス dance
れんしゅう practice ／つり fishing ／かわ river ／～がわ：みどりがわ ~ river: Midori River
しゅうまつ weekend ／としょかん library ／あさごはん breakfast ／ひ day

Conversation Scenario 💬

〈Talking with the teacher in the morning〉

Lama: Good morning.

Aoki: Good morning. Lama-san, you're always early. What time do you wake up?

Lama: 5:30.

Aoki: Wow, 5:30!

Lama: Yes. Every morning, I go jogging from 6:00 to 7:00. After that, I take a shower. It feels good.

Aoki: I see. That's great.

Aoki: Okay then, see you later.

Lama: Okay. I'm going to study from now until 9:00.

Aoki: Do your best.

4
-
1

2 まいにち りょうりを しますか

Can-do Check ✓

☐ You can talk about how you spent your day.

☐ You can ask or tell who did it, or who owns it.

Grammar Notes ✎

1 　　　　　　ました ／ 　　　　　　ませんでした

〜ました is used for the past tense of verbs, and **〜ませんでした** is used for the negative past tense.

Ex.1 けさ わたしは あさ 6じに おきました。	**Ex.1** This morning, I woke up at 6:00.
Ex.2 きのう わたしは ジョギングを しませんでした。	**Ex.2** Yesterday, I didn't go jogging.

The particle **と** is used to express that an action is being done with another person.

Ex.1 やすみの ひ、いつも たなかさんと テニスを します。	**Ex.1** On my days off, I always play tennis with Tanaka-san.
Ex.2 ともだちと えいがを みました。	**Ex.2** I saw a movie with my friends.

2 だれが 　　　　　　か

When asking who will do or has done something, **だれが 〜か** is used.

Ex.1 A：あしたの ミーティング、だれが きますか。 B：たなかさんと きむらさんと やまださんです。	**Ex.1** A: Who is coming to the meeting tomorrow? B: Tanaka-san, Kimura-san and Yamada-san.
Ex.2 A：この ケーキ、おいしいですね。だれが つくりましたか。 B：わたしです。	**Ex.2** A: This cake is delicious. Who made it? B: I did.

3 ┌─┐ ▢▢▢ の ▢▢▢▢▢ = ▢▢▢▢ の

When expressing who something belongs to, 【person】の 【thing】 is used. **だれのです**
か is used to ask who something belongs to. When the 【thing】 in question is already
understood, it may be shortened to just 【person】の.

Ex.1

A：この ほんは <u>だれのですか</u>。

B：<u>たなかさんの</u>です。

Ex.2

A：あれは <u>だれの</u> かばんですか。

B：あ、あれは <u>リンさんの</u> かばんです。

Ex.1

A: Whose book is this?

B: It's Tanaka-san's.

Ex.2

A: Whose bag is that?

B: Oh, that's Lin-san's bag.

Vocabulary and Expression 😊

りょうり cooking ／（お）べんとう bento, lunch box, packed lunch ／はは mother
まえ before, earlier ／よく often

- - -

きのう yesterday ／そうじ cleaning ／しんぶん newspaper

せんたくします wash, do the laundry ／でかけます go out ／（お）ともだち friend

でんわします call, phone ／（お）みやげ souvenir ／スキー ski

おんせんに はいります go in a hot spring ／え picture ／かきます draw, paint ／テスト test

いいます say

Conversation Scenario 💬

〈Eating lunch〉

Inoue: Oh, whose bento is this?

Lee: It's mine.

Inoue: It's yours? Who made it?

Lee: I made it.

Inoue: Wow, you did?

Lee: Yes. How about yours?

Inoue: My mother made it.

Lee: I see. That's nice.

Inoue: Lee-san, do you cook every day?

Lee: Yes. I do now. But I didn't before. I often bought my bento at convenience stores.

Inoue: Oh really?

4
-
2

3 まいしゅう つくります

Can-do Check ✓

☐ When doing something with other people, you can say what you will do.

☐ You can ask and answer questions about where a tool is.

Grammar Notes ✏

1 わたしは ＿＿＿＿ ます

When talking about what you are going to do, わたしは【verb】 or わたしは【noun】を【verb】 are used.

Conjunctive Form

わたしは	verb〈～ます〉		
	noun	を	verb〈～ます〉

Ex.1

A：6じですね。わたしは かえります。

B：わたしは もう すこし しごとを します。

Ex.2

（パーティーをします）

A：わたしは りょうりを つくります。

B：わたしは そうじを します。

C：わたしも そうじを します。

D：わたしは かいものを します。

Ex.1

A: It's 6:00. I'm going home.

B: I'm going to work a little more.

Ex.2

(Having a party)

A: I'm going to cook.

B: I'm going to clean.

C: I'm going to clean, too.

D: I'm going to go shopping.

2 ＿＿＿＿ は どこに ありますか
― ＿＿＿＿ の ＿＿ に あります

When asking where something is, 【thing】は どこに ありますか is used. 【thing】は どこ ですか can also be used. 【thing】は【place】です or【place】に あります can be used when answering. The particle に is used to show a place.

Conjunctive Form

thing	は	どこ	に	ありますか
		どこですか		

thing	は	place	に	あります
		place		です

＊The sentence format is the same as the one used when asking where a department or facility is (☞ Lesson 2-2, Lesson 3-2).

◆Words that express the location of something

みぎ right　　　ひだり left　　　うえ on　　　した under　　　なか inside　　　そと outside

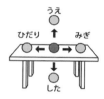 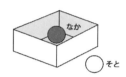

テーブルの うえ
on top of the table

テーブルの した
under the table

かばんの なか
inside the bag

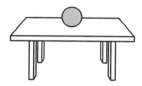 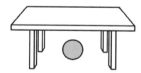

Ex.1

A：この へやの かぎは どこに ありますか。

B：ここです。この はこの なかに あります。

Ex.2

A：しおは どこに ありますか。

B：テーブルの うえです。

Ex.1

A: Where is the key for this room?

B: It's here. It's in this box.

Ex.2

A: Where is the salt?

B: It's on the table.

Vocabulary and Expression 🐛

ギョーザ gyoza, dumplings ／こんどの next time ／いっしょに together ／きります cut

わたしたち we ／（ギョーザの）かわ dumpling wrap ／ほうちょう knife ／ひきだし drawer

なか inside

のみもの drink ／もって いきます take ／きっぷ ticket ／ホテル hotel

よやくします reserve, book ／ごちそうさまでした That was delicious., Thank you for the food.

（お）さら plate, dish ／あらいます wash ／ふきます wipe, dry ／さあ well, okay ／まど window

しめます close ／でんき power, lights ／けします turn off ／はっぴょう presentation

みなさん everyone, everybody ／はっぴょうします make a presentation

アニメ anime, animation ／はなし talk, conversation ／がんばりましょう Let's do one's best

カレンダー calendar ／よこ side, horizontal ／そと outside ／みぎ right ／ひだり left

うえ top ／した bottom ／カメラ camera ／はさみ scissors ／はこ box ／レジ register

かご basket ／ほんだな book shelf ／スタンド stand ／まるい round ／テーブル table

カレー curry ／ごみぶくろ trash bag

Conversation Scenario 💬

〈Making food together〉

Lee: Here, try this.

Nakamura: Oh wow, gyoza!

Lee: I made them myself.

Inoue: What? You did?

Lee: Yes. I make them every week. Why don't we make some together this Saturday?

Nakamura and Inoue: Yeah!

Nakamura: I'll cut the vegetables.

Lee: Thank you. We'll make the gyoza wraps.

Inoue: Okay.

Nakamura: Where is the knife?

Lee: It's in that drawer.

Nakamura: Okay.

Lee: Ah, Nakamura-san. That's a little big.

Nakamura: Sorry.

1 いらっしゃいませ

Can-do Check ✓

☐ You can invite someone out to eat or drink.

☐ You can tell the restaurant how many people you are bringing and what seat you want.

Grammar Notes ✎

1 ＿＿＿＿＿ ませんか ― ＿＿＿＿＿ ましょう

When inviting others to do something, **〜ませんか** is used. When receiving an invitation, **〜ましょう** is used. **〜ましょう** is formed by changing **ます** of **〜ます** to **ましょう**, and it can be used to express your will to do something. **〜ません** is NOT used to refuse an invitation. Expressions like **すみません。ちょっと…** should be used instead.

Ex.1
A：いっしょに テニスを しませんか。
B：いいですね。しましょう。

Ex.2
A：ひるごはんを たべませんか。
B：○ すみません。わたしは もう たべました。
　　× いいえ、たべません。

Ex.1
A: Why don't we play tennis together?
B: That sounds nice. Let's!

Ex.2
A: Why don't we have lunch?
B: ○ Sorry. I already ate.
　　× No, I won't.

> **〜ましょう** is also used to make a stronger invitation.
>
> **Ex.**
> A：いっしょに おきなわへ いきませんか。
> B：おきなわですか。
> A：いきましょう。うみが きれいですよ。
> B：いいですね。いきましょう。
>
> **Ex.**
> A: Why don't we go to Okinawa together?
> B: Okinawa?
> A: Let's go. The beaches are beautiful.
> B: That sounds nice. Let's go.

5
-
1

2 ［＿＿＿＿＿＿＿＿＿］に いきます

When talking about something you are going to go do, **～に いきます** is used. The **～ます** form of verbs is called the **ます** form.

Conjunctive Form

verb ます form〈～ます〉	に いきます

Ex.1

わたしは 9じから サッカーを <u>しに</u> いきます。

Ex.1

I'm going to go play soccer from 9:00.

Ex.2

A：ひるごはんを <u>たべに いきません</u>か。

B：いきましょう。

Ex.2

A: Why don't we go eat lunch?

B: Let's go.

3 なにか・どこか・だれか ［＿＿＿＿＿＿＿＿＿＿＿＿＿＿］

When something is unclear or unknown, 【interrogative word】＋ か is used. **なにか** is used for things, **どこか** is used for places, **だれか** is used for people and **いつか** is used for time.

Ex.1

A：あついですね。<u>なにか</u> つめたい のみものを
　のみたいですね。

B：そうですね。アイスティーは どうですか。

A：いいですね。

Ex.1

A: It's hot, isn't it? I want to drink something cool.

B: Yes. How about iced tea?

A: That sounds great.

Ex.2

A：すみません。<u>なにか</u> かく ものは ありますか。

B：はい。ボールペンが ありますよ。

Ex.2

A: Excuse me. Do you have something to write with?

B: Yes. I have a ball-point pen.

なにが, なにを, どこが, どこへ, だれが, だれに or **いつが** are used when asking about a specific thing, place, person or time.

Ex.1

A：<u>なにか</u> たべたいですね。

B：<u>なにが</u> たべたいですか。

A：あまいものが たべたいです。

Ex.1

A: I want to eat something.

B: What do you want to eat?

A: I want to eat something sweet.

A：なつやすみに どこか いきませんか。

B：いいですね。どこへ いきたいですか。

A：どこか やまが いいですね。

A: Why don't we go somewhere for summer vacation?

B: Sure. Where do you want to go?

A: I'd like someplace that has mountains.

Vocabulary and Expression 😋

おなかが すきました be hungry ／なんめいさま How many people

きんえんせき non-smoking seat ／きつえんせき smoking seat ／では okay, well

こちら this way

はなび fireworks ／おでかけ going out ／くうこう airport ／むかえます pick up

ヨガ yoga ／ほんとうです really ／ききます ask ／〜にん：３にん 〜 people: three people

Conversation Scenario 💬

〈Going to a restaurant〉

Marie: I'm hungry. Why don't we go get something to eat?

Kim: Okay. Let's go.

Clerk: Welcome. How many people are there?

Marie: Two.

Clerk: We have smoking and non-smoking seats.

Kim: Non-smoking seats, please.

Clerk: Okay. This way, please.

5-1

2 ケーキに します

☐ You can talk about what you want on the menu.

☐ You can ask if you don't understand something on the menu.

Grammar Notes ✏

1 どれに しますか ―（わたしは）　　　　　　　　に します

When asking someone to make a selection from a group of things right in front of them, **どれに しますか** is used. When you have decided what you want, **〜に します** is used.

Conjunctive Form

どれ	に	しますか

（わたしは）	noun	に	します

Ex.

（アイスクリームのみせで）

A：どれに しますか。

B：わたしは チョコレートに します。Aさんは？

A：わたしは ナッツに します。

Ex.

(At an ice cream store)

A: What would you like?

B: I'll have chocolate ice cream. How about you, A-san?

A: I'll have nuts.

◆When the group of things is not limited, **なんに しますか** is used.

Ex.

（かいしゃで）

A：きょうの ひるごはん、なんに しますか。

B：カレーに しませんか。

A：いいですね。そうしましょう。

Ex.

(At work)

A: What shall we get for lunch today?

B: How about curry?

A: That sounds nice. Let's do that.

2　　　　　　　　は なんですか ― 　　　　　　　です

When asking what something is, **〜 は なんですか** is used. The form **〜、なんですか**, with the **は** omitted, can also be used.

Conjunctive Form

noun demonstrative	は 、	なんですか

Ex.1
A：きょうの おべんとうは なんですか。
B：サンドイッチですよ。

Ex.2
A：Bさんの しゅみは なんですか。
B：りょこうです。

Ex.3
A：それは なんですか。
B：これは にほんごの ほんです。

Ex.4
A：これ、なんですか。
B：ねこの おもちゃです。

Ex.1
A: What bento are you having today?
B: Sandwiches.

Ex.2
A: What are your hobbies, B-san?
B: Traveling.

Ex.3
A: What's that?
B: This is a Japanese language book.

Ex.4
A: What's this?
B: It's a cat toy.

5-2

Interrogatory Expressions

・When asking who・・・**だれですか**（☞ Lesson 1-1）
・When asking how many・・・**いくつですか**（☞ Lesson 2-1）
・When asking how much (price)・・・**いくらですか**（☞ Lesson 2-1）
・When asking where・・・**どこですか**（☞ Lesson 2-2, Lesson 3-2, Lesson 3-3, Lesson 4-3）
・When asking when・・・**いつですか**

Ex.1
A：バスていは どこですか。
B：コンビニの まえです。

Ex.2
A：たんじょうびは いつですか。
B：11がつ11にちです。

Ex.1
A: Where is the bus stop?
B: It's in front of the convenience store.

Ex.2
A: When is your birthday?
B: It's November 11.

Ex.3

A：あの ひとは <u>だれですか</u>。

B：トムさんの おにいさんです。

Ex.3

A: Who is that person?

B: That's Tom-san's older brother.

Vocabulary and Expression 😺

いろいろ many things, a lot of things, various things ／それと and

そうですねえ… Let's see... ／しょしょう おまちください One moment, please. ／こちら this

かしこまりました Understood.

おちゃ green tea ／ストロベリー strawberry ／ランチ lunch

チキン chicken ／アボカド avocado ／てんぷら tempura ／スパゲッティー spaghetti

とうふ tofu ／ハンバーグ hamburger steak ／メニュー menu ／カレーライス curry and rice

ピザ pizza ／ラーメン ramen ／そば soba, buckwheat noodles

Conversation Scenario 💬

〈Ordering〉

Kim: Wow, there are so many. What are you going to get?

Marie: I'm going to have chocolate cake. And coffee. How about you, Kim-san?

Kim: Let's see... Excuse me. What's today's cake?

Clerk: One moment, please... This is it.

Kim: Wow! What's this?

Clerk: It's apple cake.

Kim: Then I'll have this. And coffee, too, please.

Marie: I'll have this and coffee, please.

Clerk: Okay. One cake of the day, one chocolate cake and two coffees.

Marie and Kim: Right.

Clerk: Okay.

3 おいしいですね

Can-do Check ✓

☐ You can talk about how the food tastes.

☐ You can express what you want.

Grammar Notes ✎

1 ［　　　　　　　　　］は［　　　　　　　　　］です

When describing how something taste, 【noun (food)】 は 【い adjective for taste】 です is used.

Conjunctive Form

noun (food)	は	い adjective for taste	です

Here are some い adjectives that can be used to describe tastes.

い adjective	おいしい delicious	まずい bad tasting	あまい sweet	からい spicy, hot
Negative form	おいしくない not delicious	まずくない not bad tasting	あまくない not sweet	からくない not spicy, not hot

い adjective	すっぱい sour	にがい bitter	しおからい salty
Negative form	すっぱくない not sour	にがくない not bitter	しおからくない not salty

Ex.

A：どうですか。からいですか。

B：いいえ、からくないです。

Ex.

A: How is it? Is it spicy?

B: No, it's not spicy.

2 　　　X　　　 。でも、　　　Y　　　

When something (Y) is different from what expected given (X), 〜。**でも、**〜 is used.

Ex.1

ともだちの いえへ いきました。でも、ともだちは いませんでした。

Ex.1

I went to my friend's house. But my friend wasn't there.

Ex.2

きょうは てんきが いいです。でも、さむいです。

Ex.2

The weather is nice today. But it's cold.

3 　わたしは　　　　　　　　　が ほしいです

When talking about something you want, **わたしは 〜が ほしいです** is used.
〜さんは【noun】が ほしいと おもって います is used to talk about something someone else wants. However, **（あなたは）【noun】が ほしいですか** is used when asking what someone else wants.

Conjunctive Form

わたしは	noun	が	ほしいです	
〜さんは			ほしい	と おもっています

Ex.1

わたしは あたらしい かばんが ほしいです。

Ex.1

I want a new bag.

Ex.2

○ キムさんは パソコンが ほしいと おもって います。
△ キムさんは パソコンが ほしいです。

Ex.2

Kim-san wants a computer.

Ex.3

A：Bさんは いま なにが ほしいですか。
B：わたしは あたらしい じてんしゃが ほしいです。

Ex.3

A: B-san, what do you want right now?
B: I want a new bicycle.

Vocabulary and Expression 😊

いただきます Let's eat. ／しょうゆ soy sauce ／とって ください Pass ..., please.
からい spicy, hot ／わさび wasabi ／とても very, really

いちご strawberry ／あまい sweet ／すっぱい sour ／にがい bitter ／しおからい salty
さとう sugar ／ミルク milk ／なつやすみ summer holiday ／おかね money
（でんわに）でます answer the phone ／（お）たんじょうび birthday ／（お）はし chopsticks
ふきのとう butterbur sprout ／たらこ salted roe

Conversation Scenario 💬

〈Eating sushi〉

Shin: Thank you for this meal.

Inoue: Thank you for this meal.

Shin: Excuse me, could you pass the soy sauce?

Inoue: Sure. Here you are.

Shin: Thank you... Wow! This is delicious.

Inoue: Yes, it is.

Shin: But, it's spicy! What's this?

Inoue: That's wasabi.

Shin: Ooh, wasabi? It's really spicy. I want some water.

Inoue: Excuse me. Water, please.

5-3

1 りょこうします

Can-do Check ✓

☐ You can ask and answer questions about holiday plans.

☐ You can express simple reasons.

Grammar Notes 🖊

1

い ですか { はい、　　　　　　い です
　　　　　　いいえ、　　　　　　　く ないです }

When asking a question with an **い** adjective, **か** is added to the end of the sentence, as in 【noun】 は 【い adjective】 です か.

The negative form of **い** adjectives such as **おいしい** and **おおきい** is **～くない** or **おいしくない** and **おおきくない**.

Conjunctive Form

noun	は	い adjective 〈～い〉	ですか

はい、	い adjective 〈～い〉	です
いいえ、	い adjective 〈～い くない〉	

Careful !

Keep in mind that the negative form of **いい** is **よくない**.

Ex.1

A：その くつは <u>おおきいですか</u>。

B：<u>はい</u>、すこし <u>おおきいです</u>。

Ex.1

A: Are those shoes big?

B: Yes, they're a little big.

Ex.2

A：そちらの てんきは <u>いいですか</u>。

B：<u>いいえ、よくないです</u>。あめが ふって います。

Ex.2

A: Is the weather good there?

B: No, it's not. It's raining.

2　　X　から、　Y

When saying a reason for something, **から** is added after the reason. When 【sentence X】 is the reason for 【sentence Y】, 【**sentence X**】 **から、**【**sentence Y**】 is used. 【**sentence Y**】。【**sentence X**】 **から**。 can also be used.

Conjunctive Form

reason	から、	～

Ex.

あたまが いたいですから、かいしゃを やすみます。

Ex.

My head hurts, so I'm going to take the day off from work.

◆When asking a reason, **どうしてですか**。 is used. **～から**。 is used when answering with a reason.

Ex.

A：きょうは はやく かえります。

B：どうしてですか。

A：みたい ドラマが ありますから。

Ex.

A: I'm going home early today.

B: Why?

A: Because there's a TV show I want to watch.

3　どこも・なにも・だれも　　　ません

When emphasizing the negative form, 【**interrogative word**】 **も ～ません**, with **も** added after an interrogative word, is used.

Conjunctive Form

どこ		
なに	も	～ません
だれ		

Ex.1

きょうは さむかったですから、どこも いきませんでした。

Ex.1

Today was cold, so I didn't go anywhere.

Ex.2

じゅぎょうが おわりましたから、みんな かえりました。

きょうしつに だれも いません。

Ex.2

Classes ended, so everyone went home. There's no one in the classroom.

6
-
1

Vocabulary and Expression 😊

りょこうします travel ／れんきゅう long weekend, long holiday ／（お）まつり festival

とおい far ／あまり not really, not very ／しけん test ／たいへんですね That sounds tough.

ちかい close, near ／いい good ／わるい bad ／あたらしい new ／ふるい old

おおい a lot, many ／すくない few ／はやい fast ／おそい slow ／たのしい fun

むずかしい difficult, hard ／いそがしい busy ／にもつ luggage, baggage ／あね older sister

けっこんします get married ／おわります finish ／は tooth ／いたい hurt

ダイビング diving ／どうしてですか Why is that? ／へや room ／けさ this morning

きょうしつ classroom ／たいふう typhoon ／やま mountain ／のぼります climb

DVD DVD ／かります rent, borrow
ディーブイディー

Conversation Scenario 💬

〈Talking about plans for a holiday〉

Tang: Tanaka-san, what are you going to do over the extended weekend?

Tanaka: I'm going to Kyoto. I'm going to see a festival there.

Tang: Kyoto? Is that far away?

Tanaka: It's not that far. It's about two hours on the shinkansen.

Tang: Really?

Tanaka: Are you going anywhere, Tang-san?

Tang: No, I'm not. I have a test, so I'm going to study at home.

Tanaka: I see. That's tough.

Can-do Check ✓

☐ You can ask and answer questions about travel spots.
☐ You can talk about what's famous about travel spots.

Grammar Notes 🖊

1 　　　　　　な　　　　　　

Adjectives that have **な** before the noun they modify are called **な** adjectives.

ゆうめいな みせ 　famous store

げんきな 人　healthy person
　　　　ひと

きれいな へや　clean room

べんりな のりもの　convenient vehicle

しんせつな 人　kind person
　　　　　ひと

Conjunctive Form

な adjective〈～な〉	noun

Ex.1
ここは ゆうめいな みせです。

Ex.1
This is a famous store.

Ex.2
たなかさんは げんきな 人です。
　　　　　　　　　　　　ひと

Ex.2
Tanaka-san is a healthy person.

When used right before **～です**, the **な** is omitted.

Ex.1
やまださんは しんせつです。

Ex.1
Yamada-san is kind.

Ex.2
この コップは きれいです。

Ex.2
This cup is clean.

6-2

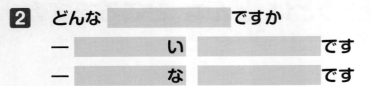

2 どんな ▢▢▢▢ですか
　　— ▢▢▢ い ▢▢▢▢ です
　　— ▢▢▢ な ▢▢▢▢ です

When asking about specific aspects of people, places or things, **どんな ～ですか** is used. When answering, **～い ～です** is used for **い** adjectives, and **～な ～です** is used for **な** adjectives.

Conjunctive Form

どんな	noun	ですか

い adjective 〈～い〉	noun	です
な adjective 〈～な〉		

Ex.1

A：とうきょうは <u>どんな</u> まちですか。

B：<u>大きい</u> まちです。<u>にぎやかな</u> まちです。
　　_{おお}

Ex.2

A：やまださんは <u>どんな</u> 人ですか。
　　　　　　　　　　　　　_{ひと}

B：<u>しんせつな</u> 人です。
　　　　　　　　_{ひと}

Ex.3

A：たなかさんの かばんは <u>どんな</u> かばんですか。

B：<u>あたらしい</u> かばんです。

Ex.1

A: What kind of city is Tokyo?

B: It's a big city. It's a lively city.

Ex.2

A: What kind of a person is Yamada-san?

B: He's a kind person.

Ex.3

A: What kind of a bag is Tanaka-san's bag?

B: It's a new bag.

3 ▢▢▢▢▢です
　　　　　▢▢▢▢▢ じゃ ありません ／ ▢▢▢▢▢ じゃ ないです

な adjectives are conjugated the same way as nouns.

げんき<u>です</u>　I'm fine.

げんき<u>じゃ ありません</u>／げんき<u>じゃ ないです</u>　I'm not fine.

げんき<u>でした</u>　I was fine.

げんき<u>じゃ ありませんでした</u>／げんき<u>じゃ なかったです</u>　I was not fine.

Conjunctive Form

な adjective 〈〜な〉	です
な adjective 〈〜な じゃ〉	ありません
	ないです

い adjectives and な adjectives

In Japanese, there are い adjectives that use 〜い to modify the nouns they come before, and な adjectives that use 〜な (☞ Lesson 2-3, Lesson 6-1).

Conjugating い adjectives and な adjectives

	い adjective	な adjective
Modifying nouns	おおきい かばん	かんたんな かんじ
Normal form	おおきいです	かんたんです
Negative form	おおきくないです	かんたんじゃ ありません かんたんじゃ ないです
Past form	おおきかったです	かんたんでした
Past negative form	おおきくなかったです	かんたんじゃ ありませんでした かんたんじゃ なかったです

6-2

Careful!

きれい and ゆうめい both end in い, but they are not い adjectives. They are な adjectives.

	きれい	ゆうめい
Modifying nouns	きれいな はな	ゆうめいな ひと
Normal form	きれいです	ゆうめいです
Negative form	きれいじゃ ありません きれいじゃ ないです	ゆうめいじゃ ありません ゆうめいじゃ ないです
Past form	きれいでした	ゆうめいでした
Past negative form	きれいじゃ ありませんでした きれいじゃ なかったです	ゆうめいじゃ ありませんでした ゆうめいじゃ なかったです

4

とても [____]
ちょっと [____]
あまり [____] **ません** / [____] **ないです**

Words can be added before or after adjectives to express their degree or quality. **とても** (very) and **ちょっと／すこし** (a little) are often used this way. **あまり 〜くないです** is used for **い** adjectives to show that the degree of the adjective is not that great, and **あまり 〜 じゃありません／ないです** is used in the same way for **な** adjectives.

Conjunctive Form

とても	い adjective	
ちょっと	な adjective	
あまり	い adjective 〈〜い く〉	ないです
	な adjective〈〜な じゃ〉	ありません
		ないです

Ex.1
きょうは とても さむいです。でかけません。

Ex.1
Today is very cold. I don't go out.

Ex.2
この りょうりは ちょっと からいです。

Ex.2
This food is a little spicy.

Ex.3
たなかさんは あまり げんきじゃ ありません。

Ex.3
Tanaka-san isn't very healthy.

Vocabulary and Expression

ところ place ／まち town ／（お）てら temple ／たくさん a lot, many

ゆうめい（な）famous ／きれい（な）pretty ／にわ yard ／たべもの food

まっちゃ Matcha, powdered green tea ／おかし candy, snacks ／にんきが あります It's popular.

げんき（な）lively, energetic ／しんせつ（な）nice, friendly ／へん（な）strange ／かお face

べんり（な）convenient ／もの things ／たいせつ（な）important ／ひま（な）free, open

じかん time ／たいへん（な）difficult, hard, tough ／かんたん（な）easy, simple

かんじ Kanji, Chinese characters ／きれい（な）clean ／て hand

にぎやか（な）lively, bustling ／しずか（な）quiet ／すき（な）favorite ／きらい（な）hate

じょうず（な）good at ／へた（な）bad at ／ちらしずし scattered sushi ／しかくい square, cubed

そふ grandfather ／プレゼント present, gift ／スポーツ sports

しゅっちょうします make a business trip ／（お）しろ castle ／たてもの building

びじゅつかん art museum ／みそかつ fried pork cutlet with miso sauce

Conversation Scenario 💬

⟨Introducing travel spots⟩

Tang: What kind of a place is Kyoto?

Tanaka: It's an old town. There are many temples.

Tang: I see.

Tanaka: There are some pictures of it here.

Tang: Ah, that's a famous temple.

Tanaka: It's Kinkaku-ji.

Tang: Wow! This is a beautiful garden.

Tanaka: Yes.

Tang: Is this a famous temple, too?

Tanaka: No, it's not that famous. But it is very beautiful.

Tang: That's great.

Tanaka: There are many delicious kinds of food, too. Matcha flavored sweets are popular.

Tang: Really? I want to go, too.

6-2

3 りょこうは どうでしたか

Can-do Check ✓

☐ You can ask and answer questions about how a trip was.

☐ You can say what you thought of a place.

Grammar Notes 🖊

1　　　　かった です
　　　　くなかった です

The past tense form of **い** adjectives is **〜かったです**, and the negative past tense form is **〜くなかったです**.

Careful !

The past tense form of the **い** adjective **いい** is **よかったです**, and its negative past tense form is **よくなかったです**.

Ex.1
きのうは とても あつかったです。

Ex.1
It was very hot yesterday.

Ex.2
きのうの テストは むずかしくなかったです。

Ex.2
Yesterday's test was not hard.

2　　　　　　　でした
　　　　じゃ ありませんでした ／ 　　　　じゃ なかったです

The past tense form of **な** adjectives is **〜でした**, and the negative past tense form is **〜じゃ ありませんでした** or **〜じゃ なかったです**.

Ex.1
きのうの おまつりは にぎやかでした。

Ex.1
Yesterday's festival was lively.

Ex.2
きのう やまださんに あいました。
やまださんは げんきじゃ ありませんでした。

Ex.2
Yesterday, I met Yamada-san.
Yamada-san was not in good spirits.

3 _____ は どうですか
_____ は どうでしたか

When asking how something is, **どうですか** is used for the present tense, and **どうでし
たか** is used for the past tense.

Conjunctive Form

noun	は	どうですか
		どうでしたか

Ex.1

A：とうきょうは <u>どうですか</u>。

B：みちが きれいです。

C：人が おおいです。
 (ひと)

Ex.2

A：きのうの おまつりは <u>どうでしたか</u>。

B：とても にぎやかでした。

Ex.1

A: How is Tokyo?

B: The streets are clean.

C: There are a lot of people.

Ex.2

A: How was the festival yesterday?

B: It was very lively.

Vocabulary and Expression 🎴

りょこう travel, trip ／ただいま I'm back., I'm home.

おかえりなさい Welcome back[home]. ／あめが ふります rain

パーティー party ／おととい the day before yesterday, two days ago ／コンサート concert

せんげつ last month ／ひっこします move ／ひろい big, wide, spacious

ゆきまつり snow festival

Conversation Scenario 💬

〈Giving impressions of a trip〉

Tanaka: I'm home.

Tang: Welcome home. How was your trip?

Tanaka: It was fun.

Tang: I see. That's great.

Tanaka: But the weather wasn't so good.

Tang: Did it rain?

6
-
3

75

Tanaka: No, it didn't rain.

Tang: That's good. Did you take any pictures?

Tanaka: Yes. I took a lot.

Tang: Wow! There are a lot of people. Is this a festival?

Tanaka: Yes. It was very lively. Here, this is a souvenir for you.

Tang: Oh! It's matcha sweets. Thank you.

1 しゅうまつ、なに する?

Can-do Check ✓

☐ You can talk about weekend plans with your teacher.
☐ You can talk about weekend plans with your friends.

Grammar Notes 🖊

〈どうしの グループわけ〉 Verb Groups

Verbs are divided into three groups based on how they are conjugated.

ら	や	ま	は	な	た	さ	か	あ
り		み	ひ	に	ち	し	き	い
る	ゆ	む	ふ	ぬ	つ	す	く	う
れ		め	へ	ね	て	せ	け	え
ろ	よ	も	ほ	の	と	そ	こ	お

1 グループ ←

→ 2 グループ

Group I

These are verbs whose **ます** form stems end in a syllable containing the vowel [i].

Ex.

あいます meet   かきます write   いそぎます hurry   はなします talk

まちます wait   しにます die   よびます call   よみます read   とります take

Group II

These are verbs whose **ます** form stems end in a syllable containing the vowel [e].

Ex.

あけます open   ねます sleep   たべます eat   しめます close

Careful !

There are Group II verbs whose **ます** form stems may end in a syllable containing the vowel [i]. There are only a few such verbs, and they are considered to be irregular.

Ex.

います exist   (シャツを) きます wear   おきます wake up   あびます take (a shower)

みます see, watch   かります borrow   おります bend

7
-
1

Group Ⅲ

There are only two verbs in this group; **します** (do) and **（がっこうへ）きます** (come). **します** can also be used with nouns as in **【noun】＋します**, like in **べんきょうします** or **かいものします**.

1️⃣ じしょ形 Dictionary Form

Up to this point, all of the verbs introduced in this book were shown as ending in **〜ます**, such as **たべます** and **のみます**. This is called the **ます** form. However, when talking with friends, family and people that are close to you, forms like **たべる** and **のむ** are used instead of **ます** form. This form is called the dictionary form (**じしょ形**), as it is the form used to list verbs in dictionaries.

Ex.

A：あした なに する？

B：えいが 見る。

Ex.

A: What are you going to do tomorrow?

B: I'm going to watch a movie.

Omission of Particles

In conversation, particles may be omitted when the meaning of the sentence can be understood without them, such as in **なに（を）する？** or **えいが（を）見る**.

Ex.1

A：あした なに（を）しますか。

B：うちで えいが（を）見ます。

Ex.1

A: What are you going to do tomorrow?

B: I'm going to watch a movie at home.

Ex.2

A：あした なに（を）する？

B：うちで えいが（を）見る。

Ex.2

A: What are you going to do tomorrow?

B: I'm going to watch a movie at home.

Ex.3

A：きのう どこ（へ）行った？

B：しんじゅく（へ）行った。

Ex.3

A: Where did you go yesterday?

B: I went to Shinjuku.

Ex.4

A：わたしが おくった メール（を）見た？

B：見たよ。

Ex.4

A: Did you see the email I sent you?

B: I saw it.

Ex.5

A：すみません。きむらさん（は）いますか。

B：はい、います。あそこです。

Ex.5

A: Excuse me. Is Kimura-san there?

B: Yes, he is. He's over there.

1-1 Dictionary Form of Group I Verbs

The syllable before **ます** ending in [i] is changed to a syllable that ends in [u].

あいます meet → あう

かきます write → かく

はなします talk → はなす

まちます wait → まつ

しにます die → しぬ

よびます call → よぶ

よみます read → よむ

とります take → とる

Ex.

A：この 本、よむ？

B：うん、よむ。

Ex.

A: Are you going to read this book?

B: Yes, I will.

1-2 Dictionary Form of Group II Verbs

ます becomes **る**.

たべます eat → たべる

みます see, watch → みる

Ex.

A：なに たべる？

B：アイスクリーム たべる。

Ex.

A: What are you going to eat?

B: I'm going to eat ice cream.

7
-
1

1-3 Dictionary Form of Group III Verbs

します becomes する, and きます becomes くる. Thus, 【noun】＋します becomes 【noun】
＋する.

べんきょうします study → べんきょうする

そうじします clean → そうじする

Ex.

A：きょう としょかんで <u>べんきょうする</u>？

B：うん、<u>する</u>。

Ex.

A: Are you going to study in the library today?

B: Yeah, I am.

2 　　　　　　　　　　に 行きます

When talking about the purpose of someone going somewhere, **〜に 行きます** is used.

Conjunctive Form

noun	に	行きます

かいもの → かいものに 行く go shopping

りょこう → りょこうに 行く go traveling

Ex.1

日よう日は 友だちと <u>かいものに 行きます</u>。

Ex.1

On Sunday, I'm going to go shopping with my friend.

Ex.2

ほっかいどうへ <u>りょこうに 行きます</u>。

Ex.2

I'm going on to Hokkaido to travel.

＊The **ます** form root of verbs can also be used in **〜に 行きます** (☞ Lesson 5-1).

Vocabulary and Expression 🐞

ジャズ jazz ／ねえ hey ／ぼく I ／カラオケ Karaoke

- -

せつめいします explain ／会います meet ／バーベキュー barbeque ／うん yeah

すわります sit ／CD CD ／さきに ahead, first ／(お) はなみ flower viewing

かいもの shopping ／ゴルフ golf ／キャンプ camp ／ミュージカル musical

いそぎます hurry (up) ／まちます wait ／よびます call ／あけます open ／おります get off

Conversation Scenario 💬

⟨Talking about the weekend⟩

Aoki: We're off of school tomorrow. Good bye.

Tang and Kim: Good bye.

Aoki: Lama-san, what are you going to do this weekend?

Lama: I'm going to play soccer with Tang-san. How about you?

Aoki: I'm going to a jazz concert on Saturday.

Lama: That sounds nice.

Marie: Hey, what are you going to do this weekend?

Lama: I'm going to play soccer with Tang-san. How about you?

Marie: I'm going to karaoke with Kim-san.

Lama: Karaoke! That's great.

7-1

2 わたしは 行かない
い

Can-do Check ✔

☐ You can tell your teacher whether you will participate in a weekend event or not.

☐ You know how to tell your friend whether you will participate in a weekend event or not.

Grammar Notes ✏

1 ない形 ない Form
けい

～ません becomes **～ない** when speaking with one's friends and family. This form is called the **ない** form (**ない形**).
けい

1 -1 ない Form of Group I Verbs

The syllable before **ます** ending in [i] is changed to a syllable that ends in [a].

かきます write → かかない

はなします speak → はなさない

まちます wait → またない

しにます die → しなない

よびます call → よばない

よみます read → よまない

とります take → とらない

Careful!

～います becomes **～わない**.

あいます meet → あわない

いいます say → いわない

Ex.

A：コンビニ、行く？
い

B：ううん、行かない。
い

Ex.

A: Are you going to the convenience store?

B: No, I'm not.

The **ない** form of **あります** is **ない**.

ます form	Dictionary form	**ない** form
あります	ある	ない

1-2　**ない** Form of Group **II** Verbs

ます becomes **ない**.

たべます eat → たべない

みます see, watch → みない

Ex.

A：えいが、見る？

B：ううん、見ない。

Ex.

A: Do you want to see a movie?

B: No, I don't.

1-3　**ない** Form of Group **III** Verbs

します becomes **しない**, and **きます** becomes **こない**. 【**noun**】＋ **します** becomes 【**noun**】

＋ **しない**.

べんきょうします study → べんきょうしない

そうじします clean → そうじしない

Ex.

A：ゲーム、する？

B：ううん、しない。

Ex.

A: Do you want to play a game?

B: No, I don't.

2　　　　　　　**ない ？** { うん、 　　　　　　　　　 ／ ううん、　　　　　　　**ない**

When inviting friends and family to do something, **〜ない？** is used instead of **〜ません**

か. **うん、**【**verb dictionary form**】 is used instead of **はい、 〜ます** to reply to an invitation.

Furthermore, **ううん、**【**verb ない form**】 is used instead of **いいえ、 〜ません**. It may be

best to follow this up with a reason for your refusal, so as not to sound rude.

Ex.1

A：日よう日、かいものに 行かない？

B：うん、行く。

Ex.1

A: Do you want to go shopping on
　Sunday?

B: Yeah, I do.

Ex.2

A：あした サッカーを <u>しない</u>？

B：<u>ううん、しない</u>。月よう日に テストが あるから。
　　ごめんね。

Ex.2

A: Do you want to play soccer
tomorrow?

B: No, I don't. I have a test on Monday.
Sorry.

3　どうして？ ― ░░░░░░░ から。

When talking with friends and family, **どうして？** is used instead of **どうしてですか**。
【verb dictionary form】から。 or **【verb ない form】から**。 is used instead of **〜ますから**。
or **〜ませんから**。 when replying.

Ex.

A：きょうは はやく ねる。

B：<u>どうして</u>？

A：あした りょこうに 行く<u>から</u>。

Ex.

A: I'm going to bed early today.

B: Why?

A: Because I'm going on a trip
tomorrow.

Vocabulary and Expression 😀

バーベキュー大会 barbeque party ／たのしみ（な）exciting

ううん No ／まんが manga, Japanese comics ／はい Here you are. ／すし sushi

しあい match, game ／こんばん tonight, this evening ／のみかい drinking party

こうりゅうパーティー (cultural) exchange party

Conversation Scenario 💬

〈Looking at a poster of a barbeque party〉

Aoki: There's a barbeque party this Sunday. Are you going, Tang-san?

Tang: Yes, I'm going. Are you?

Aoki: I'm going, too. I'm looking forward to it.

Marie: There's a barbeque party this Sunday. Are you going?

Tang: Yeah, I'm going.

Kim: I'm not going.

Marie: What? You're not going? Why not?

Kim: I have to get to my part-time job.

Tang: I see.

Can-do Check ✓

☐ You can ask a friend or a teacher about something you don't know.

☐ You can talk about how you feel.

Grammar Notes ✏

1

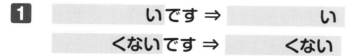

いです ⇒ 　　　　い
くないです ⇒ 　　　　くない

【い adjective】or【い adjective】くない is used instead of【い adjective】です or【い adjective】くない です when talking with friends and family.【い adjective】? with a rising intonation at the end is used when asking a question.

Ex.1

A：あつい？

B：うん、あつい。

Ex.1

A: Is it hot?

B: Yeah, it is.

Ex.2

A：いま いそがしい？

B：ううん、いそがしくない。

Ex.2

A: Are you busy now?

B: No, I'm not.

2

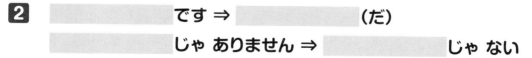

です ⇒ 　　　　　（だ）
じゃ ありません ⇒ 　　　　じゃ ない

【な adjective】or【な adjective】じゃ ない is used instead of【な adjective】です or【な adjective】じゃ ありません when talking with friends and family.【な adjective】? with a rising intonation at the end is used when asking a question.

【な adjective】だ is generally not used by women when speaking, but【な adjective】だ＋よ／ね is used by both men and women. ね is used when seeking sympathy or understanding from the listener, and よ is used when informing the listener of something they may not know.

7
-
3

Ex.1

A：あした ひま？

B：うん、<u>ひま</u>。

Ex.2

A：げんき？

B：うん、<u>げんきだ**よ**</u>。

Ex.3

A：このアプリ、<u>べんりだ**ね**</u>。

B：うん、<u>べんりだ**ね**</u>。

Ex.1

A: Are you free tomorrow?

B: Yeah, I am.

Ex.2

A: Are you doing alright?

B: Yeah, I am.

Ex.3

A: This app is convenient, isn't it?

B: Yeah, it is.

3　　　　　　です ⇒ 　　　　　　（だ）

　　　　　　じゃ ありません ⇒ 　　　　　　じゃ ない

【noun】 or 【noun】 じゃ ない is used instead of 【noun】 です or 【noun】 じゃ ありません when talking with friends and family. 【noun】？ with a rising intonation at the end is used when asking a question.

【noun】 だ is generally not used by women when speaking, but 【noun】 だ ＋ よ／ね is used by both men and women. ね is used when seeking sympathy or understanding from the listener, and よ is used when informing the listener of something they may not know.

Ex.1

A：あした 休_{やす}み？

B：うん、<u>休_{やす}み</u>。

Ex.2

A：あの 人_{ひと}、日本人_{にほんじん}？

B：ううん。<u>インドネシア人だ**よ**</u>。

A：日本_{にほん}ご、<u>じょうずだ**ね**</u>。

Ex.3

A：これ、いい <u>しゃしんだ**ね**</u>。

B：うん、<u>いい**ね**</u>。

Ex.1

A: Is tomorrow a day off?

B: Yes, it is.

Ex.2

A: Is that person Japanese?

B: No. He's Indonesian.

A: He can speak Japanese well.

Ex.3

A: This is a nice picture, isn't it?

B: Yeah, it is.

4 なんですか ⇒ なに？
　　いつですか ⇒ いつ？
　　どこですか ⇒ どこ？

【interrogative word】？ is used instead of 【interrogative word】 ですか when talking with friends and family. 【interrogative word】？ with a rising intonation at the end is used when asking a question. Particles such as は, が, を and へ are often omitted.

Ex.1

A：それ、<u>なに？</u>

B：ちゅうごくの おちゃ。

Ex.2

A：テスト、あるよ。

B：え、<u>いつ？</u>

A：あした。

B：え！

Ex.3

A：その かばん、<u>どう？</u>

B：おもい。

Ex.1

A: What's that?

B: It's Chinese tea.

Ex.2

A: There's a test.

B: What? When?

A: Tomorrow.

B: What?!

Ex.3

A: How about that bag?

B: It's heavy.

Vocabulary and Expression

わかります know ／じゃがいも potato ／バター butter ／うわあ wow ／はやく hurry, quickly
あれ Huh? ／ほんとうだ You're right., Oh yeah.

あつい hot (things) ／かたい hard ／木 wood ／グラス glass ／みんな everyone, everybody
こんしゅう this week ／あさって the day after tomorrow, two days later ／もうすぐ soon
つきます arrive ／いくら salmon roe ／もう ひとつ one more ／すじこ salted salmon roe
スポーツセンター sports center

7-3

Conversation Scenario 💬

⟨Having a barbeque⟩

Marie: What's this?

Tang: I don't know. I wonder what it could be. Sensei, what's this?

Aoki: Oh, that's a potato. You eat it with butter. It's delicious.

Tang: Wow, I want to try it now.

- -

Tang: Huh? Something is weird about this. This isn't a potato.

Marie: Yeah. Mine isn't weird.

Aoki: Tang-san, that's a potato, too. Please try it.

Tang: Oh, you're right. It's delicious.

1 友だちと サッカーしたよ
とも

Can-do Check ✓

☐ You can ask and talk to your friends about what they did at the weekend.

Grammar Notes ✏

1 た形 た Form
けい

When talking about past events with friends and family, **～た** or **～だ** is used instead of **～ました**, as in **たべた** or **のんだ**. This is called **た** form (**た形**).
けい

Ex.
A: ごはん、食べた？
　　　　た
B: うん、食べた。
　　　　　た

Ex.
A: Did you eat?
B: Yeah, I did.

1-1 た Form of Group I Verbs

た form verb conjugation varies depending on syllable ending in [i] that comes before **ます**.

┌─────────────────┐
│ **い・ち・り → った** │
└─────────────────┘

The **た** form of verbs that end in **～います**, **～ちます** and **～ります** is **～った**.

か<u>い</u>ます buy → か<u>った</u>

ま<u>ち</u>ます wait → ま<u>った</u>

と<u>り</u>ます take → と<u>った</u>

┌─────────────────┐
│ **に・び・み → んだ** │
└─────────────────┘

The **た** form of verbs that end in **～にます**, **～びます** and **～みます** is **～んだ**.

し<u>に</u>ます die → し<u>んだ</u>　（しにます is the only ～にます verb.）

あそ<u>び</u>ます play → あそ<u>んだ</u>

よ<u>み</u>ます read → よ<u>んだ</u>

8
-
1

し → した

The **た** form of **〜します** is **〜した**.

はな<u>し</u>ます speak → はな<u>した</u>

か<u>し</u>ます lend → か<u>した</u>

き → いた ／ ぎ → いだ

The **た** form of **〜きます** and **〜ぎます** is **〜いた** and **〜いだ**, respectively.

か<u>き</u>ます write → か<u>いた</u>

いそ<u>ぎ</u>ます hurry → いそ<u>いだ</u>

Ex.

A：レポート、<u>かいた</u>？

B：うん、<u>かいた</u>。

Ex.

A: Did you write the report?

B: Yeah, I did.

Careful !

The **た** form of **いきます** is **いった**. It is not **いいた**.

1-2　**た Form of Group Ⅱ Verbs**

ます becomes **た**.

たべます eat → たべ<u>た</u>

みます see, watch → み<u>た</u>

Ex.

A：きのう テレビ <u>見_みた</u>？

B：うん、<u>見_みた</u>。

Ex.

A: Did you watch TV yesterday?

B: Yeah, I did.

1-3 た Form of Group Ⅲ Verbs

します becomes した, and きます becomes きた. 【noun】＋しました becomes 【noun】＋した.

べんきょうします study → べんきょうした

そうじします clean → そうじした

Ex.1

A：きのう としょかんで べんきょうした？

B：うん、した。

Ex.2

A：けさ なんじに がっこうへ 来た？

B：8じはんに 来た。

Ex.1

A: Did you study in the library yesterday?

B: Yeah, I did.

Ex.2

A: What time did you come to school this morning?

B: I came at 8:30.

The た form of ～ませんでした is ～なかった.

かきません → かきませんでした　　かかない → かかなかった

ます form	Present negative		Past negative	
かきます write	かきません	かかない	かきませんでした	かかなかった
たべます eat	たべません	たべない	たべませんでした	たべなかった
します do	しません	しない	しませんでした	しなかった
きます come	きません	こない	きませんでした	こなかった

Ex.1

A：きのう かいものに 行った？

B：ううん、行かなかった。

Ex.2

A：きのう がっこうへ 来なかったね。

B：うん、あたまが いたかったから、休んだ。

Ex.1

A: Did you go shopping yesterday?

B: No, I didn't.

Ex.2

A: You didn't come to school yesterday.

B: Yeah, I took the day off because my head hurt.

8-1

こうりゅう会 (cultural) exchange meeting [party] ／たちます stand ／名前 name

しゅくだい homework ／出します give, assign ／エアコン air conditioner, AC

あそびます play, hang out ／うたいます sing ／もちます carry, hold

しにます die ／休みます take a break, have a holiday, rest ／かします lend ／あるきます walk

Conversation Scenario 💬

〈Talking about what you did at the weekend〉

Kim: Good morning. Did you go to the barbeque?

Tang: Yeah, I did.

Kim: How was it?

Marie: It was fun. I ate a lot.

Kim: Great. Did you go to the barbeque, too, Lama-san?

Lama: No, I didn't go. I played soccer with my friends.

Kim: I see.

Lama: What about you, Kim-san?

Kim: I worked at my part-time job. It was Sunday, so it was busy.

Tang: Oh, that sounds tough.

☐ You can talk to your friends about what you did on your day off.

Grammar Notes

1

| かった です ⇒ | かった |
| くなかった です ⇒ | くなかった |

〜かった or 〜くなかった are used instead of 〜かったです or 〜くなかったです when speaking with friends and family and using **い** adjectives in the past tense.

Ex.1
A：ごちそうさま。おいしかったね。
B：うん、おいしかった。

Ex.1
A: Thanks for the meal. It was delicious.
B: Yeah, it was good.

Ex.2
A：きのうの しけん、むずかしかった？
B：ううん、むずかしくなかった。

Ex.2
A: Was yesterday's test hard?
B: No, it wasn't.

2

| でした ⇒ | だった |
| じゃ ありませんでした
じゃ なかったです | じゃ なかった |

〜だった or 〜じゃ なかった are used instead of 〜でした or 〜じゃ ありませんでした／じゃ なかったです when speaking with friends and family and using **な** adjectives in the past tense.
どうでしたか becomes どうだった.

Ex.1
A：ひっこし、たいへんだった？
B：うん、たいへんだった。

Ex.1
A: Was moving hard?
B: Yeah, it was.

8
–
2

Ex.2

A：テスト、どうだった？ かんたんだった？

B：ううん、かんたんじゃ なかった。 むずかしかった。

Ex.2

A: How was the test? Was it easy?

B: No, it wasn't. It was hard.

3

でした ⇒	だった
じゃ ありませんでした じゃ なかったです	} じゃ なかった

〜だった or 〜じゃ なかった are used instead of 〜でした or 〜じゃ ありませんでした／じゃ なかったです when speaking with friends and family and using nouns in the past tense.

Ex.1

A：えき前の ピザの みせ、行った？

B：うん、行った。 でも、休みだった。

Ex.1

A: Did you go to the pizza shop in front of the station?

B: Yeah, I did. But it was closed.

Ex.2

A：やまださんに かさ、わたした？

B：あの かさ、やまださんのじゃ なかった。
　　たなかさんの だった。

Ex.2

A: Did you give Yamada-san an umbrella?

B: That umbrella isn't Yamada-san's. It's Tanaka-san's umbrella.

---

4 ふつう形 Plain Form

There are plain forms (ふつう形) of the positive present tense, negative present tense, positive past tense and negative past tense of verbs, い adjectives, な adjectives and nouns. These plain forms are used when speaking with friends and family.

		ふつう形 Plain form			
		Positive present	Negative present	Positive past	Negative past
verb	かきます write	かく	かかない	かいた	かかなかった
い adjective	あついです hot	あつい	あつくない	あつかった	あつくなかった
な adjective	げんきです fine	げんき（だ）	げんきじゃ ない	げんきだった	げんきじゃ なかった
noun	休みです closed	休み（だ）	休みじゃ ない	休みだった	休みじゃ なかった

Careful!

The verb **あります** and the **い** adjective **いいです** have special conjugations.

		ふつう形 Plain form			
		Positive present	Negative present	Positive past	Negative past
verb	あります exist	ある	ない	あった	なかった
い adjective	いいです good	いい	よくない	よかった	よくなかった

Ex.1

A：あした サッカーする？

B：うん、する。

Ex.2

A：ゆうびんきょく、ここから とおい？

B：ううん、とおくない。

Ex.3

A：その まんが、おもしろかった？

B：うん、おもしろかった。

Ex.4

A：アルバイト、たいへんだった？

B：ううん、たいへんじゃ なかった。

Ex.5

A：あの 人、先生？
　　　　 ひと　せんせい
B：ううん、先生じゃ ない。学生だよ。
　　　　 せんせい　　　　　　がくせい

Ex.1

A: Are you going to play soccer tomorrow?

B: Yeah, I am.

Ex.2

A: Is the post office far from here?

B: No, it's not.

Ex.3

A: Was that manga interesting?

B: Yeah, it was.

Ex.4

A: Was your part-time job a lot of work?

B: No, it wasn't.

Ex.5

A: Is that person a teacher?

B: No, she's not a teacher. She's a student.

8-2

Vocabulary and Expression 😃

ふうん Hmm.

あたたかい warm ／すずしい cool ／どうぶつえん zoo ／パンダ panda ／すごく very
かわいい cute ／えきまえ in front of the station ／レストラン restaurant
スピーチコンテスト speech contest ／〜い：1い 〜 place: first place
もうしこみしょ application form ／こども child

Conversation Scenario 💬

〈Talking about what you did at the weekend〉

Lama: Kim-san, did you work at your part-time job yesterday?

Kim: No, I was off. But I didn't go anywhere because it was cold.

Lama: I went to see a soccer game.

Kim: Oh, really? How was it?

Lama: It was interesting. It was a good match.

Kim: I see. Oh, I saw the snow festival on TV. It was really pretty.

Lama: Ah, the snow festival. We should go see it.

1 そこに すてないで ください

Can-do Check ✓

☐ You can understand instructions regarding disposal of trash and apologize if you make a mistake.

☐ You can ask your landlord about how to dispose of trash.

Grammar Notes ✎

1 ないで ください

When warning someone not to do something, **〜ないで ください** is used.

Conjunctive Form

verb ない form 〈〜ない〉	で ください

Ex.1

先生：いま テストを して いますから、大きい こえで
　　　話さないで ください。

A・B：すみません。

Ex.2

A：すみません。ここは でんきを けさないで ください。

B：はい、わかりました。

Ex.1

Teacher: We're taking a test now, so please don't speak loudly.

A, B: Sorry.

Ex.2

A: Excuse me. Please don't turn off the lights here.

B: Okay, I understand.

2 て ください て形 て Form

When asking someone to do something, **〜て ください** is used. The form of verbs that uses **〜て** or **〜で** is called **て** form (**て形**).

Conjunctive Form

verb て form 〈〜て〉 〈〜で〉	ください

Ex.1

A：ボールペンを かして ください。

B：はい。どうぞ。

Ex.1

A: Please lend me a ball-point pen.

B: Sure. Here you go.

9 -1

Ex.2

A：ここに 名前と 住所を 書いて ください。

B：はい。わかりました。

Ex.2

A: Please write your name and address here.

B: Okay. I understand.

2-1　て Form of Group I Verbs

The て form is made in the same way as the た form. The ～た or ～だ of the た form becomes ～て or ～で in the て form. The て form of verbs is conjugated differently depending on the syllable ending in [i] that comes before ます, as shown below.

い・ち・り → って

The て form of ～います, ～ちます and ～ります is ～って.

かいます buy → かって

まちます wait → まって

とります take → とって

に・び・み → んで

The て form of ～にます, ～びます and ～みます is ～んで.

しにます die → しんで

あそびます play → あそんで

よみます read → よんで

し → して

The て form of ～します is ～して.

はなします speak → はなして

かします lend → かして

き → いて ／ ぎ → いで

The て form of ～きます and ～ぎます is ～いて and ～いで, respectively.

かきます write → かいて

いそぎます hurry → いそいで

Ex.

A：これは ボールペンで 書いて ください。

B：はい。

Ex.

A: Please write this using a ball-point pen.

B: Okay.

Careful！

The て form of いきます is いって.

2-2 て Form of Group II Verbs

ます becomes **て**.

たべ<u>ます</u> eat → たべ<u>て</u>

み<u>ます</u> see, watch → み<u>て</u>

Ex.

先生：みなさん、こちらを 見て ください。
せんせい　　　　　　　　　　　み

A：はい。

Ex.

Teacher: Everyone, please look here.

A: Okay.

2-3 て Form of Group III Verbs

The **て** form of **します** is **して**, and the **て** form of **きます** is **きて**. The **て** form of 【noun】

＋**します** is 【noun】＋**して**.

べんきょう<u>します</u> study → べんきょう<u>して</u>

そうじ<u>します</u> clean → そうじ<u>して</u>

Ex.

A：あした 9時に ここに 来て ください。
　　　　　じ　　　　　　き

B：はい。

Ex.

A: Please come here tomorrow at 9:00.

B: Okay.

Conjugations for verbs you have studied previously ①

The conjugations for the verbs from previous lessons have been shown in the

ます form (**ます形**) (☞ Lesson 4-1), dictionary form (**じしょ形**)
　　　　　　　けい　　　　　　　　　　　　　　　　　　　　　　けい

(☞ Lesson 7-1), **ない** form (**ない形**) (☞ Lesson 7-2), **た** form (**た形**)
　　　　　　　　　　　　　　　けい　　　　　　　　　　　　　　　　　　　　たけい

(☞ Lesson 8-1) and **て** from (**て形**) (☞ Lesson 9-1).
　　　　　　　　　　　　　　けい

	ます form	Dictionary form	**ない** form	**た** form	**て** form
Group I	かきます write	かく	かかない	かいた	かいて
Group II	たべます eat	たべる	たべない	たべた	たべて
	みます see, watch	みる	みない	みた	みて
Group III	します do	する	しない	した	して
	きます come	くる	こない	きた	きて

3 　　　　　　　　までに

When talking about doing something within a given time period, **〜までに** is used.

Ex.1

先生：JLPTの もうしこみは 4月20日までに して
　　ください。

Ex.1

Teacher: Please register for the JLPT
by April 20.

Ex.2

りょこうがいしゃの人：しゅっぱつは 9時ですから、
　　8時45分までに ここに 来て ください。

Ex.2

Travel agent: Your departure is at 9:00,
so please come here by 8:45.

〜まで

【time】**まで** is used to show the continuation of an action until a given time.

Ex.1

まいにち がっこうで 15時まで べんきょうします。

Ex.1

I study at school everyday until
15:00.

Ex.2

来年の 5月まで 日本に います。

Ex.2

I will be in Japan until May of next
year.

までに by

15時までに 電話をして ください。

Please call by 15:00.

まで until

15時まで がっこうに います。

I will be at school until 15:00.

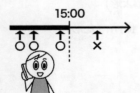

100

Vocabulary and Expression

すてます throw away ／プラスチック plastic ／生ごみ raw garbage ／ごみ garbage, trash

---

さわります touch ／入ります enter, go into ／出ます go out ／ドア door ／じしょ dictionary
わすれます forget ／ロッカー locker ／かぎ key ／なくします lose ／おなじ same
まちがえます make a mistake ／おきます put, place ／おぼえます remember, memorize
くすり medicine ／おおや landlord ／げつまつ end of the month ／やちん rent
はらいます pay ／かちょう department chief, section head ／しゃいん company employee
レポート report ／あと～ more, left ／ツアー tour ／せんたく laundry ／こえ voice

Conversation Scenario

〈Disposing of trash〉

Nishikawa: Oh, Tang-san. Please don't throw away plastic there.

Tang: Okay.

Nishikawa: Please throw it away here.

Tang: Okay, I understand. Sorry. Umm, when do we take out the raw garbage?

Nishikawa: On Tuesdays and Fridays. Please look at this.

Tang: Ah, thank you.

Nishikawa: Please bring it here by 8:00.

Tang: Okay, I understand.

9-1

2 じしょを つかっては いけません

Can-do Check ✓

☐ You can listen to and understand the test instructions.

☐ You can ask your teacher or the person in charge for simple advice regarding rules or things to do.

Grammar Notes 🖊

1 ては いけません

When telling people what they are not allowed to do, **～ては いけません** is used.

Conjunctive Form

verb て form 〈～て〉 〈～で〉	は いけません

Ex.1

A：ここで 電話を <u>しては いけません</u>。
　　　　　　でんわ

B：あ、すみません。

Ex.1

A: You can't make phone calls here.

B: Oh, sorry.

Ex.2

A：ここで しゃしんを

　　<u>とっては いけません</u>。

B：はい。

Ex.2

A: You can't take pictures here.

B: Okay.

2 ても いいです

When asking someone for or granting someone permission to do something, **～ても い いです** is used.

Conjunctive Form

verb て form 〈～て〉 〈～で〉	も いいです

Ex.1

A：ここに じてんしゃを
　　<u>おいても いいですか</u>。

B：はい、いいですよ。

Ex.1

A: May I leave my bike here?

B: Yes, you may.

Ex.2

A：あついですね。まどを <u>あけても いいですか</u>。

B：はい。 どうぞ。

Ex.2

A: It's hot. May I open the window?

B: Sure. Go ahead.

Ex.3

A：テスト、おわりました。

先生_{せんせい}：では、<u>かえっても いいですよ</u>。

Ex.3

A: I finished the test.

Teacher: Then you may go home.

3　　　　　　　　　で

で is added after the tool, process or method of transportation when asking what tool, process or method of transportation someone will use.

Ex.1

A：わたしは はし<u>で</u> ごはんを 食_たべます。

B：わたしは スプーン<u>で</u> 食_たべます。

Ex.1

A: I eat food with chopsticks.

B: I eat with a spoon.

Ex.2

A：電車_{でんしゃ}<u>で</u> かいしゃへ 行_いきます。

B：わたしは バス<u>で</u> 行_いきます。

Ex.2

A: I go to my office by train.

B: I take the bus.

Ex.3

A：ここを はさみ<u>で</u> きって ください。

B：はい。

Ex.3

A: Please cut this with scissors.

B: Okay.

Ex.4

この じてんしゃは 電_{でん}き<u>で</u> うごきます。

Ex.4

This bike is powered by electricity.

9-2

Vocabulary and Expression

つかいます use ／きょうかしょ textbook ／入れます put in
ボールペン ball-point pen ／えんぴつ pencil

たばこ cigarette ／たばこを すいます smoke ／とめます stop ／わたります cross
うんてんします drive ／かんごし nurse ／はしります run ／電話 telephone, phone
コピーします copy ／住所 address ／生年月日 date of birth ／電話番号 phone number
ひらがな hiragana

Conversation Scenario

〈Taking a test〉

Aoki: Now, we are going to take a test. Please put your textbooks in your bags. You cannot take it with a ball-point pen. Please write with a pencil. Do not talk to the person next to you.

Tang: Sensei, may we use dictionaries?

Aoki: No, you may not.

3 きょうかしょを 見て います
み

Can-do Check ✓

☐ You can listen to and understand the teacher's instructions.

☐ You can explain what other people are doing.

Grammar Notes 🖊

1　　　　　　て います

When expressing that an action is ongoing, **〜て います** is used.

Conjunctive Form

verb て form 〈〜て〉 〈〜で〉	います

Ex.1

A：たなかさん、いますか。

B：たなかさんは いま 電話を
　　でんわ
　　して います。

Ex.2

（電話で）
でんわ

A：もしもし、いっしょに ごはんを 食べに 行きませんか。
　　　　　　　　　　　　　　　た　　　い

B：すみません。いま 食べて います。
　　　　　　　　　た

Ex.1

A: Is Tanaka-san there?

B: Tanaka-san is on the phone.

Ex.2

(On the phone)

A: Hello. Why don't we go get something to eat?

B: Sorry. I'm eating now.

2　もう

　　まだ

2-1　When expressing that an action has been completed, **もう 〜ました／〜た** is used.
まだです or **まだ 〜て いません／いない** is used when answering a question about whether an action has been completed or not to express that it has not yet been completed.

Conjunctive Form

もう	verb	〈～ました〉 〈～た〉
まだ	verb	〈～て いません〉 〈～て いない〉

Ex.1

A：もう じゅぎょうは おわりましたか。

B：はい、おわりました。

Ex.2

A：もう ひるごはんを 食べましたか。

B：いいえ。まだです。

C：わたしも まだ 食べて いません。

Ex.1

A: Is class over?

B: Yes, it is.

Ex.2

A: Did you eat lunch already?

B: No, not yet.

C: I haven't eaten yet either.

When expressing that it has now become a given time or circumstance or that you will do a given action from now, **もう ～です／～だ** and **もう ～ます／～ [u]** are used. **～ [u]** means the verb dictionary form.

Conjunctive Form

もう	noun	〈～です〉 〈～だ〉
	い adjective	〈～です〉 〈～だ〉
	な adjective	〈～です〉 〈～だ〉
	verb	〈～ます〉 〈～[u]〉

Ex.

A：もう 12時です。ねましょう。

B：はい。

Ex.

A: It's already 12:00. Let's go to sleep.

B: Okay.

2 -2 When expressing that an action is still continuing, **まだ ～て います／いる** is used.

Conjunctive Form

まだ	verb	〈～て います〉 〈～て いる〉

Ex.

りょうちょう：まだ テレビを 見て いますか。

　　　　はやく ねて ください。

A：はい。

Ex.

Dorm superintendent: Are you still watching TV? Hurry up and go to bed.

A: Okay.

2 -3 When you express that something has not yet reached an expected time or condition, **まだ～です／～だ** is used.

Conjunctive Form

まだ	noun	〈～です〉 〈～だ〉
	い adjective	〈～です〉 〈～だ〉
	な adjective	〈～です〉 〈～だ〉

Ex.1

A：あ、うめのはなが さいて いますよ。もう はるですね。

B：ええ。でも、まだ さむいですね。

Ex.2

A：Bさん、おひるごはんを 食べに

　　行きませんか。

B：え、まだ 10時はんですよ。

Ex.1

A: Ah, the plum blossoms are in bloom. It's already spring.

B: Yes. But it's still cold.

Ex.2

A: B-san, why don't we go eat lunch?

B: Uh, it's only 10:30.

9 - 3

時間です Time's up. ／あつめます collect, take ／だめ（な）can't, not allowed
じかん

かたづけます pick up, clean up ／すぐ right away, quickly, be there soon ／はじめます start

やめます stop, quit ／おそい late, take too long ／はじまります start

だいじょうぶ（な）okay, no problem ／どうしよう What should I do? ／まにあいます be on time

Conversation Scenario 💬

〈After a test〉

Aoki: Time is up. Don't write anymore. The person in the back, please collect all of the tests.

Kim: Sensei, Tang-san is still writing.

Aoki: Tang-san, time is already up. Please turn in your test.

Kim: Sensei, Lama-san is looking at his textbook.

Aoki: Lama-san, you can't look at that yet.

Kim: Tang-san, hurry up!

Tang: Okay.

Can-do Check ✓

☐ You can ask about and say what a person is wearing or doing.

☐ You can introduce someone.

Grammar Notes ✏

1-1 _____ を _____ て います

When talking about what someone is wearing, **～を ～て います** is used. Different verbs are used depending on what type of clothing or item is being talking about.

Item	Verb dictionary form	Sentence
シャツ shirt コート coat セーター sweater	きる	シャツを きて います
ぼうし hat	かぶる	ぼうしを かぶって います
ズボン trouser スカート skirt くつ shoe くつした sock	はく	ズボンを はいて います
めがね glasses	かける	めがねを かけて います
ネクタイ necktie ネックレス necklace とけい watch	する	ネクタイを して います

Ex.1

たなかさんは きょう あおい シャツを きて います。

Ex.2

きむらさんは いつも ぼうしを かぶって います。

Ex.1

Tanaka-san is wearing a blue shirt today.

Ex.2

Kimura-san is always wearing a hat.

1-2　　　　　て　いる

When asking about a single person out of a group of many, **どの 人_{ひと}ですか** is used. **～て いる 人_{ひと}です** is used when answering such questions by saying what the person is wearing. **いる** is the dictionary form of **います**.

Conjunctive Form

verb て form	〈～て〉 〈～で〉	いる	人 ひと	です

Ex.1

A：たなかさんは　どの　人_{ひと}ですか。

B：あおい シャツを <u>きて いる 人_{ひと}です</u>。

Ex.2

A：いのうえさんは　どの　人_{ひと}ですか。

B：あの 人_{ひと}です。 めがねを <u>かけて いる 人_{ひと}です</u>。

Ex.1

A: Which person is Tanaka-san?

B: He's the one wearing a blue shirt.

Ex.2

A: Which person is Inoue-san?

B: That one. She's the one wearing glasses.

***～ている 人_{ひと}です** is also used when identifying a person by pointing out what they are doing (☞ Lesson 9 - 3).

Vocabulary and Expression 🍄

グレー gray ／スーツ suit ／めがねを かけます put on glasses ／システム system

～ぶ：システムぶ ～ department: system department ／しょうかいします introduce

いいですよ sure ／どうりょう coworker

コート coat ／Ｔシャツ T-shirt ／きもの kimono ／かぶります wear, put on

はきます wear, put on ／ズボン pants ／スカート skirt ／ブーツ boots

（ネクタイを）します wear a tie ／ベルト belt ／ゆびわ ring ／ネックレス necklace

ブレスレット bracelet ／マフラー scarf ／ワンピース dress ／ノート notebook

Conversation Scenario 💬

⟨Talking at a party⟩

Sarah: Lee-san, who is that person?

Lee: Huh? What person?

Sarah: The person wearing a grey suit.

Lee: Ah, the person wearing glasses.

Sarah: No, the person behind that one. The person talking to Nakamura-san.

Lee: Oh, that's Shin-san from the systems department.

Sarah: I see. Lee-san, please introduce him to me.

Lee: Okay... Shin-san, let me introduce you to my coworker. This is Sarah-san.

Sarah: Nice to meet you.

Shin: Nice to meet you, too. I'm Shin.

2 ペキンに 住んで います
す

Can-do Check ✓

☐ You can introduce your family and friends.

☐ You can ask about and describe where someone lives, their occupation and if they are married or not.

Grammar Notes ✎

1 ｜｜｜｜｜ て います

When talking about where you live, your job or whether you are married or not, ～て います is used.

Conjunctive Form

verb て form	⟨～て⟩ ⟨～で⟩	います

Ex.1

とうきょうに 住んで います。
す

えいごを おしえて います。

けっこんして います。

Ex.1

I live in Tokyo.

I teach English.

I'm married.

Ex.2

A：Bさんは どこに 住んで いますか。
す

B：わたしは さくらしに 住んで います。
す

Ex.2

A: B-san, where do you live?

B: I live in Sakurashi.

Ex.3

A：どんな しごとを して いますか。

B：わたしは 日本語を おしえて います。
にほんご

C：わたしは 車を うって います。
くるま

Ex.3

A: What kind of job do you do?

B: I teach Japanese.

C: I sell cars.

Ex.4

A：わたしは けっこんして います。

　きょねん けっこんしました。

B：そうですか。

　わたしは まだ けっこんして いません。

Ex.4

A: I'm married. I got married last year.

B: Oh, really? I'm not married.

＊～て います is also used when an action is ongoing (☞ Lesson 9-3).

112

2

は	くて、	です
は	で、	です

~くて is used when using multiple い adjectives in a series, and ~で is used for な adjectives.

Conjunctive Form

い adjective 〈~い く〉	て
な adjective 〈~な〉	で

Ex.1

わたしの いえは 大きくて、ひろくて、あたらしいです。

Ex.2

あの みせは りょうりが おいしくて、てんいんが
しんせつです。

Ex.3

トムさんは げんきで、しんせつで、あかるいです。

Ex.4

びじゅつかんの にわは きれいで、ひろいです。

Ex.1

My house is big, spacious and new.

Ex.2

The food at that store is delicious, and the employees are kind.

Ex.3

Tom-san is energetic, kind and cheerful.

Ex.4

The art museum's garden is beautiful and spacious.

Vocabulary and Expression

住みます live ／こいびと boyfriend, girlfriend, lover, partner, significant other ／かのじょ she
あかるい bright, lively ／まじめ（な） serious ／やさしい nice, kind ／いもうと little sister
おねえさん older sister ／よく にて います really look alike
おとうと little brother ／はたらきます work ／男の子 boy ／女の子 girl

りょうしん parents ／父 dad, father ／あに older brother ／ぼうえきがいしゃ trading company
けいえいします manage, operate ／ざっし magazine ／イラスト illustration ／セールス sales
高校 high school ／おしえます teach ／ごけっこんは？ Are you married?
どくしん bachelor, single ／きっさてん coffee shop ／イケメン handsome ／かれ he
かぞく family

Conversation Scenario 💬

⟨Introducing your family⟩

Nakamura: Lee-san, who is this?

Lee: Ah!

Nakamura: Is this your girlfriend?

Lee: Uh, yes.

Nakamura: Huh. She's pretty.

Lee: Yes. She's cheerful and hard-working. She's good at cooking and kind.

Nakamura: That's great. Is this your younger sister?

Lee: No, she's my older sister.

Nakamura: Your older sister?

Lee: Yes. She lives in Beijing.

Nakamura: I see.

Inoue: Who is this? He looks a lot like you.

Lee: That's my younger brother. He works at a hotel.

Inoue: I see.

Lee: My brother is married. He has two kids.

Inoue: A boy and a girl, right? They're cute.

Can-do Check ✓

☐ You can simply introduce your town.
☐ You can describe how you feel.

Grammar Notes 🖊

1　　　　　　 は　　　　　　 が　　　　　　 です

When describing the condition of people or things, adjectives are used, as in **きょうは あついです**. **〜が 〜です** is used when explaining something in detail, as in **きょうは てんきが いいです**.

Conjunctive Form

noun	は	noun	が	adjective	です

Ex.1
たなかさんは せが 高_{たか}いです。

たなかさん

Ex.1
Tanaka-san is tall.

Ex.2
うちの ねこは 目_めが 大_{おお}きいです。

Ex.2
My cat's eyes are big.

2　　　　　　 が、

When expressing two things in opposition to one another, **〜が、 〜** is used.

Conjunctive Form

い adjective 〈〜い〉	です	が、	い adjective 〈〜い〉	です
な adjective 〈〜な〉			な adjective 〈〜な〉	
			〜ます	

Ex.1
びじゅつかんの にわは せまいですが、きれいです。

Ex.1
The art museum's garden is small but beautiful.

Ex.2
バスは べんりですが、時間_{じかん}が かかります。

Ex.2
The bus is convenient, but it takes a long time.

**10
‐
3**

115

3 （わたしは） _____ と おもいます

When expressing your own opinion （わたしは）～と おもいます is used. わたしは can be omitted.

Conjunctive Form

（わたしは）	～	と	おもいます

Ex.1
わたしは 日本語の べんきょうは たのしいと おもいます。
<small>にほんご</small>

Ex.1
I think studying Japanese is fun.

Ex.2
きょうの テストは かんたんだったと おもいます。

Ex.2
I think yesterday's test was easy.

【person】は ～と おもって います is used when expressing someone else's opinion.

Ex.
トムさんは 日本語の べんきょうは
<small>にほんご</small>
たのしいと おもって います。

Ex.
Tom-san thinks that studying Japanese is fun.

Vocabulary and Expression 😊

南 south ／りっぱ（な） splendid, handsome, beautiful ／うるさい noisy, loud
<small>みなみ</small>
ぜひ please, feel free to

- - - - - - - - - -

ビル building ／くうき air ／きたない dirty ／人口 population ／高い high ／せが 高い tall
<small>じんこう</small> <small>たか</small> <small>たか</small>
ひくい low ／せが ひくい short ／うた song ／かみ hair ／目 eye ／ねだん price
<small>め</small>

Conversation Scenario 💬

〈Introducing my town〉

Tanaka: Ah, is this Vietnam?

Tang: Yes. It's Ho Chi Minh. It's a city in the south of Vietnam. It's an old city with many beautiful buildings.

Tanaka: Really? Is this Ho Chi Minh, too?

Tang: Yes.

Tanaka: There are a lot of motorbikes.

Tang: It's a little loud, but the people that live there are very kind. I think it's a great city. Please come visit.

Tanaka: Yes. I'd like to.

1 ありがとうございます

Can-do Check ✓

☐ You can ask about what to give as a gift.
☐ You can express your gratitude for a gift.

Grammar Notes ✎

1 -1 ＿＿＿＿＿ は ＿＿＿＿＿ に ＿＿＿＿＿ を あげます

When talking about giving someone a present or some other item, 【person X】は【person Y】に【thing】を あげます is used. 【person X】 refers to the giver, and 【person Y】 refers to the receiver.

person X   person Y

Conjunctive Form

person X	は	person Y	に	noun (thing)	を	あげます

Ex.1

あしたは トムさんの たんじょう日です。
リンさんは トムさんに ケーキを あげます。

リンさん   トムさん

Ex.1

Tomorrow is Tom-san's birthday.

Lin-san is going to give Tom-san a cake.

Ex.2

トムさんが けっこんを します。
キムさんは トムさんに とけいを あげました。

キムさん   トムさん

Ex.2

Tom-san is going to get married.

Kim-san gave Tom-san a clock.

1-2 ＿＿＿＿ は ＿＿＿＿ に ＿＿＿＿ を もらいます

When talking about receiving a present or some other item from someone, 【person X】 は 【person Y】 に 【thing】 を もらいます is used. 【person X】 refers to the receiver, and 【person Y】 refers to the giver.

person Y ✕ わたし | person X

Conjunctive Form

person X	は	person Y	に	noun (thing)	を	もらいます

Ex.1

トムさんは リンさんに ケーキを もらいました。

リンさん ・ トムさん

Ex.2

トムさんは キムさんに とけいを もらいました。

キムさん ・ トムさん

Ex.1

Tom-san got a cake from Lin-san.

Ex.2

Tom-san got a clock from Kim-san.

Careful !

わたし is not used in place of 【person Y】.

Ex.

✕ トムさんは わたしに ケーキを もらいました。

○ わたしは トムさんに ケーキを あげました。

Ex.

✕ Tom-san got a cake from me.

○ I gave Tom-san a cake.

2 　　　　　　　　　　ましょうか
　　　　　　　　　　は どうですか

When asking someone how they feel about what you are asking them, **〜ましょうか** or **〜は どうですか** is used.

Conjunctive Form

verb ます form 〈〜ます しょう〉	か

noun	は	どうですか

Ex.1

A：きょうは 何を 食べましょうか。

B：すしは どうですか。

A：いいですね。

Ex.2

A：もう6時ですね。かえりましょうか。

B：そうですね。

Ex.3

A：つぎの ミーティング、いつに しましょうか。

B：来しゅうの 火よう日は どうですか。

A：いいですね。

Ex.1

A: What shall we eat today?

B: How about sushi?

A: That sounds good.

Ex.2

A: It's already 6:00. Shall we go home?

B: Yes, let's.

Ex.3

A: When shall we have the next meeting?

B: How about next Tuesday?

A: That sounds good.

3 　　　　た とき、　　　ました

When talking about what you did at the time of another action being done, **〜たとき、〜ました** is used.

Conjunctive Form

verb た form 〈〜た〉〈〜だ〉	とき、	verb 〈〜ました〉

Ex.1

大学に 入った とき、父に とけいを もらいました。
だいがく　はい　　　　　ちち

Ex.2

けさ 電車に のった とき、クラスの 友だちに 会いました。
　　でんしゃ　　　　　　　　　　とも　　　あ

Ex.3

きょねん 日本へ 来た とき、ほっかいどうへ 行きました。
　　　　にほん　き　　　　　　　　　　　　い

4　　　　　　とか　　　　　　（とか）

When listing several nouns as an example of something, 〜とか 〜（とか）〜 is used.

Conjunctive Form

noun	とか	noun	（とか）	noun

Ex.1

日本語学校で はつおんとか ぶんぽうとか かんじを
にほんごがっこう
べんきょうして います。

Ex.2

きのうの パーティーで 日本しゅとか ワインとか
　　　　　　　　　　にほん
いろいろな さけを のみました。

Ex.1

When I got into college, my father gave me a watch.

Ex.2

When I got on the train this morning, I met a friend from my class.

Ex.3

When I came to Japan last year, I went to Hokkaido.

Ex.1

I'm studying things like pronunciation, grammar and kanji at my Japanese language school.

Ex.2

At yesterday's party, I drank many kinds of alcohol like Japanese sake and wine.

Vocabulary and Expression

（お）いわい congratulations, congratulatory gift ／しゃしんたて picture frame

おめでとうございます Congratulations. ／おしあわせに may you find happiness

たいせつに します take good care of ...

そぼ grandmother ／すてき（な）lovely ／さいふ wallet ／大学 university
　　　　　　　　　　　　　　　　　　　　　　　　　　　　　だいがく

（学校に）入ります enter school ／しゅうしょく getting a job
がっこう　はい

きまります be decided ／しょくじ meal ／うまれます be born ／おもちゃ toy

すごい amazing ／テニス tennis ／バスケットボール basketball ／たっきゅう table tennis

チケット ticket

Conversation Scenario 💬

⟨Giving marriage congratulations⟩

Sarah: Inoue-san said he is going to get married.

Ogawa: I heard, too.

Sarah: I want to give him something to celebrate the occasion.

Ogawa: Yes. What shall we get him?

Sarah: Hmm... What did you get when you got married?

Ogawa: I got things like a clock and a picture frame.

Sarah: Oh, a clock! That sounds good. Let's get him a clock.

Ogawa: But, why don't we ask him what he wants?

Sarah: Ah, you're right.

Sarah and Ogawa: Inoue-san, congratulations on your marriage! May you find happiness.

Inoue: Thank you. I'll take good care of it.

2 母に つくって もらいました
はは

☐ You can express your thanks for a compliment about your possessions or clothing.

☐ You can simply explain about something you have received.

Grammar Notes 🖋

1-1   わたし は   に   て もらいます

When talking about how someone has saved or helped you, **わたしは ～に ～て もらいます** is used.

Conjunctive Form

わたし	は	person	に	what they did for you verb て form ⟨～て⟩ ⟨～で⟩	もらいます

Ex.1
わたしは リンさんに 中国語を おしえて もらいました。
　　　　　　　　ちゅうごくご

Ex.2
わたしは トムさんに にもつを もって もらいました。

Ex.1
Lin-san taught me Chinese.

Ex.2
Tom-san carried my luggage for me.

Ex.3

わたしは 友だちに びょういんへ つれて 行って
　　　　とも　　　　　　　　　　　　　　い
もらいました。

Ex.3

My friend took me to the hospital.

1-2　　　　　は　　　　に　　　　て もらいます

When talking about what someone else did to help another person, 〜は 〜に 〜て もら
います is used. 【person X】 is the receiver, and 【person Y】 is the person giving.

Conjunctive Form

person X	は	person Y	に	what they did for the other person verb て form 〈〜て〉 〈〜で〉	もらいます

Ex.1

やまださん**は** たなかさん**に** お金を かして もらいました。
　　　　　　　　　　　　　　　　かね

ありがとう

Ex.1

Tanaka-san lent Yamada-san some
money.

Ex.2

なかむらさん**は** アントニオさんに イタリア語を
　　　　　　　　　　　　　　　　　　　　ご
おしえて もらいました。

イタリア

Ex.2

Antonio-san taught Nakamura-san
Italian.

Careful !

わたし is not used in place of 【person Y】 (☞ Lesson 11 - 1).

× なかむらさんは わたしに イタリア語を
　　　　　　　　　　　　　　　　　ご
　おしえて もらいました。

× Nakamura-san was taught
　 Italian by me.

123

2 　じしょ形 とき、 ます／ました

When talking about when you will do or did an action, 【**verb dictionary form**】**とき、**
〜ます／ました is used. When talking about doing something after the first action has
been completed, the verb that comes before **とき** is used in its **た** form (☞ Lesson
11-1). When talking about doing something before the first action begins, the verb
that comes before **とき** is used in its dictionary form.

Conjunctive Form

verb dictionary form	とき、	verb 〈〜ます〉 〈〜ました〉

Ex.1

ごはんを 食べる とき、「いただきます」と 言います。
ごはんを 食べた とき、「ごちそうさま」と 言います。

Ex.1

When eating a meal, we say
"itadakimasu".

After eating a meal, we say
"gochisousama".

Ex.2

日本へ 来る とき、国の 友だちに 「さようなら」と
言いました。
日本へ 来た とき、ルームメートに 「はじめまして」と
言いました。

Ex.2

Before coming to Japan, I said, "good
bye" to my friends in my own country.

After I came to Japan, I said, "nice to
meet you", to my roommate.

Vocabulary and Expression 🐛

バティック batik ／〜まい：1まい (counter for flat objects): one ／にあいます suit someone, look good

---

にんぎょう doll ／つれて いきます take someone along ／てつだいます help
（めがねを）なおします repair glasses ／クラス class ／かぜ cold ／なおります recover
サングラス sunglasses ／せんす folding fan ／ゆかた Japanese summer kimono
おばあさん grandmother

⟨Wearing a nice shirt⟩

Nakamura: Budi-san, your shirt is an Indonesian batik. It's wonderful.

Budi: Thank you. My mother made it for me.

Nakamura: Wow, your mother?!

Budi: Yes. Before I came to Japan, she made three for me.

Nakamura: Three! That's great. Your mother is really good at making them. They look really good on you.

Budi: Thank you.

Can-do Check ✓

☐ You can offer to help someone.

☐ You can express your gratitude to someone for helping you.

Grammar Notes ✏

1 　　　　　　　　　　ましょうか

When offering help or assistance to someone, **～ましょうか** is used. **ありがとうございます。** or **おねがいします。** is used to accept someone's offer to help. **だいじょうぶです。** or **けっこうです。** is used to decline someone's offer to help. **ありがとうございます** can also be used when declining.

Conjunctive Form

verb ます form 〈～ます しょう〉	か

Ex.1

A：あついですね。

B：まど、<u>あけましょうか</u>。

A：ありがとうございます。

Ex.2

A：かばん、<u>もちましょうか</u>。

B：ありがとうございます。おねがいします。

Ex.3

A：しょうゆ、<u>とりましょうか</u>。

B：ありがとうございます。けっこうです。

Ex.1

A: It's hot, isn't it?

B: Shall I open a window?

A: Thank you.

Ex.2

A: Shall I carry your bag?

B: Thank you. Yes, please.

Ex.3

A: Shall I get you some soy sauce?

B: No, thank you.

~ましょうか can also be used to ask someone what they think about something
(☞ Lesson 11 - 1).

Ex.

A：しごと、たくさん ありますね。<u>どうしましょうか</u>。

B：みんなに てつだって もらいましょう。

Ex.

A: We have a lot of work. What
should we do?

B: Let's have everyone help us.

2　　　　　　て あげて ください

When asking another person to help someone, **~て あげて ください** is used.

Conjunctive Form

verb て form 〈～て〉 〈～で〉	あげて ください

Ex.1

A：Bさん、たなかさんの しごとを <u>てつだって あげて</u>
　<u>ください</u>。

B：はい、わかりました。

Ex.1

A: B-san, could you help Tanaka-san
with his work?

B: Sure, I understand.

Ex.2

A：Bさん、リンさんに コップを <u>とって あげて ください</u>。

B：はい。

Ex.2

A: B-san, could you give Lin-san a cup?

B: Okay.

When talking about something someone will do for another person, **【person
X】は 【person Y】に 【what they did for the other person】 ～て あげます** is
used.

Ex.

たなかさん**は** やまださん**に** お金を <u>かして あげました</u>。

Ex.

Tanaka-san lent Yamada-san some
money.

If **わたし** is used in place of 【person X】, it may overemphasize the act of giving
and sound patronizing.

Ex.

△ わたしは やまださんに お金を かして あげました。

○ わたしは やまださんに お金を かしました。

Ex.

I lent Yamada-san some money.

When the 【person Y】 の 【thing】 を ～て あげます form of 【what they did for the other person】 ～て あげます is used, 【person Y】 に in 【person Y】 に ～て あげます is omitted.

Ex.1

× たなかさんは <u>トムさんに</u> トムさんの しごとを てつだって あげました。

○ たなかさんは トムさんの しごとを てつだって あげました。

Ex.2

○ タンさんは マリさんの にもつを もって あげました。

Ex.1

Tanaka-san helped Tom-san with his work.

Ex.2

Tang-san carried Mari-san's bag.

3　　　て　いただいて、ありがとうございました

When thanking someone for helping you, ～ていただいて、ありがとうございました is used. いただいて（いただく）is the humble speech form of もらって（もらう）(☞ Lesson 16-3).

Conjunctive Form

verb て form 〈～て〉〈～で〉	いただいて、	ありがとうございました

Ex.

A：しごとを <u>てつだって いただいて、ありがとうございました</u>。

B：いいえ、どういたしまして。

Ex.

A: Thank you for helping me with my work.

B: You're welcome.

4　　　　　　て、

When expressing a reason for something, the ～て／～で form can be used.

Conjunctive Form

verb て form	⟨～て⟩ ⟨～で⟩	～
verb ない form ⟨～ない くて⟩		

Ex.1

雨が やんで、よかったです。
あめ

Ex.2

A：びょうきが なおって、よかったですね。

B：ありがとうございます。

Ex.1

I'm glad it stopped raining.

Ex.2

A: I'm glad you've recovered from your illness.

B: Thank you.

Vocabulary and Expression 🥟

とります take ／～本・2本 (counter for long objects): two ／見せます show
ほん　ほん　　　　　　　　　　　　　　　　　　　　　み

どういたしまして You're welcome. ／さくぶん essay, composition

（さくぶんを） なおします correct a composition ／せきを かわります trade seats

おくります escort, take ／いろいろ（な） various ／つかれます be tired

Conversation Scenario 💬

⟨Tidying up⟩

Lee: Do you need some help?

Nakamura: No, I'm fine. Please help Sarah-san.

Lee: Okay. Sarah-san, do you need help?

Sarah: Oh, are you sure? Sorry. Thank you.

Sarah: Thank you for helping me, everyone.

Lee: No problem.

Nakamura: I'm glad we finished so quickly.

1 おしえて ください

Can-do Check ✓

☐ You can give a reason and make a simple request.

☐ You can ask about and understand a simple procedure.

Grammar Notes ✎

1 ［　　　　　　］んですが、［　　　　　］て ください

When explaining a reason or circumstances and then making a request, 〜んですが、〜てください is used.

Conjunctive Form

verb plain form	んですが、	**verb て form** 〈〜て〉〈〜で〉	**ください**
い adjective plain form〈〜い〉			
な adjective plain form〈〜だ な〉			
noun plain form〈〜だ な〉			

Ex.1

A：すみません。えきへ 行きたいんですが、みちを おしえて ください。

B：はい。

Ex.1

A: Excuse me. I want to get to the station, so could you tell me how to get there?

B: Okay.

Ex.2

A：きょうの かいぎの ばしょが わからないんですが、おしえて ください。

B：はい。

Ex.2

A: I don't know where today's meeting is going to be held, so could you tell me?

B: Okay.

Ex.3

A：すみません。このいすを はこぶんですが、てつだって ください。

B：はい。

Ex.3

A: Excuse me. I'm going to carry this chair, so could you help me?

B: Okay.

2　　　　　　　方 (かた)

When expressing a method of doing an action, **方 (かた)** is added to the end of the verb.

Conjunctive Form

verb ます form 〈～ます〉	方 (かた)

読 (よ) みます read → 読 (よ) み方 (かた)
書 (か) きます write → 書 (か) き方 (かた)
食 (た) べます eat → 食 (た) べ方 (かた)

Ex.1

A：JLPTの もうしこみ方 (かた) を おしえて ください。

B：はい、わかりました。

Ex.2

A：入口 (いりぐち) の ドアの あけ方 (かた) を しって いますか。

B：はい、しって います。たなかさんに おしえて
　　もらいました。

Ex.1

A: Please tell me how to apply for the JLPT.

B: Okay.

Ex.2

A: Do you know how to open the entrance door?

B: Yes, I do. Tanaka-san taught me.

3　　　　　　　て 、　　　　　　　て 、

When explaining a sequence of actions, the **て** form of verbs can be used.

Conjunctive Form

verb X て form 〈～て〉〈～で〉	、	verb Y て form 〈～て〉〈～で〉	、	verb Z

Ex.1

毎朝 (まいあさ) 6時 (じ) に おきて、ジョギングを して、
シャワーを あびて、朝 (あさ) ごはんを 食 (た) べます。

Ex.2

カレーを 作 (つく) ります。はじめに やさいを あらって、
きって、なべに 入 (い) れます。つぎに、……。

Ex.1

Every morning, I wake up at 6:00, go jogging, take a shower and eat breakfast.

Ex.2

I make curry. First, I wash the vegetables, then I cut them, then I put them in a pot. Next, ...

Vocabulary and Expression 🐹

来月 next month ／帰国します return to one's country ／きゅうかとどけ vacation request form
らいげつ　　　　　　　　　　きこく

かみ paper ／理由 reason ／はんこ personal seal, name seal ／おします press, stamp
　　　　　りゆう

東北しんかんせん Tohoku shinkansen, Tohoku bullet train ／のりば platform ／よてい plan
とうほく

メール email ／ミーティング meeting ／とっきゅうけん express ticket ／ことば word

いみ meaning ／はこびます carry ／こわれます break ／とりかえます replace

しゅっぱつ departure ／電話を かけます make a call ／ボタン button ／でんげん electrical power
　　　　　　でんわ

スタート start ／しって います know ／しりません don't know ／まわします turn

コーヒーマシン coffee machine ／カップ cup ／どうやって how ／ゆでます boil

（バターを）つけます spread butter on ／けっせきとどけ absence request ／じむしょ office

JLPT・日本語のうりょくしけん Japanese Language Proficiency Test
ジェイエルビーティー　にほんご

もうしこみ application ／Web the web, the internet ／ゆうびん post, postal service ／ID identification
　　　　　　　　ウェブ　　　　　　　　　　　　　　　　　　　　　　　アイディー

Conversation Scenario 💬

〈Writing a vacation request〉

Shin: Lee-san, I'm going back to my country next month for one week.

Lee: That's great. Did you submit a vacation request form?

Shin: Huh? A vacation request form?

Lee: Yes. You submit them to Nakamura-san.

Shin: I see.

Shin: Nakamura-san, I'm going back to my country next month, so could you show me how to fill out a vacation request form?

Nakamura: Yes. Write your reason on this sheet of paper, stamp it with your name seal and then submit it.

Shin: Okay. I understand... Nakamura-san, is this okay? Please take a look at it.

Nakamura: Okay.

2 見て いただけませんか
み

Can-do Check ✓

☐ You can give a reason and make a polite request.

☐ You can explain a problem and ask for help.

Grammar Notes ✏

1 ＿＿＿＿んですが、＿＿＿＿て いただけませんか

When politely explaining a reason or circumstances and then making a request, **〜んで
すが、〜ていただけませんか** is used.

Conjunctive Form

verb plain form			
い adjective plain form 〈〜い〉	んですが、	verb て form 〈〜て〉	いただけ
な adjective plain form 〈〜だ な〉		〈〜で〉	ませんか
noun adjective plain form 〈〜だ な〉			

Ex.1

（えきで）

A：あのう、すみません。きっぷを 買いたいんですが、
　　きっぷの 買い方を おしえて いただけませんか。
　　　　　か　　かた

B：はい。

Ex.2

（学校で じゅぎょうの あとに）
　がっこう

A：先生、すみません。アルバイトの もうしこみ書を
　せんせい　　　　　　　　　　　　　　　　しょ
　　書いたんですが、見て いただけませんか。
　　か　　　　　　　み

先生：はい。いいですよ。
せんせい

Ex.1

(At a station)

A: Umm, excuse me. I'd like to buy a
　ticket, so could you show me how
　buy one?

B: Okay.

Ex.2

(After class at school)

A: Excuse me, Sensei. I wrote an
　application for a part-time job, so
　could you take a look at it?

Teacher: Sure, I'll take a look.

2 -1　　dictionary form　まえに、

When talking about two actions in sequential order, **～まえに、～** is used. This expresses that 【verb Y】 will be done after 【verb X】.

Conjunctive Form

verb Y dictionary form	まえに、	verb X

Ex.1

（小学校で）
しょうがっこう

先生：ねる まえに はを みがきましょう。
せんせい

小学生：は〜い。
しょうがくせい

Ex.2

（レストランで）

A：この みせは 食べる まえに チケットを 買うんですよ。
　　　　　　　　　た　　　　　　　　　　　　か

B：わかりました。

Ex.1

(At am elementary school)

Teacher: Brush your teeth before you go to sleep.

Student: Okay.

Ex.2

(At a restaurant)

A: At this store, you buy a ticket before you eat.

B: Okay.

2 -2　　　　　　　　　の まえに、

When talking about two actions in sequential order, **～の まえに、～** is used. This is used with a noun in place of the 【verb Y】 from the above **2-1**. This expresses that 【noun】 will be done after 【verb】.

Conjunctive Form

noun ＋ の	まえに、	verb

Ex.1

しょくじの まえに てを あらいます。

Ex.2

りょこうの まえに ホテルを よやくします。

Ex.1

I wash my hands before eating.

Ex.2

I make hotel reservations before going on a trip.

3 ＿＿＿＿＿ て みます

When expressing trying to do something, **〜てみます** is used.

Conjunctive Form

verb て form 〈〜て〉 〈〜で〉	みます

Ex.1

A：これは 何ですか。どんな あじですか。

B：わたしの 国の おちゃです。<u>のんで みて ください</u>。

A：ありがとうございます。あ、おいしいですね。

Ex.2

（デパートの くつうりばで）

てんいん：この くつは いかがですか。

A：ああ、いいですね。<u>はいて みます</u>。

Ex.1

A: What's this? What does it taste like?

B: It's tea from my country. Please try some.

C: Thank you. Oh, it's delicious.

Ex.2

(In the shoe section of a department store)

Store clerk: How do you like these shoes?

A: Oh, they're nice. I'll try them on.

12 - 2

Vocabulary and Expression

おねがい request ／おしらせ notification ／むり（な）impossible ／れんしゅうします practice
やります do

─────────────────────────

ホール hall ／ばしょ place ／ちず map ／イベント event ／こと what, things

そうだんします discuss ／（アルバイトを）かわります take one's shift

しょくじします have a meal ／たいそうします exercise ／そうじします clean

ホーム platform ／せっけん soap ／におい smell ／ガス gas ／こうじ construction

てんちょう store manager, restaurant manager

Conversation Scenario

〈Receiving a notification〉

Tang: Excuse me, Sensei. I have a favor to ask.

Aoki: Okay. What is it?

Tang: I got a notice from the post office. Could you take a look at it?

Aoki: Sure, I'll look at it. You have a package at the post office, so please call this number.

Tang: What? Call them? No way. Can't you call them for me?

Aoki: It's okay. Let's practice before you call them.

Tang: Okay. I'll try.

3 けしゴム、かして

Can-do Check ✓

☐ You can make a simple request to your friend.

☐ You can ask your friend for a favor that may be difficult for the friend to do.

Grammar Notes

1 て 。

〜て。 is used when asking friends, family or people close to you to do a favor.

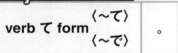

Conjunctive Form

verb て form 〈〜て〉〈〜で〉	。

Ex.1

（友だちに）
とも
A：その ペン、とって。
B：はい。
A：ありがとう。

Ex.1

(Talking with a friend)
A: Hand me that pen.
B: Here.
A: Thanks.

Ex.2

あに：ちょっと 来て。
き
おとうと：何？
なに

Ex.2

Older brother: Come here.
Younger brother: What?

2 て くれない？

〜て くれない？ is used when asking friends, family or people close to you to do a favor that may be difficult to do. くれない？ is said with a rising intonation at the end.

Conjunctive Form

verb て form 〈〜て〉〈〜で〉	くれない？

Ex.1

（友<small>とも</small>だちに）

A：あ、さいふを わすれた！ Bさん、ごめん。

　すこし お金<small>かね</small>、<u>かして くれない？</u>

B：うん、いいよ。いくら？

A：1,000円<small>えん</small>。

B：うん、いいよ。

Ex.2

（アルバイトで）

A：Bさん、わるいんだけど、こんどの 日<small>にち</small>よう日<small>び</small>、

　アルバイト <u>かわって くれない？</u>

B：うん、いいよ。

Ex.1

(To a friend)

A: Ah, I forgot my wallet. Sorry, B-san.
　Could you lend me some money?

B: Yeah, okay. How much?

A: A thousand yen.

B: Okay.

Ex.2

(At a part-time job)

A: B-san, sorry, but could you cover my
　shift for me this Sunday?

B: Yeah, okay.

The following words are used before asking someone to do something difficult.

・すみません。

・あのう、おねがいが あるんですが

・わるいんですが

・もうしわけありませんが

The following words are used before asking friends, family or people close to you to do something difficult.

・ごめん。

・ねえ、おねがいが あるんだけど

・わるいんだけど

・もうしわけないんだけど

3　plain form　noun

The plain form (☞ Lesson 8 - 2) of verbs can be placed in front of nouns to describe people, places or things.

Conjunctive Form

verb plain form	noun

Ex.1

A：いい とけいですね。

B：これは、父に もらった とけいです。

Ex.2

A：あの 人、きのう テレビで 見た 人です。

B：あ、あの 人は ゆうめいな サッカーせんしゅですよ。

Ex.3

A：この しゃしんの ばしょは どこですか。

B：これは わたしが 住んで いた ところです。

Ex.1

A: That's a nice watch.

B: My father gave it to me.

Ex.2

A: That's the person I saw on TV yesterday.

B: Ah, that person is a famous soccer player.

Ex.3

A: What's the place in this picture?

B: That's where I used to live.

Vocabulary and Expression

けしゴム eraser ／ひどい awful ／ちゃんと properly ／かえします return

ねこ cat ／（でんきを）つけます turn on ／わたします pass ／クイズ quiz

おとな adult ／ニュース news ／ばんぐみ TV program

（テレビに）出ます appear on a TV program ／かしゅ singer ／デザイン design

デザイナー designer ／外国人 foreigner ／うります sell

Conversation Scenario

〈Borrowing an eraser〉

Tang: Kim-san, lend me an eraser.

Kim: Okay.

Tang: Thanks.

Tang: Oh! Kim-san, sorry, but I have a favor to ask.

Kim: What?

Tang: I forgot my eraser again. Can you lend me one?

Kim: Uh, what happened to the eraser I lent you yesterday?

Tang: I forgot that one, too.

Kim: That's terrible! Here. Give it back this time.

Tang: Okay, I will. Sorry. Thanks.

Can-do Check ✔

☐ You can explain that you feel unwell and go home early or take a rest.

☐ You can give a reason and receive permission (to leave early).

Grammar Notes ✏

1-1　　　　　　　　　ので、　　　　　て も いいですか

When giving a reason and ask for permission to do something, **~ので、~てもいいです
か** is used.

Conjunctive Form

～	ので、	verb て form 〈～て〉 〈～で〉	も いいですか

Ex.1

A：先生、テストがおわったので、帰っても いいですか。
せんせい　　　　　　　　　　　　　　　　かえ
先生：はい、いいですよ。
せんせい

Ex.1

A: Sensei, I finished the test, so may I
　 go home?

Teacher: Yes, you may.

Ex.2

しゃいんA：ミーティングを するので、この へやを
　 つかっても いいですか。
しゃいんB：はい。どうぞ。

Ex.2

Employee A: We're going to have a
　 meeting, so can we use this room?

Employee B: Sure. Go ahead.

Ex.3

A：さむいので、まどを しめても いいですか。
B：はい。どうぞ。

Ex.3

A: It's cold, so may I close the window?

B: Sure. Go ahead.

1-2　　　　　　　　　から、　　　　　て も いい?

When talking to friends, family or people close to you to give a reason and ask for
permission to do something, **~から、~てもいい?** is used.

Conjunctive Form

～	から、	verb て form 〈～て〉 〈～で〉	も いい?

Ex.1

A：雨が ふっているから、この かさ、かりても いい？
あめ

B：うん、いいよ。

Ex.2

A：ちょっと くらいから、電気、つけても いい？
でんき

B：うん、いいよ。

Ex.3

子ども：お母さん、おなかが すいたから、この ケーキ、
こ　　　かあ

食べても いい？
た

母：だめよ。もうすぐ ごはんだから。
はは

Ex.1
A: It's raining, so may I borrow this umbrella?
B: Yeah, sure.

Ex.2
A: It's a little dark, so may I turn on the light?
B: Yeah, sure.

Ex.3
Child: Mom, I'm hungry, so may I eat this cake?
Mother: No, you may not. We're going to have dinner soon.

1-3　　　　　　　ので、

When talking about your actions and your reasons for them, **～ので、～** is used. **ので** is added after the reason (X), and this is followed by whatever actions (Y) happened because of them.

Conjunctive Form

sentence X	ので、	sentence Y

Ex.1

あたまが いたいので、しごとを 休みました。
やす

Ex.2

時間が なかったので、ひるごはんを 食べませんでした。
じかん　　　　　　　　　　　　　　　た

Ex.3

来年 りゅうがくするので、ちょきんを して います。
らいねん

Ex.4

きょうは ひまだったので、友だちと えいがを 見に 行き
とも　　　　　　　　み　い
ました。

Ex.5

あしたは テストなので、きょうは べんきょうします。

Ex.1

My head hurts, so I took the day off from work.

Ex.2

I didn't have time, so I didn't eat lunch.

Ex.3

I'm going to study abroad next year, so I'm saving money.

Ex.4

I'm free today, so I went to see a movie with my friend.

Ex.5

I have a test tomorrow, so I'm going to study today.

The reasons that come before **ので** may also be put in the polite form.

Ex.1 A：時間が ありませんので、タクシーで 行きましょう。 　　 じかん　　　　　　　　　　　　　　　　　　い B：わかりました。	**Ex.1** A: We don't have much time, so let's take a taxi. B: Okay.
Ex.2 A：雨が ふって いますので、タクシーを よびました。 　　あめ B：ありがとうございます。	**Ex.2** A: It's started raining, so I called a taxi. B: Thank you.

2 -1　どうしたんですか。 —　　　　　　　　　んです

When asking someone what is troubling them or what is out of the ordinary, **どうした んですか。** is used. **〜んです** is used when answering. **〜んです** is used to express the feeling of asking about or describing the situation (☞ Lesson 8 - 2 **ふつう形**).
けい

Conjunctive Form

どうしたんですか。	——	**verb plain form**	んです。
		い adjective plain form 〈〜い〉	
		な adjective plain form 〈〜だ な〉	
		noun plain form 〈〜だ な〉	

Ex.1 えきいん：どうしたんですか。 A：きっぷが ないんです。		**Ex.1** Station employee: What's the matter? A: I don't have a ticket.
Ex.2 A：どうしたんですか。 B：あたまが いたいんです。		**Ex.2** A: What's wrong? B: My head hurts.

2 -2　どうして　　　　　　　んですか。 —　　　　　　　　んです

When asking the reason why someone else do something, **どうして 〜んですか** is used.
〜んです is used when answering (☞ Lesson 8 - 2 **ふつう形**).
けい

Conjunctive Form

どうして	verb plain form	んですか。	——	〜んです。

141

Ex.1

A：どうして 帰らないんですか。

B：あしたまでの しごとが あるんです。

Ex.2

先生：どうして 日本語を べんきょうしたいんですか。

A：日本の 会社で はたらきたいんです。

Ex.1

A: Why aren't you going home?

B: I have some work that needs to be done by tomorrow.

Ex.2

Teacher: Why do you want to study Japanese?

A: I want to work at a Japanese company.

Vocabulary and Expression 🙂

おちます fall ／（テストを）うけます take a test ／おだいじに Get well soon.

くらい dark ／おなか stomach ／ゆうびん番号 post code, zip code ／れんらくします contact

くわしく detailed, in detail ／たくはいびん home delivery service

いんかん personal seal, name seal ／サイン signature ／けっこうです That's okay.

よります drop by, come by ／さくら cherry blossom ／さきます bloom ／あ〜 Oh no!

データ data ／きえます be deleted ／なきます cry ／ちこくします be late for

Conversation Scenario 💬

〈Going to the hospital〉

Lama: Excuse me, Sensei.

Aoki: Yes? Oh, Lama-san, what's wrong?

Lama: Well, I fell down the stairs.

Aoki: What?!

Lama: I'll be going to the hospital today, so may I leave early?

Aoki: Yes. Will you be okay going to the hospital on your own?

Lama: Yes. Umm, is it okay if I don't take the kanji test today?

Aoki: Yes, you can take it next week.

Lama: Okay.

Aoki: Get well soon.

Lama: Thank you.

1 わしょくは どうですか

Can-do Check ✓

☐ You can invite a coworker out to a meal.

☐ You can accept an invitation and discuss where to go.

Grammar Notes 🖊

1 　　　　　　ませんか

When inviting someone to do something, **〜ませんか** is used. **〜ない?** is used when talking to friends or people close to you.

Conjunctive Form

verb ます form〈〜ます せん〉	か

Ex.1

A：12時ですよ。おひるを 食べに 行きませんか。

B：行きましょう。でも、ちょっと まって ください。

Ex.1

A: It's 12:00. Why don't we go have lunch?

B: Let's go. But please wait a little.

Ex.2

A：こんどの 日よう日 いっしょに サッカーを しない?

B：ごめん。こんどの 日よう日は ちょっと。

Ex.2

A: Why don't we play soccer together this Sunday?

B: Sorry. I can't this Sunday.

2 　　　　　　たら、

When talking about what you will do (Y) after completing a first action (X), **〜たら、 〜** is used. The verb's **た** from is used, but here it is used to talk about future events rather than the past.

Conjunctive Form

verb X た form 〈〜た〉〈〜だ〉	ら、	verb Y

Ex.1

A：しごとが おわったら、いっしょに 飲みに 行きませんか。

B：いいですね。行きましょう。

Ex.1

A: After we're done with work, why don't we go for a drink?

B: That sounds great. Let's go.

Ex.2

先生：レポートを 書いたら、見せて ください。

A：はい。

Ex.2

Teacher: After you write the report, please show it to me.

A: Okay.

3　░░░░░░░░░ ─ ░░░░░░░░ なら、░░░░░░░░

When adding on something that you know to something that someone else is talking about, 〜なら、〜 is used.

Conjunctive Form

noun	なら、	〜

Ex.1

A：おいしい カレーが 食べたいですね。

B：カレーなら、わたしが 作りますよ。食べに 来て
　　ください。

Ex.2

A：あれ、きむらさん、いませんね。

B：きむらさんなら、ロビーに いますよ。

A：ロビーですか。ありがとうございます。

Ex.1

A: I want eat some delicious curry.

B: If it's curry you want, I can make some. Please come and have some.

Ex.2

A: Huh? Kimura-san isn't here.

B: If you're looking for Kimura-san, he's in the lobby.

A: The lobby, huh? Thank you.

Vocabulary and Expression 😊

わしょく Japanese food ／やきとり yakitori, chicken skewers ／じゃ well

少し a little ／（せきが）あきます a seat be available ／もどします return ／かいぎ meeting
しりょう document(s) ／かいぎしつ meeting room ／ええ？ Oh, really?
コーヒーを いれます make coffee ／ちゅうかりょうり Chinese food ／デザート dessert

Conversation Scenario 💬

〈Inviting a coworker〉

Inoue: After work today, why don't we go get some drinks?

Lee: Oh, that sounds nice. Let's go. I want to eat Japanese food today.

Inoue: Great.

Lee: How about sushi or yakitori?

Inoue: Well, if you want yakitori, I know a great place. The food is good and the restaurant is clean. They also have many different kinds of Japanese sake.

Lee: Great. Then, let's go there.

2 その日は ちょっと
ひ

Can-do Check ✓

☐ You can invite a coworker to hang out.

☐ You can discuss the date and time when your coworker asked you to go out together.

Grammar Notes ✏

1 _____ — _____ なら、_____

When suggesting a different idea when something someone else suggested does not work for you, **～なら、～** is used.

Conjunctive Form

noun	なら、	～

In the following examples, the part underlined with _____ is a suggestion to do something other than the previously stated action underlined with _____.

Ex.1

A：こんどの 日よう日、みんなで ふじ山へ
　　 にち　　び　　　　　　　　　　　　さん
　　行きませんか。
　　い

B：こんどの 日よう日は よていが ありますが、
　　　　　　にち　　び
　　来週なら 行きたいです。
　らいしゅう　い

Ex.2

(デパートのくつうりばで)

A：この くつ、くろは ありますか。

てんいん：すみません。あおなら あります。

Ex.1

A: Why don't we all climb Mt. Fuji this Sunday?

B: I've got plans this Sunday, but I would love to go next weekend.

Ex.2

(At the shoe section in a department store)

A: Do you have these shoes in black?

Employee: I'm sorry. We have them in blue.

2　　　　　たり、　　　　たり

When giving several examples of actions, **〜たり、 〜たり 〜** is used.

Conjunctive Form

verb X た form 〈〜た〉〈〜だ〉	り、	verb Y た form 〈〜た〉〈〜だ〉	り	します

Ex.1

A：いつも 日よう日は 何を しますか。

B：そうですね。テニスを したり、
　友だちと あそびに 行ったり します。

Ex.1

A: What do you usually do on Sundays?

B: Let's see. I do things like playing tennis or hanging out with my friends.

Ex.2

A：きょうとの りょこう、どうでしたか。
　何を しましたか。

B：とても たのしかったです。わしょくを 食べたり、
　きものを きたり しました。

Ex.2

A: How was your trip to Kyoto? What did you do?

B: It was really fun. I did things like eating Japanese food and wearing a kimono.

3-1　　　　　　　　の あとで、

When talking about what you are going to do after a given action that is described using a noun, **〜のあとで、 〜** is used.

Conjunctive Form

noun ＋ の	あとで、	verb

Ex.1

ジョギングの あとで、シャワーを
あびます。

Ex.1

After jogging, I'm going to take a shower.

Ex.2

しょくじの あとで、さらを あらいます。

Ex.2

After eating, I'm going to wash the dishes.

3-2　　　　　　た あとで、

When expressing doing 【action Y】 after 【action X】, ～ （**X**） たあとで、～ （**Y**） is used.

Conjunctive Form

verb X た form 〈～た〉 〈～だ〉	あとで、	verb Y

Ex.1
ジョギングを した あとで、シャワーを あびます。

Ex.2
しょくじを した あとで、さらを あらい
ます。

Ex.1
After I go jogging, I'm going to take a shower.

Ex.2
After I eat, I'm going to do the dishes.

~まえに~ or ~の まえに~ are used to express that 【verb Y】 will be done before 【verb X】 (☞ Lesson 12-2).

Conjunctive Form

verb X dictionary form	まえに、	verb Y

Ex.
ごはんを 食べる まえに、てを あらいます。
　　　　た

Ex.
Before I eat, I wash my hands.

Conjunctive Form

noun ＋ の	まえに、	verb

Ex.
しょくじの まえに、てを あらいます。

Ex.
Before eating, I wash my hands.

4　　　　　　　か　　　　　　　（か）、

When asking someone to choose one thing out of a group of two, **Xか Y（か）、どちらが ～か** is used. **どっち** is used instead **どちら** of when talking to friends and people close to you.

Conjunctive Form

X	か	Y	（か）、	どちらが	～	か

Ex.1

A：パン<u>か</u> ごはん<u>か</u> どちらが いいですか。

B：パンを おねがいします。

Ex.2

A：この あかい ネクタイ<u>か</u> あの あおい ネクタイ<u>か</u> どっちが いい？

B：あの あおいのが いいよ。

Ex.1

A: Which would you like, bread or rice?

B: Bread, please.

Ex.2

A: Which is better, this red tie or this blue tie?

B: That blue tie is nice.

・**Aか Bか C（か）、どれが ～か**：for a group of three or more things

・**Aか Bか C（か）、いつが ～か**：for dates or times

・**Aか Bか C（か）、どこが ～か**：for places

・**Aか Bか C（か）、だれが ～か**：for people

Ex.1

A：ごはんを 食べに 行きましょう。
　日本りょうり<u>か</u> ちゅうかりょうり<u>か</u> イタリア りょうり<u>か</u>、どれが いいですか。

B：イタリアりょうりが いいです。

Ex.2

A：この しごと、たなかさん<u>か</u> やまかわさんに たのみましょう。

B：そうですね。わたしは たなかさんが いいと 思います。

Ex.1

A: Let's go get something to eat. What would you prefer, Japanese, Chinese or Italian food?

B: I'd like Italian food.

Ex.2

A: Let's ask either Tanaka-san or Yamakawa-san to do this job.

B: Let's see. I think Tanaka-san would be good for it.

Vocabulary and Expression

さんぽ taking a walk ／（お）ひるごはん lunch ／リボン ribbon

Conversation Scenario

〈Discussing going to play golf〉

Inoue: Why don't we play golf together this Sunday?

Shin: This Sunday? I'd love to, but I already have plans that day.

Inoue: I see. Then, how about next Saturday or Sunday?

Shin: Great. Sunday would be good.

Inoue: Then, next Sunday. After golf, let's go to a hot spring or go drinking.

Shin: That sounds good. I'm looking forward to it.

13-1-2

Can-do Check ✓

☐ You can invite a friend to an event.

☐ You can turn down a friend's invitation to an event.

Grammar Notes 🖊

1　　　　　　　て みない？

When suggesting trying something to someone, **～て みませんか** is used. **～て みない？** is used instead when talking with friends, family and people close to you.

Conjunctive Form

verb て form	〈～て〉	みませんか
	〈～で〉	みない？

Ex.1

（ケーキやで）

A：これ、新しい ケーキだね。食べて みない？
　　　あたら　　　　　　　　た

B：うん。食べて みる。
　　　　た

A：すみません。これ、2つ ください。

Ex.2

A：えき前に 新しい カフェが できたね。
　　　まえ　あたら

B：うん。あとで 行って みない？
　　　　　　　い

A：いいね。

Ex.1

(At a cake store)

A: This is a new cake. Why don't you try some?

B: Okay, I will.

A: Excuse me. Two of these, please.

Ex.2

A: There's a new café in front of the station.

B: Yeah. Why don't we go there later?

A: Okay.

＊～て みます is used to express that you are going to try doing something

（☞ Lesson 12 - 2）.

2　**いこう形**　Volitional Form
　　　　けい

The volitional form of verbs is used instead of **～ましょう**, as in **かえりましょう** or **食べま**
た
しょう（☞ Lesson 5 - 1）when talking to friends, family or people close to you. This conjugation of verbs where the verb ending is changed to a syllable ending in **う** is called the volitional form（**いこう形**）.
けい

Ex.1

（アルバイトで）

A：そうじ、おわった。 Bさん、帰ろう。
　　　　　　　　　　　　　　かえ

B：うん、帰ろう。
　　　　　かえ

Ex.2

A：あした 買いもの、行かない？
　　　　　か　　　　い

B：いいね。行こう。
　　　　　　い

Ex.1

(At a part-time job)

A: I'm done with the cleaning. B-san, let's go home.

B: Yeah, let's go home.

Ex.2

A: Why don't we go shopping tomorrow?

B: Sure. Let's go.

2 -1 Volitional Form of Group I Verbs

The volitional form is made by changing the syllable that comes before **ます** to one that ends with [o] and adding **う**.

> **〜い → 〜おう**

The volitional form of verbs that end in **〜います** is **〜おう**.

か います buy → か おう

> **〜き → 〜こう ／ 〜ぎ → 〜ごう**

The volitional form of verbs that end in **〜きます** is **〜こう**, and for verbs that end in **〜ぎます**, it is **〜ごう**.

か きます write → か こう

いそ ぎます hurry → いそ ごう

> **〜し → 〜そう**

The volitional form of verbs that end in **〜します** is **〜そう**.

はな します talk → はな そう

か します lend → か そう

> **〜ち → 〜とう**

The volitional form of verbs that end in **〜ちます** is **〜とう**.

ま ちます wait → ま とう

> **〜に → 〜のう**

The volitional form of verbs that end in **〜にます** is **〜のう**.

し にます die → し のう

～び → ～ぼう

The volitional form of verbs that end in **～びます** is **～ぼう**.

あそびます play → あそぼう

～み → ～もう

The volitional form of verbs that end in **～みます** is **～もう**.

よみます read → よもう

～り → ～ろう

The volitional form of verbs that end in **～ります** is **～ろう**.

とります take → とろう

2-2　Volitional Form of Group Ⅱ Verbs

ます becomes **よう**.

たべます eat → たべよう

みます see, watch → みよう

2-3　Volitional Form of Group Ⅲ Verbs

The volitional form of verbs that end in **～します** is **～しよう**. 【noun】＋**します** becomes 【noun】＋**しよう**.

べんきょうします study → べんきょうしよう

そうじします clean → そうじしよう

3　　　　　うと 思って います

When expressing that you are considering doing something, ～（よ）うと 思って います is used. In conversation, 思って います becomes 思って ます, and 思って いる is often shortened to 思ってる.

Conjunctive Form

verb volitional form	と 思って います

152

Ex.1

A：Bさん、きょう しごとが おわったら、何を しますか。

B：ジムへ 行こうと 思って います。

A：そうですか。よかったら、コンサートに 行きませんか。チケットが あるんですが。

B：え、だれの コンサートですか。

Ex.2

A：かんじ、たくさん あるね。どうする？

B：わたしは 毎日 かんじを 5つ おぼえようと 思ってる。

Ex.3

A：あしたから ダイエットしようと 思って います。

B：そうですか。がんばって ください。

Ex.1

A: B-san, what are you going to do after work today?

B: I think I might go to the gym.

A: I see. If you'd like, why don't we go to a concert? I have tickets.

B: Huh? Whose concert?

Ex.2

A: There are a lot of kanji. What are you going to do?

B: I think I'm going to try memorizing five kanji each day.

Ex.3

A: I think I'm going to go on a diet starting tomorrow.

B: Really? Please do your best.

13 - 3

Vocabulary and Expression

フェスティバル festival ／いや (な) unfavorable, unpleasant

ざんねん (な) too bad, unfortunate

もって きます bring (a thing) ／そつぎょうします graduate

ぼんおどり bon odori, bon dancing ／ぶんかさい culture festival

Conversation Scenario

⟨Inviting a friend⟩

Tang: Hey, did you know? The Thai Festival is going to be held in Midori Park this Saturday and Sunday.

Kim: Oh yeah?

Tang: Why don't we go? They're going to have things like Thai singers and Thai food.

Kim: Hmm. But I don't like crowded places.

Tang: Aw, let's go. I think it'll be fun.

Kim: Hmm. I was thinking I would spend this weekend quietly at home. Sorry.

Tang: I see. That's too bad.

Lesson 14

1 びょういんへ 行った ほうが いいですよ
い

Can-do Check ✓

☐ You can ask an unwell person how they are doing.

☐ You can give simple advice.

Grammar Notes 🖊

1-1　　　　　　　ない　ほうが　いいです

When suggesting not doing something to someone, **〜ない ほうが いいです** is used.

〜ほうが いいですよ is often used when making a suggestion.

Conjunctive Form

verb ない form 〈〜ない〉	ほうが いいです

Ex.1

（プールでせきをしている人に）
　　　　　　　　　　　　ひと

A：かぜですか。およがない ほうが いいですよ。

B：そうします。

Ex.2

（たばこをすっている人に）
　　　　　　　　　ひと

A：たばこを すわない ほうが いいですよ。

　　からだに わるいですから。

B：はい。

Ex.1

(To someone coughing at the pool)

A: Do you have a cold? You shouldn't go swimming.

B: I won't.

Ex.2

(To someone smoking)

A: You shouldn't smoke. It's bad for you.

B: Okay.

1-2　　　　　　　た　ほうが　いいです

When suggesting doing something to someone, **〜た ほうが いいです** is used.

Conjunctive Form

verb た form 〈〜た〉 〈〜だ〉	ほうが いいです

154

Ex.1

（ねつがある人に）

A：だいじょうぶですか。くすりを <u>飲んだ ほうが</u>
　　<u>いいです</u>よ。

B：はい。

Ex.2

（テレビを見ている人に）

A：1時ですよ。もう <u>ねた ほうが</u>
　　<u>いいです</u>よ。

B：はい。

Ex.1

(To someone with a fever)

A: Are you okay? You should take some
　medicine.

B: Okay.

Ex.2

(To someone watching TV)

A: It's 1:00. You should go to bed.

B: Okay.

---

2 [　　] く なります
[　　] に なります

When explaining how something has changed, **〜なります** is used. **〜く なります** is used
for **い** adjectives, **〜に なります** for **な** adjectives and **〜に なります** for nouns.

Conjunctive Form

い adjective 〈〜い く〉	
な adjective 〈〜な に〉	**なります**
noun ＋ に	

Ex.1

A：<u>さむく なりました</u>ね。

B：そうですね。11月ですからね。

Ex.2

A：<u>くらく なりました</u>。電気を つけて ください。

B：はい。

Ex.3

A：かぜ、どうですか。

B：くすりを 飲んだので、<u>げんきに なりました</u>。

Ex.1

A: It's gotten cold, hasn't it?

B: Yes. Because it's November.

Ex.2

A: It's gotten dark. Please turn on the
　light.

B: Okay.

Ex.3

A: How is your cold?

B: I took some medicine and now I'm
　feeling better.

Ex.4

A：ひさしぶりですね。おとうとさん、せが 高く

　　なりましたね。

B：はい。中学生に なりました。

A：そうですか。

Ex.5

（雨の あと）

A：いい 天気に なりましたね。

B：そうですね。

Ex.4

A: Long time no see. Your younger
brother has gotten tall.

B: Yes. He's a junior high school
student.

A: I see.

Ex.5

(After it has rained)

A: The weather has cleared up.

B: Yes, it has.

Vocabulary and Expression 🎭

かおいろ complexion ／つめたい cold (things)

かぜを ひきます catch a cold ／（お）ふろに 入ります take a bath ／マスク mask

花に 水を やります water the flower ／ねむい sleepy ／だんだん gradually

（コンビニが）できます a new convenience store is going to open ／いろんな various

Conversation Scenario 💬

〈Having a cold〉

Sarah: Lee-san, you look pale. Are you okay?

Lee: My stomach hurts.

Sarah: Well, if your stomach hurts, then you shouldn't drink cold beverages.

Lee: Okay.

Sarah: I think you should go to a hospital before it gets worse.

Lee: Okay. I understand.

2 ネットで さがせば、いろいろ あるよ

Can-do Check ✓

☐ You can give advice to someone who is looking for a solution of problems.

☐ You can talk about what you can and can't do.

Grammar Notes 🖊

1 ば 、 じょうけん形 Conditional Form

When expressing that 【action Y】 will occur in the condition that 【action X】 occurs, **〜ば、 〜** is used. The form of verbs that ends in **〜ば** is known as the conditional form (**じょうけん形**).

Conjunctive Form

verb X conditional form	action Y

Ex.1

A：あたまが いたいです。

B：くすりを 飲めば、よく なりますよ。
　　　　　の

Ex.2

A：かんじの べんきょうが たいへんです。

B：友だちと いっしょに べんきょうすれば、たのしいですよ。
　　とも

Ex.1

A: My head hurts.

B: If you take some medicine, you'll get better.

Ex.2

A: Studying kanji is hard.

B: It can be fun if you study with your friends.

1 -1　Conditional Form of Group Ⅰ Verbs

The conditional form of verbs is formed by changing the part that comes before **ます** to a syllable that ends in [e] and adding **ば**.

〜い → 〜えば

The conditional form of verbs that end in **〜います** is **〜えば**.

かいます buy → かえば

157

~き → ~けば ／ ~ぎ → ~げば

The conditional form of verbs that end in **~きます** is **~けば**, and for verbs that end in **~ぎます**, it is **~げば**.

か<u>き</u>ます write → か<u>け</u>ば

いそ<u>ぎ</u>ます hurry → いそ<u>げ</u>ば

~し → ~せば

The conditional form of verbs that end in **~します** is **~せば**.

はな<u>し</u>ます talk → はな<u>せ</u>ば

か<u>し</u>ます lend → か<u>せ</u>ば

~ち → ~てば

The conditional form of verbs that end in **~ちます** is **~てば**.

ま<u>ち</u>ます wait → ま<u>て</u>ば

~に → ~ねば

The conditional form of verbs that end in **~にます** is **~ねば**.

<u>し</u>にます die → <u>し</u>ねば

~び → ~べば

The conditional form of verbs that end in **~びます** is **~べば**.

あそ<u>び</u>ます play → あそ<u>べ</u>ば

~み → ~めば

The conditional form of verbs that end in **~みます** is **~めば**.

よ<u>み</u>ます read → よ<u>め</u>ば

~り → ~れば

The conditional form of verbs that end in **~ります** is **~れば**.

と<u>り</u>ます take → と<u>れ</u>ば

1-2　Conditional Form of Group II Verbs

ます becomes **れば**.

たべ<u>ます</u> eat → たべ<u>れば</u>

み<u>ます</u> see, watch → み<u>れば</u>

■-3 Conditional Form of Group Ⅲ Verbs

The conditional form of **します** is **すれば**. The conditional form of **きます** is **くれば**.

【noun】＋ **します** becomes 【noun】＋ **すれば**.

べんきょうします study → べんきょうすれば

そうじします clean → そうじすれば

Conjugations for verbs you have studied previously ②

Conjugations for verbs include the **ます** form (**ます形**) and dictionary form (**じしょ形**), as well as the **ない** form (**ない形**) (☞ Lesson 7-2), **た** form (**た形**) (☞ Lesson 8-1), **て** form (**て形**) (☞ Lesson 9-1), volitional form (**いこう形**) (☞ Lesson 13-3) and conditional form (**じょうけん形**) (☞ Lesson 14-2).

	ます form	Dictionary form	**ない** form	**た** form	**て** form	Volitional form	Conditional form
Group Ⅰ	かきます write	かく	かかない	かいた	かいて	かこう	かけば
Group Ⅱ	たべます eat	たべる	たべない	たべた	たべて	たべよう	たべれば
	みます see, watch	みる	みない	みた	みて	みよう	みれば
Group Ⅲ	します do	する	しない	した	して	しよう	すれば
	きます come	くる	こない	きた	きて	こよう	くれば

■ _____ が できます

When talking about something that you are able to do, **〜が できます** is used.

Conjunctive Form

noun	が	できます

Ex.1

A：Bさんは ドイツ語が できますか。

B：いいえ、できません。わたしは 中国語と 英語が できます。

A：すごいですね。

Ex.1

A: B-san, can you speak German?

B: No, I can't. I can speak Chinese and English.

A: That's amazing.

Ex.2

A：Bさん、テニス、<u>できる</u>？

B：うん、<u>できる</u>。Aさんは？

A：ううん、<u>できない</u>。でも、して みたい。おしえて。

B：いいよ。

Ex.2

A: B-san, can you play tennis?

B: Yes, I can. How about you?

A: No, I can't. But I want to try it. Please teach me.

B: Sure.

Vocabulary and Expression

ネット internet ／さがします search for ／バイト part-time job ／ほら hey, look

- -

やせます lose weight ／うんどうします exercise ／もんだい question, problem

アプリ app, application ／うんてん driving ／つうやく interpretation ／スケート skating

りょうほう both ／せつめいかい information session ／オープンキャンパス open campus

Conversation Scenario

〈Looking for a part-time job〉

Lama: I want a part-time job. I wonder if there are any good ones.

Kim: There are a lot out there if you look on the Internet.

- -

Kim: Hey, how about this?

Lama: What kind of job is it?

Kim: It's a job where you make phone calls.

Lama: I can't do that. The Japanese used in phone calls is difficult.

Kim: Then, how about working at a convenience store?

Lama: A convenience store.

Kim: It's okay. You can do that.

Lama: Hmm, I don't know.

3 行って みたら どうですか
い

Can-do Check ✔

☐ You can ask if someone has or hasn't been somewhere.

☐ You can explain, give advice and make suggestions regarding a travel destination.

Grammar Notes 🖋

1 ⬜⬜⬜⬜⬜ **なら、** ⬜⬜⬜⬜⬜ **が いいです**

When making a suggestion to someone after hearing what they want, **〜なら、〜がいい です** is used.

Conjunctive Form

verb dictionary form	なら、	noun	がいいです

Ex.1

A：ほっかいどうへ 行って みたいです。
い

B：ほっかいどうへ 行くなら、7月が いいですよ。
い　　　　がつ

Ex.2

A：新しい カメラを 買いたいんですが、どこが いいですか。
あたら　　　　　　か

B：カメラを 買うなら、えき前の 電気やが いいですよ。
か　　　　　まえ　でんき

Ex.1

A: I want to try going to Hokkaido.

B: If you want to go to Hokkaido, July is a good time.

Ex.2

A: I want to buy a new camera. Where should I go?

B: If you want to buy a camera, the electronics store in front of the station is good.

When you give advice or making suggestions, **〜なら、〜** is used.

Ex.1

A：日本の 大学へ 行きたいです。
に　ほん　だいがく　い

B：日本の 大学へ 行くなら、日本りゅうがくしけんを
に　ほん　だいがく　い　　　　　　にほん
うけてください。

Ex.2

A：日本語の 本を 買いたいです。
に　ほん　ご　ほん　か

B：本を 買うなら、インターネットが べんりですよ。
ほん　か

Ex.1

A: I want to go to a Japanese university.

B: If you want to go to a Japanese university, please take the Examination for Japanese University Admission.

Ex.2

A: I want to buy a Japanese language book.

B: If you want to buy a book, the Internet can be useful.

2　　　たら、どうですか

When expressing ideas to solve a problem, **〜たら、どうですか** is used. **〜たら、どう?** is used instead when talking with friends and people close to you.

Conjunctive Form

verb た form 〈〜た〉 〈〜だ〉	ら、	どうですか
		どう?

Ex1.

（ねつがある人に）

A：びょういんへ <u>行ったら、どうですか</u>。

B：はい。そうします。

Ex.2

A：ああ、つかれた。

B：少し <u>休んだら、どう?</u>

A：そうだね。休もう。

Ex.1

(To someone with a fever)

A: Why don't you go to the hospital?

B: Okay, I will.

Ex.2

A: Ah, I'm tired.

B: Why don't you rest a bit?

A: Yeah. Let's rest.

＊〜た ほうが いいです or **〜ない ほうがいいです** is used to suggest that someone do or not do something that you think is a good or bad idea (☞ Lesson 14-1).

3　　　た ことが あります

When talking about something you have the experience of doing, **〜た ことが あります** is used.

Conjunctive Form

verb た form 〈〜た〉 〈〜だ〉	ことが	あります

Ex.1

A：さしみを <u>食べた</u> ことが ありますか。

B：いいえ、ありません。生の さかなは
<u>食べた</u> ことが ありません。

Ex.1

A: Have you ever had sashimi?

B: No, I haven't. I've never eaten raw fish.

Ex.2

A：日本の アニメを 見た ことが ある？

B：うん、ある。おもしろいから、よく 見るよ。

Ex.3

A：アメリカへ 行った ことが ありますか。

B：はい、あります。

A：いつ 行きましたか。

B：3年前です。友だちと りょこうしました。

Ex.2

A: Have you ever seen Japanese anime?

B: Yes, I have. It's interesting, so I watch it often.

Ex.3

A: Have you ever been to America?

B: Yes, I have.

A: When did you go?

B: Three years ago. I traveled with my friend.

Vocabulary and Expression 🐛

あき autumn, fall ／もみじ maple tree

ふね boat, ship ／（めがねが）できます glasses be made ／ちかく close

ざいりょう ingredients, materials ／たのみます order ／インターネット internet

しらべます look up, research ／さいきん recently ／こし lower back

しんぱい（な）worry, worrying ／やっきょく drug store ／スノーボード snow-boarding

そんなに not really, not so much ／さあ… I'm not sure ／なっとう natto, fermented soybeans

すもう sumo (wrestling) ／スピーチ speech

Conversation Scenario 💬

〈Talking while watching TV〉

Ati: Wow! It's beautiful. Where is this temple?

Sarah: It's Kinkakuji in Kyoto. I went last year. Have you ever been to Kyoto?

Ati: No, I've never been. I want to go.

Sarah: If you want to go to Kyoto, you should go in the fall.

Ati: I see.

Sarah: Because the autumn foliage is beautiful and the weather is good.

Ati: Really?

Sarah: There's an extended weekend next month, so why don't you try going then?

Ati: Okay.

1 こわして しまって、すみません

Can-do Check ✓

☐ You can apologize politely for something you did.

☐ You can give a simple explanation of what happened.

Grammar Notes 🖉

1-1 　　　　　て しまいました

When expressing that you have made a mistake, ～て しまいました is used.

Conjunctive Form

verb て form 〈～て〉 〈～で〉	しまいました

Ex.1

A：どうしたんですか。

B：けさ ちこくを して しまいました。

A：それは いけませんね。

Ex.2

A：あ、かばんを わすれて しまいました。

B：え、どこに？

Ex.1

A: What's wrong?

B: I was late this morning.

A: That's not good.

Ex.2

A: Ah, I forgot my bag.

B: Huh? Where?

1-2 　　　　　て しまって、すみませんでした

When apologizing for doing something bad, ～てしまって、すみません／すみませんでした is used. ～て しまって、もうしわけありません／もうしわけありませんでした is a more polite form of this. ～て しまって、ごめんなさい／ごめん is used when speaking with friends and people that are close to you.

Conjunctive Form

		すみません
verb て form 〈～て〉 〈～で〉	しまって、	すみませんでした
		もうしわけありません
		もうしわけありませんでした
		ごめんなさい
		ごめん

Ex.1

A：あのう、それ、わたしの かさです。

B：あ、まちがえて しまって、すみません。

A：いいえ。

Ex.2

A：おくれて、ごめん。

B：うん。まってたよ。

Ex.3

しゃいん：きのうは きゅうに 休んで しまって、
　　　　もうしわけありませんでした。

かちょう：あ、だいじょうぶですか。もう よく なりましたか。

しゃいん：はい、よく なりました。

Ex.1

A: Umm, that's my umbrella.

B: Oh, sorry I made a mistake.

A: It's no problem.

Ex.2

A: Sorry I'm late.

B: Yeah, I've been waiting.

Ex.3

Employee: Sorry for taking the day off suddenly yesterday.

Manager: Are you okay? Are you feeling better now?

Employee: Yes, I'm better.

15-1

2-1　　ければ　、

～ければ、～ is used with **い** adjectives to express that something will happen given a certain condition.

Conjunctive Form

い adjective 〈～い ければ〉、	～

Ex.1

A：いそがしければ、てつだいますよ。

B：ありがとうございます。

Ex.2

A：あした 天気が よければ、お花見に 行きませんか。

B：いいですね。行きましょう。

Ex.1

A: If you're busy, I'll help.

B: Thank you.

Ex.2

A: If the weather is good tomorrow, why don't we go flower viewing?

B: That sounds great. Let's go.

*When using verbs to express a condition for something, the conditional form of verbs is used (☞Lesson 14-2).

2-2　　　　　　なら、

〜なら、〜 is used with **な** adjectives or nouns to express that something will happen given a certain condition.

Conjunctive Form

な adjective 〈〜な〉	なら、	〜
noun		

Ex.1
A：あした ひまなら、びじゅつかんへ えを 見に 行こうと
思って います。
B：いいですね。

Ex.2
A：テニス、かんたんなら、やって みたいです。
B：やって みましょう。

Ex.3
A：なつ休み、いっしょに りょこうに 行かない?
B：いいね。アルバイトが あるけど、8月の はじめなら、
だいじょうぶだよ。

Ex.1
A: If I'm free tomorrow, I'm thinking I might go to an art museum to look at paintings.
B: Great.

Ex.2
A: If tennis is simple, I want to try it.
B: Let's try.

Ex.3
A: Why don't we go on a trip together during summer vacation?
B: Great. I have to work at my part-time job, but early August would be okay.

🍡 **Vocabulary and Expression** 🍡

こわします break ／けります kick ／あてます hit
もうしわけ ありません I'm very sorry.

しょるい documents ／よごします make ... dirty ／かびん vase ／わります break
おとします drop ／ぶつかります hit ／たおします knock over ／気を つけます take care
山のぼり mountain climbing ／サーフィン surfing ／へいじつ weekday
すいています not crowded

Conversation Scenario 💬

⟨Apologizing to a teacher⟩

Lama: Oh no, what should I do?

Lama: Aoki-sensei.

Aoki: Yes?

Lama: Oh, if you're busy, I'll come back later.

Aoki: No, it's okay. What's wrong?

Tang: Sensei, sorry. We broke the class clock.

Aoki: What? The clock? What happened?

Lama: I kicked a soccer ball and it hit the clock.

Aoki: So, you kicked a ball in the classroom?

Lama: Yes. Sorry.

Tang: Sorry we broke the clock.

15 - 1

2 ごめんなさい

Can-do Check ✓

☐ You can apologize to a friend.

☐ You can explain what happened to a friend.

Grammar Notes ✐

1 ［　　　　　　　　　］ちゃった

When talking to friends, family and people you are close to about something you did on accident, **〜ちゃった** is used. **〜ちゃった** is a contraction of **〜て しまいました**.

Conjunctive Form

verb て form 〈〜て〉 〈〜で〉	ちゃった

Ex.1

A：けさ、スマホ、おとしちゃった。

B：え、だいじょうぶ?

A：われちゃった。

Ex.1

A: I dropped my smartphone this morning.

B: Oh, was it okay?

A: It cracked.

Ex.2

A：どうしたの?

B：かさ、まちがえちゃった。これ、わたしのじゃない。

Ex.2

A: What's wrong?

B: I took the wrong umbrella. This isn't mine.

◆When talking to friends, family and people that are close to you to apologize for doing something bad, **ごめんなさい** or **ごめん** is used. **〜ちゃって、ごめんね** may also be used. **うん。** is used to respond to an apology. **ううん。** can also be used to mean "don't worry about it".

Ex.1

A：あ、かりた 本、わすれちゃった。ごめん。
　　あした もって くる。

B：うん。いいよ。あしたで。

Ex.1

A: Ah, I forgot the book I borrowed from you. Sorry. I'll bring it tomorrow.

B: It's okay. Tomorrow is fine.

Ex.2

A：ノートを よごしちゃって、ごめんね。

B：うん。

Ex.2

A: Sorry I got your notebook dirty.

B: It's okay.

Ex.3

A：あ、これ、Bさんの けしゴムだ。

　<u>つかっちゃって、ごめんなさい</u>。

B：<u>ううん</u>。だいじょうぶ。

Ex.3

A: Ah, this is your eraser. Sorry for
　using it.

B: That's okay.

2　　　　　　**ながら**

When expressing that two actions (X, Y) are being done at the same time, **～ながら ～** is used.

Conjunctive Form

verb X ます form〈～ます〉	ながら	verb Y

Ex.1

A：<ruby>毎朝<rt>まいあさ</rt></ruby> おんがくを <u><ruby>聞<rt>き</rt></ruby>きながら</u> <ruby>朝<rt>あさ</rt></ruby>ごはんを <ruby>食<rt>た</rt></ruby>べます。

B：いいですね。どんな おんがくですか。

Ex.1

A: Every morning, I eat breakfast while
　listening to music.

B: That's nice. What kind of music?

Ex.2

A：<ruby>電話<rt>でんわ</rt></ruby>を <u>しながら</u> うんてんしては
　いけません。

B：はい。

Ex.2

A: Don't talk on the phone while
　driving.

B: Okay.

15 - 2

Vocabulary and Expression 😊

あのね Well... ／え〜 Oh gosh! ／しかたが ありません There is nothing you can do.

あぶない dangerous

Conversation Scenario 💬

〈Apologizing to a friend〉

Kim: Lama-san, I'm sorry.

Lama: Huh, what?

Kim: Well... I got the book I borrowed from you dirty.

Lama: What?

Kim: I was reading it while eating ice cream...

Lama: Uh huh.

Kim: And I dropped the ice cream.

Lama: What?!

Kim: I'm really sorry.

Lama: Well... I guess there's nothing to be done about it now.

Can-do Check ✓

☐ You can use formal language to have a simple conversation with someone of a higher status.

Grammar Notes ✓

1 尊敬語 Honorific Speech
　　そんけい ご

When speaking to people of a higher status (teachers, company presidents, department managers, section managers, elderly people, etc.), honorific speech (尊敬語) is used.
そんけい

Verb	Honorific speech verb	Example sentence
行きます い go	いらっしゃいます	先生は明日京都へいらっしゃいます。 せんせい　あした きょうと My teacher is going to Kyoto tomorrow.
来ます き come	いらっしゃいます	先生は毎日8時に学校へいらっしゃいます。 せんせい　まいにち　じ　がっこう My teacher comes to school every day at 8:00.
います be	いらっしゃいます	先生は今教室にいらっしゃいます。 せんせい　いま きょうしつ My teacher is in the classroom now.
〜ています is doing	〜ていらっしゃいます	先生は今本を読んでいらっしゃいます。 せんせい　いま ほん　よ My teacher is reading a book now.
食べます た eat	めしあがります	先生はいちごのケーキをめしあがりました。 せんせい My teacher ate strawberry cake.
飲みます の drink	めしあがります	先生はコーヒーもめしあがりました。 せんせい My teacher drank coffee, too.
見ます み see, watch	ごらんになります	先生は毎朝テレビのニュースをごらんになります。 せんせい　まいあさ My teacher watches the news on TV every morning.
言います い say	おっしゃいます	先生は「これからテストをします」とおっしゃいました。 せんせい My teacher said, "Now, we will have a test".
します do	なさいます	先生は毎週テニスをなさいます。 せんせい　まいしゅう My teacher plays tennis every week.
知っています し know	ごぞんじです	先生はベトナム料理の店をごぞんじですか。 せんせい　　　　りょう り　みせ Sensei, do you know any Vietnamese restaurants?

Polite Speech (敬語)・Honorific Speech (尊敬語)・Humble Speech (謙譲語)

When talking to people in public places like a company, the **ます** form of verbs is used and **です** is added to **い** adjectives, **な** adjectives and nouns. However, when speaking with friends, family and people that are close to you, casual speech, which uses the plain forms of verbs, **い** adjectives, **な** adjectives and nouns, is used. In addition, there is also polite speech (**敬語**), which is used when speaking to people of a higher status than you. Within polite speech, there is honorific speech (**尊敬語**), which is used to talk with or about people of a higher status. There is also humble speech (**謙譲語**), which is used to talk about oneself to people of a higher status.

Ex.1

（どうりょうと話すとき）

A：Bさん、コンビニへ行きますか。

B：はい、行きます。

Ex.2

（友だちと話すとき）

A：Bさん、コンビニへ行く？

B：うん、行く。

Ex.3

（上司と話すとき）

A：課長、コンビニへいらっしゃいますか。

課長：はい、行きます。

Ex.4

課長：Aさん、会議室に来てください。

A：はい、まいります。

Ex.1

(Talking to a coworker)

A: B-san, are you going to go to a convenience store?

B: Yes, I am.

Ex.2

(Talking to a friend)

A: B-san, are you going to go to a convenience store?

B: Yeah, I am.

Ex.3

(Talking to a section manager)

A: Manager, are you going to go to a convenience store?

Section manager: Yeah, I am.

Ex.4

Section manager: A-san, please come to the meeting room.

A: Okay. I'll be there soon.

16
-
1

People of a higher status may use either **ます** forms or plain forms of verbs.

Ex.1

A：社長、今日はA社へいらっしゃいますか。
　　しゃちょう　きょう　　しゃ

社長：うん、<u>行く</u>。
しゃちょう　　　い

Ex.2

A：社長、明日は何時に会社へいらっしゃいますか。
　　しゃちょう　あした　なんじ　かいしゃ

社長：8時に<u>来ます</u>。
しゃちょう　じ　き

Ex.1

A: President, are you going to A Company today?

President: Yeah, I am.

Ex.2

A: President, what time are you going to come to work tomorrow?

President: I'm going to come at 8:00.

There are words other than verbs that are also used to express respect.

Plain expression	Polite expression
人 ひと	方 かた
さん	さま
だれ	どなた

Ex.

A：あの<u>方</u>はどなたですか。
　　かた

B：課長のおくさまです。
　　かちょう

Ex.

A: Who is that person?

B: The section manager's wife.

2　（もし）　　　　たら、

When expressing a hypothetical condition, （もし）〜たら、〜 is used.

Conjunctive Form

verb た form	〈〜た〉 〈〜だ〉	ら、	〜
い adjective	〈〜かった〉		
な adjective	〈〜だった〉		
noun	だった		

172

Ex.1

A：もしたからくじが<u>あたったら</u>、何をしますか。

B：旅行したいです。

Ex.2

A：今度の日曜日、<u>天気がよかったら</u>、お花見に行きませんか。

B：いいですね。行きましょう。

Ex.3

A：今度の日曜日、<u>ひまだったら</u>、お花見に行きませんか。

B：いいですね。行きましょう。

Ex.4

A：<u>明日雨だったら</u>、映画を見に行きましょう。<u>はれだったら</u>、テニスをしましょう。

B：いいですね。そうしましょう。

Ex.1

A: If you won the lottery, what would you do?

B: I want to travel.

Ex.2

A: If the weather is nice this Sunday, why don't we go flower viewing?

B: That sounds good. Let's go.

Ex.3

A: If you're free this Sunday, why don't we go flower viewing?

B: That sounds good. Let's go.

Ex.4

A: If it rains tomorrow, let's go see a movie. If it is sunny, let's play tennis.

B: That sounds good. Let's do that.

Vocabulary and Expression

いらっしゃいます be present 〈honorific〉 ／いらっしゃいます come 〈honorific〉

この間 the other day ／ごらんになります take a look 〈honorific〉 ／おっしゃいます say 〈honorific〉

みずうみ lake ／ごぞんじです know 〈honorific〉 ／しんこん旅行 honeymoon

もし～ if, perhaps ／なさいます do 〈honorific〉

いらっしゃいます go 〈honorific〉 ／めしあがります eat, drink 〈honorific〉

研究します research ／～ていらっしゃいます be doing 〈honorific〉 ／ペット pet

かいます own, have ／のりまき nori roll ／～社：X社 ～ Company : X Company

新商品 new product ／出します release ／新年会 New Year's party ／たからくじ lottery

あたります win (the lottery) ／かちます win ／さびしい lonely ／入学試験 entrance exam

おちます fail (at the exam) ／～さい：10さい ～ year(s) old: ten years old ／わかい young

おくれます be late ／～てん：0てん ～ point(s): zero point ／注意します be careful of

はいしゃ dentist ／上げます raise ／登山 mountain climbing ／中止 stop

だいぶつ Buddhist statue ／はしらくぐり passing through a pillar for luck ／びょうき disease, sickness

Conversation Scenario 💬

⟨Speaking to a teacher⟩

Lama: Excuse me. Is Aoki-sensei here?

Hayashi: Please wait one moment.

- -

Hayashi: She'll be here very soon.

Lama: Okay.

Aoki: Hello, Lama-san.

Lama: Hello. Sensei, look at this. The other day, you said you wanted to see it, so I brought it.

Aoki: Thank you. Oh, that's a famous lake.

Lama: Yes. Did you know? There are a lot of people there on their honeymoons.

Aoki: Really? I didn't know that. I want to go there for my honeymoon, too.

Lama: Sensei, when are you going to get married?

Aoki: I don't know. I mean if I get married.

Lesson 16 | 2 何時ごろおもどりになりますか
なんじ

Can-do Check ✓

☐ You can ask about your superior's plans and communicate them to others.

Grammar Notes 🖊

1-1 お _____ になります

When talking about actions of people of a higher status (teachers, company presidents, department managers, section managers, elderly people, etc.), **お～になります** is used.

Conjunctive Form

お	verb ます form 〈～ます〉	になります

Verb	Honorific speech form	Example sentence
書きます か write	お書きになります か	これは先生がお書きになった本です。 せんせい か ほん This is a book that my teacher wrote.
読みます よ read	お読みになります よ	先生、この新聞をお読みになりますか。 せんせい しんぶん よ Sensei, will you read this newspaper?
とります take	おとりになります	これは社長がおとりになった写真です。 しゃちょう しゃしん This is a picture that the company president took.
待ちます ま wait	お待ちになります ま	おきゃくさまがお待ちになっています。 ま The customers are waiting.

1-2 ご _____ になります

In addition to **～なさいます**, **ご～になります** can also be used with verbs in the 【noun】＋ **します** form, as in **説明します** or **案内します**.
せつめい あんない

Conjunctive Form

ご	noun	になります

175

Verb	Honorific speech form	Example sentence
説明します せつめい explain	ご説明になります せつめい	これは先生がご説明になります。 せんせい　　　　　せつめい My teacher will explain this.
到着します とうちゃく arrive	ご到着になります とうちゃく	おきゃくさまがご到着になりました。 とうちゃく The customer has arrived.
出発します しゅっぱつ depart	ご出発になります しゅっぱつ	社長は明日 9 時にご出発になります。 しゃちょう　あす　じ　　　しゅっぱつ The company president will depart tomorrow at 9:00.
出席します しゅっせき attend	ご出席になります しゅっせき	社長、パーティーにご出席になりますか。 しゃちょう　　　　　　　しゅっせき President, will you be coming to the party?

Careful!

電話します, 料理します and そうじします cannot be used with ご〜になります. They should
でんわ　　りょうり
be used with （お）〜なさいます instead.

Conjunctive Form

（お）	noun	なさいます

Ex.1

A：先生、トムさんにお電話なさいましたか。
せんせい　　　　　　でんわ

先生：はい、しました。でも、つながりませんでした。
せんせい

Ex.2

A：課長は料理なさいますか。
かちょう　りょうり

課長：はい、しますよ。
かちょう

Ex.1

A: Sensei, did you call Tom-san?

Teacher: Yes, I did. But he didn't
answer.

Ex.2

A: Do you cook?

Section manager: Yes, I do.

2-1　お＿＿＿＿＿

お can be added before nouns used in daily life to make them more polite.

Ex.

お名前 name ／お手紙 letter ／お電話 telephone
なまえ　　　　てがみ　　　　でんわ

お電話番号 telephone number ／お天気 weather ／お話 talking, story
でんわばんごう　　　　　　　　てんき　　　　　　はなし

お仕事 work ／おべんきょう studying ／お食事 meal ／お料理 cooking
しごと　　　　　　　　　　　　しょくじ　　　　りょうり

お水 water ／おさら plate ／おはし chopsticks ／お花 flower ／おかばん bag
みず　　　　　　　　　　　　　　　　　　　　はな

おくつ shoes ／おつくえ desk ／おいす chair ／おさけ alcohol

2 -2　ご

For some words, **ご** is added before them instead.

Ex.

ご住所 address ／ご家族 family ／ご相談 consultation ／ご連絡 contact
　じゅうしょ　　　　　か ぞく　　　　　　　そうだん　　　　　　　　れんらく

ご説明 explanation ／ご案内 guidance ／ごけっこん marriage ／ご旅行 travel
　せつめい　　　　　　　あんない　　　　　　　　　　　　　　　　　　りょこう

ご予定 schedule ／ご本 book
　よ てい　　　　　　ほん

Careful !

There are some words that do not use **お** nor **ご**.

Ex.

× お／ご学校　　× お／ご会社　　× お／ご会議　　× お／ご電気
　　　　がっこう　　　　　　　かいしゃ　　　　　　　かい ぎ　　　　　　　てん き

× お／ご映画　　× お／ご音楽
　　　　えい が　　　　　　　おんがく

Words that are written in katakana do not use **お** nor **ご**.

Ex.

× お／ごコップ　× お／ごテレビ　× お／ごナイフ

3　こちら・そちら・あちら・どちら

The polite forms of **ここ**, **そこ**, **あそこ** and **どこ** are **こちら**, **そちら**, **あちら** and **どちら**, respectively.

Ex.1

（電話で）
　でん わ

社員A：そちらに課長はいらっしゃいますか。
しゃいん　　　　　　か ちょう

社員B：いいえ、こちらにはいらっしゃいません。
しゃいん

社員A：そうですか。
しゃいん

社員B：会議室にいらっしゃいます。
しゃいん　　かい ぎ しつ

Ex.1

(On the phone)

Employee A: Is your section manager there?

Employee B: No, he isn't here.

Employee A: I see.

Employee B: He's in the meeting room.

Ex.2

A：すみません。レジはどこですか。

店員：あちらです。
てんいん

Ex.2

A: Excuse me. Where is the checkout counter?

Store clerk: Over there.

Vocabulary and Expression 😊

～ころ: 何時ごろ around ～ : around what time ／もどります return ／部長 department manager
なんじ   ぶちょう

ぼうえきセンター trading center, center of trade ／午前中 in the morning ／出席 attendance
                                            ごぜんちゅう   しゅっせき

- -

考えます think ／おきゃくさま customer 〈honorific〉／きゃく customer
かんが

～さま: 山田さま Mr., Mrs., Ms., Miss: Mr. Yamada ／フォーク fork ／スプーン spoon
       やまだ

出発します depart ／到着します arrive ／出席します attend ／欠席します be absent
しゅっぱつ   とうちゃく   しゅっせき   けっせき

参加します participate, join ／社長 company president ／支社 branch office ／連絡 contact
さんか   しゃちょう   ししゃ   れんらく

手紙 letter ／相談 consultation ／説明 explanation ／案内 guidance ／送ります send
てがみ   そうだん   せつめい   あんない   おく

そろそろ soon ／じゅんびします prepare ／ゆうがた evening

Conversation Scenario 💬

〈Asking about the department manager's plans〉

Mimura: Excuse me. Is the department manager here?

Sarah: He's at the trading center right now.

Mimura: I see. What time will he be back?

Sarah: He should be back around 5:00.

Mimura: I see. Then does he have any time tomorrow?

Sarah: He has a meeting in the morning, but he'll be here in the afternoon.

Mimura: Okay. Thank you. Sorry for bothering you.

Sarah: It's no problem.

3 アントニオともうします

Can-do Check ✔

☐ You can greet people when meeting them for the first time in professional or formal situations.

Grammar Notes ✎

1 謙譲語 Humble Speech
けんじょうご

When talking about something you are going to do to people of a higher status (teachers, company presidents, department managers, section managers, elderly people, etc.), humble speech (謙譲語) is used.
けんじょうご

Verb	Humble speech verb	Example sentence
行きます go	まいります	課長：リさん、会議室に来てください。 リ：はい、すぐまいります。 Section manager: Lee-san, please come to the meeting room. Lee: Okay. I'll be there soon.
言います say	もうします	キム：はじめまして。キムともうします。韓国のソウルからまいりました。
来ます come	まいります	課長：はじめまして。田中です。 Kim: Nice to meet you. I'm Kim. I'm from Seoul, Korea. Section manager: Nice to meet you. I'm Tanaka.
います be	おります	課長：キムさんのご家族は日本にいらっしゃいますか。 キム：いいえ。ソウルにおります。 Section manager: Is your family in Japan? Kim: No, they're in Seoul.
～ています is doing	～ております	キム：私は今海外プロジェクトを担当しております。 Kim: I'm in charge of an overseas project now.
食べます eat	いただきます	社員：課長のお宅でおくさまの手作りのケーキをいただきました。 Employee: I ate a homemade cake from the section manager's wife at his house.
飲みます drink	いただきます	課長：これ、インドネシアのコーヒーです。飲みませんか。 A：ありがとうございます。いただきます。 Section manager: This is Indonesian coffee. Why don't you try some? A: Thank you. I will.

16-3

見ます see, watch	はいけんします	課長：昨日送ったメール、見ましたか。 A：はい。はいけんしました。 Section manager: Did you see the email I sent yesterday? A: Yes, I saw it.
します do	いたします	課長：だれか、A社の山田さんに連絡してくれない？ A：私がいたします。 Section manager: Can someone contact Yamada-san at A Company for me? A: I'll do it.
知っています know	ぞんじています	課長：社長が入院なさることを知っていますか。 A：はい、ぞんじています。 Section manager: Did you know the president is going to be hospitalized? A: Yes, I know.
もらいます receive	いただきます	社員：課長にけっこんいわいをいただきました。 Employee: I got a wedding gift from my section manager.
あげます give	さしあげます	社員：課長に中国のお茶をさしあげました。 Employee: I gave my section manager some Chinese tea.
会います meet	お目にかかります	社員：課長のご家族にお目にかかったことがあります。 Employee: I have met my section manager's family.

Careful!

Humble speech is not used when the actions of people of a lower status are not directly related to people of a higher status.

Ex.

課長：Aさん、休みの日は何をしていますか。

A：うちでテレビを見ます。ゲームもよくします。

Ex.

Section manager: A-san, what do you do on your days off?

A: I watch TV at home. I also often play video games.

2 こちら・そちら・あちら・どちら

The polite forms of **この人**, **その人**, **あの人** and **どの人** are **こちら**, **そちら**, **あちら** and **どちら**, respectively.

Ex.1

A：Bさん、こちらは山田さんです。

山田：はじめまして。山田です。

B：はじめまして。Bです。よろしくおねがいします。

Ex.1

A: B-san, this is Yamada-san.

Yamada: Nice to meet you. I'm Yamada.

B: Nice to meet you, too. I'm B.

Ex.2

A：大山課長はどの方ですか。

B：あちらです。めがねをかけていらっしゃる方です。

Ex.2

A: Which person is Oyama-kacho?

B: That person. He's the one wearing glasses.

Vocabulary and Expression 🐱

もうします say 〈honorific〉 ／まいります come 〈honorific〉 ／お目にかかります meet 〈honorific〉

人事 human resources ／〜ていただきます have someone do[done] 〈honorific〉

けんしゅう training ／がんばります do one's best

はいけんします see 〈honorific〉 ／まいります go 〈honorific〉 ／うかがいます come 〈honorific〉

しつもんします ask a question ／うかがいます ask (a question) 〈honorific〉

いただきます receive, eat, drink 〈honorific〉 ／（ここに）おります be (here) 〈honorific〉

いたします do 〈honorific〉 ／うれしい happy ／かんげい会 welcome party

しゅっちょう business trip ／りれき書 resume ／こうし室 instructor's room ／紹介 introduce

どなた who 〈honorific〉

Conversation Scenario 💬

〈Greeting a manager〉

Yamamoto: Manager, this is Antonio-san from the Milano branch company.

Antonio: Hello. I'm Antonio. I'm from Italy. Nice to meet you.

Mita: Antonio-san, right? I'm Mita. Nice to see you again. We met this morning.

Antonio: Yes, we met. You showed me where the personnel department room was.

Yamamoto: Oh, did he?

Mita: Please do your best with the training.

Antonio: Okay, thank you.

16 - 3

4 おにもつ、お持ちします
も

Can-do Check ✓

☐You can welcome a superior, greet them and guide them.

Grammar Notes 🖉

1-1　お [   ] します

When talking about actions that you do or things you do for people of a higher status (teachers, company presidents, department managers, section managers, elderly people, etc.), **お〜します** is used.

Conjunctive Form

お	verb ます form〈〜ます〉	します

Verb	Honorific speech form	Example sentence
持ちます も have	お持ちします も	おきゃくさま、おにもつをお持ちします。 も Ma'am, I'll carry your luggage.
とります take	おとりします	ケーキ、おとりします。どれがよろしいですか。 I'll get the cake. Which one would you like?
とどけます deliver	おとどけします	今週中におにもつをおとどけします。 こんしゅうちゅう Your package will be delivered this week.
送ります おく send	お送りします おく	先生に写真をお送りしました。 せんせい　しゃしん　おく I sent a picture to my teacher.

1-2　ご [   ] します

ご is added to the front of nouns that are used to form verbs using **【noun】＋します**, such as **説明します** or **案内します**.
せつめい　　　　　　あんない

Conjunctive Form

ご	noun	します

Verb	Honorific speech form	Example Sentence
説明します せつめい explain	ご説明します せつめい	おきゃくさま、こちらの使い方をご説明します。 つか かた せつめい Ma'am, I'll explain how to use this.
案内します あんない guide	ご案内します あんない	おきゃくさまを会場にご案内します。 かいじょう あんない I'll show the customers to the venue.
連絡します れんらく contact	ご連絡します れんらく	ひこうきの時間が決まりましたら、ご連絡します。 じ かん き れんらく I'll contact you once the time of the flight has been decided.
紹介します しょうかい introduce	ご紹介します しょうかい	私の国の料理をご紹介します。 わたし くに りょうり しょうかい I'll introduce some food from my country.

Careful!

お is used instead of **ご** in front of the verbs **電話します**, **料理します** and **そうじします**.
でん わ りょう り

Ex.

先生：明日の午前中に私に電話をしてください。
せんせい あした ご ぜんちゅう わたし でん わ
A：はい、わかりました。明日、先生にお電話します。
あした せんせい でん わ

Ex.

Teacher: Please call me tomorrow
morning.

A: Okay, I understand. I'll call you
tomorrow.

The humble speech form of **します** is **いたします**, and it can be used as **お〜いた**
します or **ご〜いたします**.

Conjunctive Form

お	verb ます form 〈〜ます〉	いたします
ご	noun	

Ex.1

A：このかばん、黒いのはありますか。
くろ
店員：はい。すぐにお持ちいたします。
てんいん も

Ex.1

A: Do you have this bag in black?

Store clerk: Yes. I'll bring it right
away.

Ex.2

A：このシャツ、少しよごれているんですが。
すこ
店員：もうしわけございません。おとりかえいたします。
てんいん

Ex.2

A: This shirt is a little dirty.

Store clerk: I'm very sorry. I'll get
another one.

Ex.3

A：すみません。このエアコンの使い方を教えてくだ
つか つか おし
さい。
店員：はい。ご説明いたします。
てんいん せつめい

Ex.3

A: Excuse me. Please show me how
to use this air conditioner.

Store clerk: Okay. I'll explain.

16
-
4

2 [____] のとき、[____] た

When talking about what you did at a certain time, 〜のとき、〜た is used.

Conjunctive Form

noun	のとき、	verb た form 〈〜た〉 〈〜だ〉
		〜ました

Ex.1
24さいのとき、けっこんしました。

Ex.1
I got married when I was 24 years old.

Ex.2
入学しきのとき、みんなで写真をとった。
にゅうがく　　　　　　　　　しゃしん

Ex.2
During the school entrance ceremony, we all took a picture.

Ex.3
中学生のとき、テニスをはじめた。
ちゅうがくせい

Ex.3
I started playing tennis when I was in junior high school.

When talking about what you did after another given action was done, 〜【verb た form】とき、〜ました／〜た is used (☞ Lesson 11 - 1).

Ex.1
大学の入学試験にごうかくしたとき、父に時計をもらいました。
だいがく　にゅうがく しけん　　　　　　　　　ちち　とけい

Ex.1
My father gave me a watch when I passed my college entrance exam.

Ex.2
山田さんに会ったとき、借りたかさをかえした。
やまだ　　　あ　　　　　　か

Ex.2
When I met Yamada-san, I returned the umbrella I borrowed.

When talking about what you did before doing another given action, 【verb dictionary form】とき、〜ました／た is used (☞ Lesson 11 - 2).

Ex.1
アメリカへ行くとき、パスポートをつくりました。
い

Ex.1
Before I went to America, I got my passport made.

Ex.2
映画を見に行くとき、インターネットでチケットを買いました。
えいが　み　い　　　　　　　　　　　　　　か

Ex.2
Before going to see a movie, I bought my ticket online.

3 こちら・そちら・あちら・どちら

When talking about directions, **こちら**, **そちら**, **あちら** and **どちら** are used.

Ex.1

A：すみません。

　　ちかてつにのりたいんですが。

B：ちかてつの駅はこちらです。

　　あるいて５分ぐらいです。

Ex.1

A: Excuse me. I'm trying to get to the metro.

B: The metro station is this way. It's about a five-minute walk.

Ex.2

A：すみません。みどり公園は

　　どちらですか。

B：そちらです。今いらっしゃった

　　ほうこうです。

Ex.2

A: Excuse me. Which way is Midori Park?

B: It's that way. It's in the direction you just came from.

こちら, **そちら**, **あちら** and **どちら** are also polite speech forms of **ここ**, **そこ**, **あそこ** and **どこ** (☞ Lesson 16-2) .

Ex.1

（外国にいる人と話す）

A：そちらは今何時ですか。

B：こちらは朝の９時です。

Ex.1

(Talking with someone in a different country)

A: What time is it there?

B: It's 9:00 in the morning here.

Ex.2

（大学で）

A：すみません。山田先生のお部屋はどちらですか。

事務員：あちらです。ドアがあいているお部屋です。

Ex.2

(At a university)

A: Excuse me. Where is Yamada-sensei's room?

Office staff: It's that way. It's the room with the open door.

こちら, そちら, あちら and **どちら** are also polite speech forms of **これ, それ, あれ** and **どれ**.

Ex.1

A：このくつ、ワンサイズ<ruby>大<rt>おお</rt></ruby>きいのはありませんか。

<ruby>店員<rt>てんいん</rt></ruby>：はい、ございます。<u>こちら</u>です。いかがですか。

Ex.2

A：このシャツ、いくらですか。

<ruby>店員<rt>てんいん</rt></ruby>：<u>そちら</u>は2,500<ruby>円<rt>えん</rt></ruby>でございます。

Ex.1

A: Do you have these shoes in a larger size?

Store clerk: Yes, we do. Here they are. How do you like them?

Ex.2

A: How much is this shirt?

Store clerk: That's 2,500 yen.

こちら, そちら, あちら and **どちら** are also polite speech forms of **この<ruby>人<rt>ひと</rt></ruby>, その<ruby>人<rt>ひと</rt></ruby>, あの<ruby>人<rt>ひと</rt></ruby>** and **どの<ruby>人<rt>ひと</rt></ruby>** (☞ Lesson 1‑1).

Ex.

（パーティーで）

A：<u>そちら</u>はおくさまですか。

B：あ、いいえ。<ruby>大学<rt>だいがく</rt></ruby>のときの<ruby>友人<rt>ゆうじん</rt></ruby>です。

C：はじめまして。<ruby>田中<rt>たなか</rt></ruby>ともうします。

A：はじめまして。Bさんのどうりょうの<ruby>大山<rt>おおやま</rt></ruby>ともうします。

Ex.

(At a party)

A: Is that your wife?

B: Ah, no. She's a friend of mine from college.

C: Nice to meet you. I'm Tanaka.

A: Nice to meet you. I'm B-san's coworker, Oyama.

Vocabulary and Expression 🐛

ひさしぶり It's been a while. ／<ruby>世話<rt>せわ</rt></ruby>になります Thank you for looking over me.

いえいえ Not at all. ／セミナー seminar ／<ruby>会場<rt>かいじょう</rt></ruby> venue ／スケジュール schedule

- -

<ruby>問題集<rt>もんだいしゅう</rt></ruby> workbook ／<ruby>案内<rt>あんない</rt></ruby>します guide ／<ruby>用意<rt>ようい</rt></ruby>します prepare

<ruby>今<rt>いま</rt></ruby>よろしいですか Do you have a minute? ⟨honorific⟩ ／へんこう change ／<ruby>先方<rt>せんぽう</rt></ruby> other party

はじめて first ／<ruby>海外旅行<rt>かいがいりょこう</rt></ruby> overseas vacation ／<ruby>小学生<rt>しょうがくせい</rt></ruby> elementary school student

なくなります pass away ／おじ uncle ／お<ruby>手<rt>て</rt></ruby>あらい bathroom, restroom

エレベーター elevator ／<ruby>本日<rt>ほんじつ</rt></ruby> today ⟨formal⟩

〈Going to pick up the manager〉

Ati: Uchida-buchou, I've been waiting for you.

Uchida: Oh, Ati-san, it's been a while. Thank you for your help at last year's business trip to Indonesia.

Ati: Not at all. You have a lot of bags. I'll help carry them.

Uchida: They're materials for tomorrow's seminar. Thank you.

Ati: Then I'll show you to the seminar venue.

Uchida: Okay. And tomorrow's schedule?

Ati: Right. I'll explain in the car. This way, please.

Uchida: Thank you.

16 - 4

1 ぼくよりじょうずだね

Can-do Check ✓

☐You can compare and talk about who is better.

☐You can say who or what is the best.

Grammar Notes ✎

1 ╎ X ╎ は ╎ Y ╎ より ╎

When comparing two things and express that X is more something than Y, **〜は〜より〜** is used.

Conjunctive Form

noun X	は	noun Y	より	い adjective plain form	です
				な adjective plain form 〈〜だ〉	

Ex.1

[Land area: Canada $9,984,670$ km^2

> the United States $9,629,091$ km^2]

カナダ<u>は</u>アメリカ<u>より</u>広いです。
　　　　　　　　　　　ひろ

カナダ
9,984,670㎢

アメリカ
9,629,091㎢

Ex.2

[Population: China $1,383,920,000$ people

> India $1,311,050,000$ people (2017)]

中国<u>は</u>インド<u>より</u>人口が多いです。
ちゅうごく　　　　　　　じんこう　おお

インド<u>は</u>中国<u>より</u>人口が少ないです。
　　　　ちゅうごく　　じんこう　すく

Ex.3

[Famous old city in Japan: Kyoto > Nara]

京都は奈良よりゆうめいです。
きょうと　なら

Ex.1

Canada is bigger than America.

Ex.2

China's population is larger than India's.

India's population is smaller than China's.

Ex.3

Kyoto is more famous than Nara.

2 ━━━━━━━━━ ことができます

When talking about things that you have the ability to do, **～ことができます** is used. **～こ とができません** is used to talk about things that you do not have the ability to do. **～こと ができますか** is used to ask what someone has the ability to do. **はい、できます。** and **いい え、できません。** are used when answering questions about what you can or cannot do.

Conjunctive Form

verb dictionary form	ことが	できます

Ex.1
田中さんはおよぐことができます。私はおよぐことができ
ません。

Ex.1
Tanaka-san can swim. I can't swim.

Ex.2
あには料理をすることができますが、おとうとはできませ
ん。

Ex.2
My older brother can cook, but my younger brother can't.

Ex.3
私は日本語を話すことができますが、書くことができま
せん。

Ex.3
I can speak Japanese, but I can't write it.

Ex.4
A：Bさんはかんじを読むことができますか。
B：はい、できます。

Ex.4
A: B-san, can you read kanji?
B: Yes, I can.

～ができます is used with nouns.

Ex.
A：Bさんはスポーツで何ができますか。
B：私はテニスができます。
C：私はサッカーとやきゅうができます。

Ex.
A: B-san, what sports can you play?
B: I can play tennis.
C: I can play soccer and baseball.

---

3 ━━━ X ━━ が ━━ range ━━ で 一番

When talking about the top thing out of a wider range of things, **～が～で一番～** is used. The order of **Xが** and **～で** may be reversed.

Conjunctive Form

noun X	が	～で	一番 _{いちばん}	い adjective plain form	です
				な adjective plain form 〈～だ〉	

Ex.1

トムさんがクラスで一番せが高いです。
_{いちばん} _{たか}

Ex.2

クラスで田中さんが一番うたがじょうずです。
_{たなか} _{いちばん}

Ex.3

中国がせかいで一番人口が多いです。
_{ちゅうごく} _{いちばんじんこう} _{おお}

Ex.4

せかいでロシアが一番広いです。
_{いちばんひろ}

Ex.5

A：１年でいつが一番すきですか。
_{ねん} _{いちばん}
B：夏です。
_{なつ}

Ex.1

Tom-san is the tallest person in class.

Ex.2

In our class, Tanaka-san is the best at singing.

Ex.3

China has the largest population in the world.

Ex.4

The biggest country in the world is Russia.

Ex.5

A: What is your favorite time of the year?

B: Summer.

Vocabulary and Expression 🎭

くるくる round and round ／回ります turn around ／リンク skating rink
_{まわ}

せ height ／おいくつですか How old are you? 〈honorific〉 ／年下 younger person
_{としした}

今年 this year ／毎年 yearly, annually ／がっき instrument ／ギター guitar ／ひきます play
_{ことし} _{まいとし}

ピアノ piano ／習います learn ／止まります stop ／工場 factory
_{なら} _と _{こうじょう}

～台：１，０００台 ～ unit(s): a thousand units ／自動車 automobile ／きせつ season ／春 spring
_{だい} _{だい} _{じどうしゃ} _{はる}

せいかつ life ／サーブ serve ／うちます hit, strike ／ならびます align, line up

Conversation Scenario 💬

〈Skating〉

Marie: Lama-san, that's amazing!

Tang: Lama-san, you're better than I am. Is this really your first time?

Lama: Yeah, it is. Skating sure is fun. Whoa! Kim-san can spin around and around.

Tang: Yeah, Kim-san is the best in this rink.

Marie: I see.

2 これかこれにするつもりです

Can-do Check ✓

☐You can compare information about property and part-time jobs and speak about it.

Grammar Notes ✎

1 ＿＿＿＿＿＿つもりです

When talking about something you intend to do, **〜つもりです** is used.

Conjunctive Form

verb dictionary form	つもりです
verb ない form 〈〜ない〉	

Ex.1

A：今年の夏休みは北海道へ行くつもりです。

B：いいですね。いつですか。

A：まだチケットは買っていませんが、８月のはじめに行くつもりです。

Ex.2

大学をそつぎょうしたら、国へ帰って、父の仕事を手伝うつもりです。

Ex.3

明日仕事がありますから、今日は早くねるつもりです。

Ex.4

大学の試験があるので、今年の夏休みは国へ帰らないつもりです。

Ex.1

A: I intend to go to Hokkaido for summer vacation this year.

B: That's great. When?

A: I haven't bought my ticket, but I intend to go in early August.

Ex.2

After I graduate from university, I intend to go back to my country and help my father with his work.

Ex.3

I have work tomorrow, so I intend to go to bed early today.

Ex.4

I have a university test, so I don't intend to go back to my country this summer vacation.

17
-
2

When talking about something you plan to do, **～予定です** is used.

Conjunctive Form

verb dictionary form	**予定です**
verb ない form 〈～ない〉	

Ex.

A：来月国へ帰りますか。
　らいげつくに　かえ

B：はい。12月1日に国へ帰って、12月10日に日
　　がつついたち　くに　かえ　　　　がつとおか　に
本にもどる予定です。
ほん　　　　よてい

Ex.

A: Are you going back to your country next month?

B: Yes. I plan to go back to my country on December 1 and come back to Japan on December 10.

2　　　　　　　　　ができます

～ができます is used to talk about something that you are allowed to do or it is possible for you to do.

Conjunctive Form

noun	が	できます

Ex.1

この公園でサッカーができます。
　こうえん

Ex.1

I can play soccer in this park.

Ex.2

学校のカフェは食事ができます。
がっこう　　　　しょくじ

Ex.2

I can eat in the school café.

Ex.3

私のうちのにわでバーベキューができます。
わたし

Ex.3

I can barbeque in my house's yard.

＊～ができます and **～ことができます** is used to talk about things that you have the ability to do (☞ Lesson 17 - 1).

3 　のに、

When talking about when something unfortunate or unexpected happens that is different than what was expected, **〜のに、〜** is used.

Conjunctive Form

verb plain form	のに、	〜
い adjective plain form		
な adjective plain form 〈〜だ な〉		
noun plain form 〈〜だ な〉		

Ex.1

明日テストがある<u>のに</u>、おとうとはゲームをしています。
_{あした}

Ex.1

My younger brother is playing video games even though he has a test tomorrow.

Ex.2

ご飯を食べた<u>のに</u>、おなかがすいています。
_{はん} _た

Ex.2

I'm hungry even though I already ate.

Ex.3

名前を聞いた<u>のに</u>、わすれました。
_{な まえ} _き

Ex.3

I forgot her name even though I asked her what it was.

Ex.4

天気がいい<u>のに</u>、雨がふっています。
_{てん き} _{あめ}

Ex.4

It's raining even though the weather is clear.

Ex.5

雨な<u>のに</u>、テニスをしています。
_{あめ}

Ex.5

He's playing tennis even though it's raining.

Ex.6

日曜日じゃない<u>のに</u>、公園に人がたくさんいました。
_{にちよう び} _{こうえん} _{ひと}

Ex.6

There were a lot of people in the park even though it's not Sunday.

17 - 2

Vocabulary and Expression 😀

ひっこし moving ／こっち this one ／まわり surrounding ／それに besides

かんきょう environment

めんきょ license ／（めんきょを）とります get (a license) ／（お）正月 New Year's
_{しょうがつ}

やめます quit ／予約 appointment, reservation ／カード credit card, cash card
_{よ やく}

しはらい payment ／現金 cash ／ねつ fever ／うわ Whoa! ／じきゅう hourly wage
_{げんきん}

チャンス chance ／ボーナス bonus ／試食 food samples
_{し しょく}

〈Moving〉

Sarah: Have you decided where you're going to move to?

Lee: Not yet, but I'm going to see some places this Sunday, and I intend to go with this one or this one.

Sarah: Wow.

Lee: This is close to the station and very convenient. But it's a little old. This one is new and the area around it is quiet, but it's far from the station.

Sarah: Wow. This is spacious. And you can play tennis in the nearby park.

Lee: Yeah. It's new and spacious, the area around it is pretty good even though it's cheap.

Sarah: That's nice. How about buying a bike?

Lee: Yeah.

3 どちらが物価が高いですか
ぶっか　たか

Can-do Check ✓

☐ You can speak about prices while comparing your country with others.

Grammar Notes ✎

1 ＿＿＿＿＿＿＿＿ ことができます

When talking about something that you are allowed to do or it is possible for you to do, **～ことができます** is used. The negative form of this is **～ことができません**.

Conjunctive Form

verb dictionary form	ことができます

Ex.1

ここでたばこをすうことができます。

Ex.1

You can smoke here.

Ex.2

じゅぎょうのとき、飲んだり食べたりすることができません。
の　　　　た

Ex.2

You can't eat or drink during class.

Ex.3

スマホを持っていますから、インターネットでしらべること
も
ができます。

Ex.3

I have a smartphone, so I can look it up on the Internet.

*【noun】＋ができます can also be used (☞ Lesson 17 - 2).

Ex.

この公園でコンサートができます。
こうえん

Ex.

They can hold concerts in this park.

2 -1 ＿＿＿ X と Y とどちらが ＿＿＿＿＿ か

When comparing two things and asking something about them, **～と～とどちらが～か** is used.

17
‒
3

195

Conjunctive Form

noun X	と	noun Y	と	どちらが	い adjective 〈～い〉	ですか
					な adjective 〈～な〉	

Ex.1

A：にくとさかなとどちらがすきですか。

B：にくです。

Ex.1

A: Which do you like more, meat or fish?

B: Meat.

Ex.2

A：中国とインドとどちらが人口が多いですか。
　　ちゅうごく　　　　　　　　　じんこう　おお

B：中国です。
　　ちゅうごく

Ex.2

A: Which has a larger population, China or India?

B: China.

2 -2　　　X　　　より　　　Y　　　のほうが

When comparing X to Y and say that Y is more of something than X, **～より～のほうが ～** is used (X< Y).

Conjunctive Form

noun X	より	noun Y	のほうが	い adjective 〈～い〉	です
				な adjective 〈～な〉	

Ex.1

A：にくとさかなとどちらがすきですか。

B：さかなよりにくのほうがすきです。

　（さかな ＜ にく）

Ex.1

A: Which do you like more, meat or fish?

B: I like meat more than fish.
　(fish < meat)

Ex.2

インドより中国のほうが人口が多いです。
　　　　ちゅうごく　　　　じんこう　おお

（インド ＜ 中国）
　　　　　ちゅうごく

Ex.2

China has a larger population than India. (India < China)

Ex.3

バスよりちかてつのほうがはやいです。

（バス ＜ ちかてつ）

Ex.3

The metro is faster than the bus.
(bus < metro)

The order of 【noun X】より and 【noun Y】のほうが may also be switched (Y > X).

Ex.

このゲームのほうがあのゲームよりおもしろいです。

（このゲーム ＞ あのゲーム）

Ex.

This game is more interesting that that game.

(this game ＞ that game)

Vocabulary and Expression

物価 price ／マンゴー mango ／かわります There is a difference.
ぶっか

～はい：1ぱい ～ bowl(s) of, ～ cup(s) of: one bowl, one cup ／きおん temperature

とんこつ pork bone broth ／～てん：タイゾーてん ～ exhibition: the Taizo Exhibition

ヒール heel ／うどん udon

Conversation Scenario

〈Shopping at the supermarket〉

Ati: Whoa, this orange is 400 yen!

Sarah: This mango is 800 yen.

Ati: Japanese fruit is expensive.

Sarah: Yes.

Ati: In my country, you can buy a mango for about 80 yen.

Sarah: That's cheap!

Ati: Which has higher prices, Japan or your country?

Sarah: Let's see... I don't think it's that different. But fruit is cheaper in my country than in Japan.

Ati: Oh, really?

1 使い方がわからないんですが
つか　かた

Can-do Check ✓

☐You can ask how to use machines and tools, and give simple explanations.

Grammar Notes 🏷

1 ＿＿＿＿＿ X ＿＿＿＿＿ と、＿＿＿＿ Y ＿＿＿＿＿

When expressing that Y always happens right after X, 〜と、〜 is used.

Conjunctive Form

		verb ます form
verb dictionary form	と、	verb dictionary form
		verb ない form 〈〜ない〉

Ex.1

春になると、さくらがさきます。
はる

Ex.2

ビールを飲むと、かおがあかくなる。
の

Ex.3

A：この部屋の電気をつけたいんですが、どうしたらいい
　　へ や　　でんき
ですか。

B：ドアを開けると、電気がつきますよ。
　　あ　　　　でんき

Ex.1

When it becomes spring, the cherry blossoms bloom.

Ex.2

When I drink beer, my face turns red.

Ex.3

A: I want to turn the lights on in this room, so what should I do?

B: The light comes on when you open the door.

2 ＿＿＿＿＿＿＿に使います
　　　　　　　　　　つか
　　＿＿＿＿＿＿のに使います
　　　　　　　　　　　つか

When explaining what a given tool is used to do, 〜に使います or 〜のに使います are
　　　　　　　　　　　　　　　　　　　　　　　　　　つか　　　　　　　　　　つか
used. 何に使いますか is used to ask what a tool is used to do.
　　　なに　つか

Conjunctive Form

noun		に使います
		つか
verb dictionary form	の	

Ex.1

このはさみは料理に使います。

Ex.1

These scissors are used when cooking.

Ex.2

このくつはダンスに使います。

Ex.2

These shoes are for dancing.

Ex.3

A：このナイフは何に使いますか。

B：パンを切るのに使います。

Ex.3

A: What is this knife used for?

B: It's used to cut bread.

Ex.4

A：私の国ではご飯を食べるのにはしを使います。

B：私の国ではスプーンを使います。

Ex.4

A: In my country, we use chopsticks to eat.

B: In my country, we use spoons.

When asking how to do something, **どうやって～か** is used (☞ Lesson 12 - 1).

Ex.1

A：どうやってきっぷを買いますか。

B：ここにお金を入れて、きんがくのボタンをおして
ください。

Ex.1

A: How do I buy a ticket?

B: Put your money in here, and press the button for the price.

Ex.2

A：どうやってくうこうへ行きますか。

B：バスで行きます。

Ex.2

A: How do you get to the airport?

B: I go by bus.

When talking about the order in which you are going to do multiple actions,
まず、【first action】。つぎに、【second action】。それから、【third action】。 is
used.

Ex.

この料理の作り方を説明します。

まず、やさいをあらいます。つぎに、なべに水を入
れます。それから、肉とやさいを入れてにます。

Ex.

I'm going to explain how to make this dish.

First, wash the vegetables. Next, put water in the pot. Then, put the meat and vegetables into the pot and cook them.

まず first ／入ります turn, switch on ／つぎに next ／セットします set (a time)

それから from that point on, from there ／ストレッチします stretch

かいさつ ticket gate ／開きます open ／クリックします click ／ろくおん audio recording

ながれます flow ／正しい correct ／えらびます select ／しょっけん meal voucher

マイク microphone ／音 sound ／ＡＴＭ ATM (automated teller machine)

あんしょう番号 PIN (personal identification number) ／入力します input

きんがく amount of money ／かくにん confirmation ／ろせんず route map ／かけます hang

バッグハンガー bag hanger ／なべ pot ／なべつかみ oven mitt ／ホッチキス stapler

はり needle ／はずします remove ／ホッチキスリムーバー stapler remover

バッテリー battery ／けいたい電話 cell-phone, mobile phone ／じゅうでんします charge

Conversation Scenario 💬

〈Asking someone how to use machines and tools〉

Sarah: Excuse me. I don't know how to use this, so can you show me?

Instructor: Okay. First, please press this button. That turns it on.

Sarah: So, if I press this button, it turns on.

Instructor: Yes. Next, press this and set a time.

Sarah: Okay.

Instructor: Then, please press the start button.

Sarah: Okay. I got it. Thank you. Umm, what is that for?

Instructor: Ah, that's used for stretching. It feels good.

Sarah: Wow, really?

2 どこで買ったの？
か

Can-do Check ✓

□You can explain the location of a store or place when asked.

Grammar Notes ✏

1 -1 ＿＿＿＿＿＿ やすいです

When expressing that a given action is easy to do, 〜やすいです is used.

Conjunctive Form

verb ます form〈〜ます〉	やすいです

Ex.1
この車は運転しやすいです。
くるま　うんてん

Ex.2
このテレビは大きくて見やすいです。
おお　　　み

Ex.3
このカメラは使いやすいです。
つか

Ex.1
This car is easy to drive.

Ex.2
This TV is big and easy to see.

Ex.3
This camera is easy to use.

1 -2 ＿＿＿＿＿＿ にくいです

When expressing that a given action is difficult to do, 〜にくいです is used.

Conjunctive Form

verb ます form〈〜ます〉	にくいです

Ex.1
この車は運転しにくいです。
くるま　うんてん

Ex.2
このパソコンは小さくて見にくいです。
ちい　　　み

Ex.3
このけいたい電話は使いにくいです。
でんわ　　つか

Ex.1
This car is hard to drive.

Ex.2
This computer is small and hard to see.

Ex.3
This cell phone is hard to use.

18
-
2

2 　　　　　と、　　　　　　があります

When pointing out landmarks when giving directions, 〜と、〜があります is used.

Conjunctive Form

verb dictionary form	と、	noun	があります

Ex.1

A：バスていはどこですか。

B：この道_{みち}をまっすぐ行_いくと、ゆうびんきょくがあります。
　　バスていはゆうびんきょくの前_{まえ}にあります。

Ex.2

A：この近_{ちか}くに病院_{びょういん}がありますか。

B：はい。あそこにしんごうがありますね。あのしんごうを
　　左_{ひだり}にまがると、コンビニがあります。病院_{びょういん}はコンビニ
　　のとなりです。

Ex.1

A: Where is the bus stop?

B: Go straight down this street and there will be a post office. The bus stop is in front of the post office.

Ex.2

A: Is there a hospital around here?

B: Yes. There's a traffic light over there. Turn left at that traffic light and there will be a convenience store. The hospital is next to the convenience store.

Phrases used when giving directions

まっすぐ行_いく
go straight

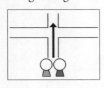

右_{みぎ}にまがる
turn right

左_{ひだり}にまがる
turn left

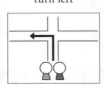

つきあたり
end of a street

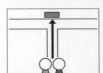

1つ目_めのこうさてん
first intersection

2つ目_めのしんごう
second traffic light

3つ目_めのかど
third corner

こうさてんをわたる
cross at the intersection

道_{みち}をわたる
cross the street

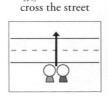

はしをわたる
cross the bridge

ほどうきょうをわたる
cross the pedestrian bridge

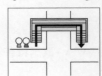

Vocabulary and Expression

１００円ショップ 100-yen shop ／まっすぐ straight, upright

ペン pen ／せなか back ／ボタン button ／いかがですか How is it? 〈honorific〉

ファスナー fastener ／道 road, street, way ／かど corner ／まがります turn

こうさてん intersection ／〜つ目 ：２つ目 ordinal number: the second

西区役所 west ward office

Conversation Scenario

〈Explaining the location of a store〉

Lama: Kim-san, that's nice.

Kim: Isn't it?

Lama: Is it easy to use?

Kim: Yeah. This is for homework, this is for tests and this is for essays.

Lama: I want one, too. Where did you buy it?

Kim: They sell them at the 100-yen shop.

Lama: Wow. Near here?

Kim: Yeah. Turn right when you leave the station, and there will be a karaoke place.

Lama: Right.

Kim: The 100-yen shop is across from that.

Lama: Ah, I got it. Thanks.

18 - 2

Can-do Check ✔

☐You can give a simple explanation of how to make a dish when asked.

Grammar Notes 🖊

1-1 　　　 X 　　 し、 　　 Y 　　 から、 　　 Z

When listing two or more reasons for something, **Xし、Yから、Z** is used, with **し** being used to connect the two reasons. X and Y are the reasons and Z is the conclusion. When Z is in plain form, X and Y should also be in plain form.

Conjunctive Form

sentence X 〈～です〉〈～ます〉	し、	sentence Y 〈～です〉〈～ます〉	から、	sentence Z 〈～です〉〈～ます〉
sentence X plain form		sentence Y plain form		sentence Z 〈～です〉〈～ます〉

sentence X plain form	し、	sentence Y plain form	から、	sentence Z plain form

Ex.1
北海道は遠いですし、さむいですから、行きたくないです。
ほっかいどう　とお　　　　　　　　　　　　　　い

Ex.2
時間もないし、お金もないから、旅行に行きません。
じかん　　　　かね　　　　　　りょこう　い

Ex.3
駅から近いし、店がたくさんあるから、ここはべんりだ。
えき　ちか　　みせ

Ex.1
Hokkaido is far away and cold,
so I don't want to go.

Ex.2
I don't have the time or the money,
I don't travel.

Ex.3
It's close to the station and there are a lot of stores, so this place is convenient.

1-2 　　　 X 　　 し、 　　 Y 　　 から。

When giving two or more reasons for something after being asked to do so, **～し、～から。** or **～し、～からです。** are used. X and Y can be used either with **です** and **ます** or in plain form. 【plain form sentence X】**し、**【plain form sentence Y】**から。** is used when talking to friends or family.

Ex.1

A：アルバイト、行かないんですか。

B：はい。あたまがいたいです<u>し</u>、ねつもあります<u>から</u>。

Ex.2

A：どうして日本にりゅうがくしようと思ったんですか。

B：日本の会社ではたらきたいです<u>し</u>、あにが日本にいます<u>から</u>。

Ex.3

A：どうして貯金をしているんですか。

B：バイクを買いたい<u>し</u>、旅行もしたい<u>から</u>です。

Ex.4

A：夏休み、国へ帰らないの？

B：うん。アルバイトもある<u>し</u>、大学の試験もある<u>から</u>。

Ex.1

A: Are you not going to your part-time job?

B: Yes (I'm not going). Because my head hurts and I have a fever.

Ex.2

A: Why did you decide to study abroad in Japan?

B: Because I want to work at a Japanese company and my older brother is in Japan.

Ex.3

A: Why are you saving money?

B: Because I want to buy a bike and travel.

Ex.4

A: Are you not going back to your country for summer vacation?

B: Yeah (I'm not going). I have to work at my part-time job, and I have tests at university.

2 どうやって ＿＿＿＿＿＿＿ か

When asking how to do something **どうやって～か** is used (☞ Lesson 12 - 1 , 18 - 1).

Ex.1

A：<u>どうやって</u>きっぷを買うんです<u>か</u>。

B：ここにお金を入れて、きんがくのボタンをおしてください。

Ex.2

A：<u>どうやって</u>くうこうへ行くんです<u>か</u>。

B：バスで行きます。

Ex.3

A：<u>どうやって</u>日本語を勉強しました<u>か</u>。

B：日本のアニメを見たり、まんがを読んだりしました。

Ex.1

A: How do you buy a ticket?

B: Put your money in here and press the button for the price of your ticket, please.

Ex.2

A: How do you get to the airport?

B: I go by bus.

Ex.3

A: How did you study Japanese?

B: I did things like watching Japanese anime and reading manga.

18-3

3 ＿＿＿ X ＿＿ てから、＿＿ Y ＿＿

When expressing that you will do 【action X】 first, then do 【action Y】, **～から、～** is used.

Conjunctive Form

verb て form	〈～て〉 〈～で〉	から、	～

Ex.1

手をあらってから、ご飯を食べます。

Ex.1

I eat after I wash my hands.

Ex.2

朝ご飯を食べてから、くすりを飲みます。

Ex.2

I take medicine after I eat breakfast.

Ex.3

ジョギングをしてから、シャワーをあびます。

Ex.3

I take a shower after I go jogging.

Vocabulary and Expression

いためます stir fry ／にます simmer ／フォー Pho (name of a dish)

かっこいい good-looking ／けっこん marriage ／バインセオ Bánh xèo (name of a dish)

レタス lettuce ／のせます put on top ／まきます roll ／おび Japanese belt for yukata and kimono

むすびます tie, entwine ／おりがみ origami ／おります fold ／牛肉 beef ／受付 reception

入館証 entry permit ／たまねぎ onion ／ミキサー blender

おやこどん rice bowl with chicken and egg

Conversation Scenario

〈Explaining how to make food〉

Tang: Tanaka-san, this is delicious.

Tanaka: Really? Great. Curry rice is easy to make and delicious, so I make it often.

Tang: Huh? It's easy to make? How do you make it?

Tanaka: Cut the meat and the vegetables, put them into the pot, sauté them a bit and then simmer them. It's easy, right?

Tang: I see.

Tanaka: Vietnamese food is really good, too. I like pho. How do you make that?

Tang: Uh, sorry. I can't cook.

1 明日来られますか
あした こ

Can-do Check ✓

☐You can make a phone call in response to a part-time job ad and determine an interview date and time.

Grammar Notes ✎

1 可能形 Potential Form
か のうけい

When talking about something that you are able to do or are permitted to do, **～ことができます** is used (☞ Lesson 17-3). The potential form of a verb [-emasu] can be used, as in **すうことができます → すえます** or **食べることができます → 食べられます**, for
た　　　　　　　　　　　　　　　　た
example. The potential form of verbs can also use the [-eru] form, as in**すえる** and **食べ
た
られる**.

Ex.1

A：ここでたばこをすえますか。

店員：すみません。ここはちょっと。
てんいん

Ex.2

（としょかんで）

A：本を借りたいんですが、何さつ借りられますか。
ほん か　　　　　　　　なん か
としょかん員：1週間に5さつ、借りられます。
いん　しゅうかん　　　　か

Ex.3

（ホテルで）

A：朝ご飯は何時から食べられる？
あさ はん なんじ　　た
B：6時からだよ。
じ

Ex.4

A：今日何時に帰れる？
きょうなんじ かえ
B：6時に帰れるよ。
じ かえ
A：じゃあ、いっしょに食事しない？
しょくじ
B：いいね。

Ex.1

A: Can I smoke here?

Store clerk: Sorry, not here.

Ex.2

(At the library)

A: I want to borrow some books. How many can I borrow?

Librarian: You can borrow five books each week.

Ex.3

(At a hotel)

A: From what time can we eat breakfast?

B: From 6:00.

Ex.4

A: What time can you go home today?

B: I can go home at 6:00.

A: Then why don't we go eat together?

B: Sure.

19-1

1-1 Potential Form of Group I Verbs

The potential form of verbs is made by changing the syllable that comes before **ます** to one that ends in [e], then adding **ます**.

～い → ～え

The potential form of **～います** is **～えます**.

かいます buy → かえます

～き → ～け ／ ～ぎ → ～げ

The potential form of **～きます** is **～けます**, and for **～ぎます**, it is **～げます**.

かきます write → かけます

いそぎます hurry → いそげます

～し → ～せ

The potential form of **～します** is **～せます**.

はなします talk → はなせます

かします lend → かせます

～ち → ～て

The potential form of **～ちます** is **～てます**.

まちます wait → まてます

～に → ～ね

The potential form of **～にます** is **～ねます**.

しにます die → しねます

～び → ～べ

The potential form of **～びます** is **～べます**.

あそびます play → あそべます

～み → ～め

The potential form of **～みます** is **～めます**.

よみます read → よめます

～り → ～れ

The potential form of **～ります** is **～れます**.

とります take → とれます

1-2 Potential Form of Group Ⅱ Verbs

ます becomes **られます**.

たべます eat → たべられます

みます see, watch → みられます

かります borrow → かりられます

1-3 Potential Form of Group Ⅲ Verbs

します becomes **できます**, and **きます** becomes **こられます**. 【noun】+ **します** becomes 【noun】+ **できます**.

べんきょうします study → べんきょうできます

そうじします clean → そうじできます

2　　　　　　でいいですか

When asking someone if something is convenient for them, **～でいいですか** is used.

Conjunctive Form

noun	でいいですか

Ex.1

A：今度のミーティング、来週の火曜日の2時<u>でいいです</u>
　<u>か</u>。

B：はい、いいです。

Ex.2

A：コーヒー、ありますか。

B：すみません。コーヒーはありませんが、こうちゃはあり
　ます。こうちゃ<u>でいいですか</u>。

A：こうちゃはちょっと。

B：すみません。

Ex.1

A: Is 2:00 next Tuesday okay for the next meeting?

B: Yes.

Ex.2

A: Do you have coffee?

B: I'm sorry. We don't have any coffee, but we do have black tea. Would black tea be okay?

A: I'd rather not have black tea.

B: I'm sorry.

19-1

ぼしゅう recruiting ／たんとう person in charge ／留学生 international student
りゅうがくせい

めんせつ interview ／身分証明書 personal identification ／パスポート passport
みぶんしょうめいしょ

服 clothes ／通ります pass (through) ／ずいぶん very ／欠席 absent ／せまい narrow
ふく　　　　　　　とお　　　　　　　　　　　　　　　　　　　　　　けっせき

れいぞうこ refrigerator ／メモします take a memo

Conversation Scenario 💬

〈Applying via phone〉

Lama: Hello. I'm calling because I saw the ad for a part-time job. May I speak with the person in charge?

Employee: Yes. Please wait one moment.

Manager: Hello? This is the manager, Kimura.

Lama: My name is Lama Vijay. Umm, I'm studying abroad, so will I be able to work there?

Manager: Yes, you can.

Lama: Really? Thank you.

Manager: Well then, we'll interview you. Can you come tomorrow?

Lama: Yes, I can.

Manager: Then, please come tomorrow at 6:00 in the evening.

Lama: Okay.

Manager: When you do, please bring personal identification.

Lama: Is a passport okay?

Manager: Yes, it is.

Lama: Okay. Thank you. Good bye.

2 かんたんな会話はできます

Can-do Check ✓

☐You can talk about what you can do and when you can work at part-time job interviews.

Grammar Notes ✎

1 可能形 Potential Form
かのうけい

When you want to express that you have the ability to do something, the verb potential form (可能形) is used. ～ことができます can also be used (☞ Lesson 17-1, 19-1).

Ex.1

A：Bさんはおよげますか。

B：いいえ、およげません。

Ex.2

A：日本語の歌が歌えますか。
にほんご うた うた

B：はい、歌えます。
うた

Ex.1

A: B-san, can you swim?

B: No, I can't.

Ex.2

A: Can you sing Japanese songs?

B: Yes, I can.

2 なくて はいけません

When you want to talk about something you have to do, ～なくてはいけません is used.

Conjunctive Form

verb ない form 〈～ない くて〉	はいけません

Ex.1

先生：みなさん、試験を受けるときは、受験ひょうと身
せんせい しけん う じゅけん み
分証明書を持って行かなくてはいけませんよ。わす
ぶんしょうめいしょ も い
れないでください。

A：はい。

Ex.1

Teacher: Everyone, when taking the test, you must bring your admission ticket for the examination and personal identification. Please don't forget.

A: Okay.

Ex.2

母：もう10時よ。はやくねなくてはいけませんよ。
はは じ

子ども：は〜い。
こ

Ex.2

Mother: It's already 10:00. You have to go to bed now.

Child: Okay.

19-2

3　でも

When talking about an unspecified time or thing, 【interrogative word】＋でも～ is used.

Conjunctive Form

interrogative word	でも	～

Ex.1

A：クラスのかかりをきめましょう。Bさんは何がやりたいですか。

B：私は何でもいいです。

Ex.2

A：いつ映画を見に行きましょうか。

B：いつでもいいです。

Ex.3

A：この仕事、だれにたのみましょうか。

B：だれでもできますよ。

Ex.4

A：Bさんの帰国の前に、みんなでいっしょに食事をしましょう。どこがいいですか。

B：ありがとうございます。私はどこでもけっこうですよ。

A：じゃあ、みんなに聞いてみます。

Ex.1

A: Let's decide our class roles. What do you want to do, B-san?

B: Anything is okay with me.

Ex.2

A: When shall we go see a movie?

B: Anytime is okay.

Ex.3

A: Who shall we ask to do this job?

B: Anyone is okay.

Ex.4

A: Before you go back to your own country, let's all have a meal together. Where shall we go?

B: Thank you. Anywhere is okay with me.

A: Then I'll try asking everyone.

Vocabulary and Expression 🐝

会話 conversation ／～字：100字 ～ letter(s): a hundred letters

今週中 during the week, by the end of the week

なれます get used to ／こまります be troubled ／自分 myself, yourself

着せます put clothes on (someone) ／ほうこくします report ／分けます separate

リサイクル recycle ／いっしょにします put together ／おどります dance

Conversation Scenario 💬

〈Interviewing for a job〉

Manager: Lama-san, how well can you speak Japanese?

Lama: I can have simple conversations.

Manager: What about kanji?

Lama: I can read about 100 characters.

Manager: I see. Can you work in the morning?

Lama: Yes, I can. But I have classes from 1:00, so I have to go to school by then.

Manager: I see. What about weekends?

Lama: I can work until any time on weekends.

Manager: Okay. Then, I'll contact you sometime this week.

Lama: Okay. Thank you.

19 - 2

Can-do Check ✓

☐You can talk about what you were asked at the interview.

Grammar Notes 🖊

1 受身形　Passive Form
うけ み けい

When X calls Y, Y is said to be **よばれました**. When verbs are used to describe actions passively, it is called the verb passive form. The [-remasu] form of verbs, as in **よばれます**, **聞かれます** and **見られ** き み **ます**, is called the passive form (**受身形**). There is also a passive うけ み けい form that ends in [-reru], as in **よばれる**, **聞かれる** and **見られる**. き み

〇〇さん

よびます　よばれます

Ex.1

先生：これから名前をよびます。
せんせい　　　　　　　　　　なまえ

　　　よばれた人はここに来てください。
　　　　　　　ひと　　　　　き

A：はい。

Ex.2

駅で知らない人にきっぷの買い方を聞かれました。
えき　し　　　ひと　　　　　　か　かた　き

Ex.3

友だちにバーベキューにさそわれました。
とも

Ex.1

Teacher: Now I'm going to call names. If your name is called, please come here.

A: Okay.

Ex.2

At the station, I was asked how to buy a ticket by a stranger.

Ex.3

I was invited to a barbeque by my friend.

1-1　Passive Form of Group I Verbs

The passive form is made by changing the syllable before **ます** to one that ends in [a] and adding **れます**.

〜い → 〜わ

The passive form of **〜います** is **〜われます**.

いいます say → いわれます

さそいます invite → さそわれます

～き → ～か

The passive form of **～きます** is **～かれます**.

ききます ask, hear ➡ きかれます

～し → ～さ

The passive form of **～します** is **～されます**.

はなします talk ➡ はなされます

～ち → ～た

The passive form of **～ちます** is **～たれます**.

まちます wait ➡ またれます

～に → ～な

The passive form of **～にます** is **～なれます**.

しにます die ➡ しなれます

～び → ～ば

The passive form of **～びます** is **～ばれます**.

よびます call ➡ よばれます

えらびます choose ➡ えらばれます

～み → ～ま

The passive form of **～みます** is **～まれます**.

よみます read ➡ よまれます

たのみます ask ➡ たのまれます

～り → ～ら

The passive form of **～ります** is **～られます**.

とります take ➡ とられます

■-2 Passive Form of Group II Verbs

ます is changed to **られます**.

たべます eat ➡ たべられます

みます see, watch ➡ みられます

ほめます praise ➡ ほめられます

1-3 Passive Form of Group Ⅲ Verbs

します becomes されます and きます becomes こられます. 【noun】＋します becomes 【noun】＋されます.

しょうたいします invite → しょうたいされます

案内します guide → 案内されます
あんない　　　　　　　あんない

Vocabulary and Expression 🍡

ぜんぶ everything

さそいます invite ／ほめます praise ／たすけます save ／しょうたいします invite

てつだい help ／クリスマス Christmas ／けっこんしき wedding

スピーチ大会 speech contest ／代表 representative ／せんもん学校 vocational school
　　　　たいかい　　　　　　　　　だいひょう　　　　　　　　　　　がっこう

Conversation Scenario 💬

〈Speaking to a friend the day after the interview〉

Kim: Lama-san, your part-time job interview was yesterday, right?

Lama: Yeah.

Kim: So, what kind of things were you asked?

Lama: Well... I was asked things like "How well can you speak Japanese?" and "Can you work on weekends?"

Kim: Did you say everything in Japanese?

Lama: Yeah. It wasn't that hard.

Kim: That's great!

1 さくらがさいていますよ

Can-do Check ✓

☐ You can talk about your surroundings and the scenery.

Grammar Notes ✎

1 _____ が _____ て います

When talking about things that are happening in nature, such as **雨がふる**, **花がさく** or
ほしが出る, **〜が〜ています** is used.

Conjunctive Form

noun	が	verb て form 〈〜て〉 〈〜で〉	います

Ex.1

朝から雨がふっています。

Ex.1

It's been raining since morning.

Ex.2

ふじ山にゆきがつもっています。

Ex.2

There is snow on Mt. Fuji.

Ex.3

さくらの花がさいています。

Ex.3

The cherry blossoms are in bloom.

Verbs that are used with **〜を** to indicate an object of the action, such as **りんご
を食べます** or **テレビを見ます**, are called transitive verbs (**他動詞**). Verbs that are
not used with **〜を**, such as **学校へ行きます** or **雨がふります**, are called
intransitive verbs (**自動詞**). Intransitive verbs use a 【noun】が 【intransitive
verb】construction, and transitive verbs use 【noun】を 【transitive verb】
(☞ Lesson 20 - 2).

自動詞 （intransitive verb）	他動詞 （transitive verb）
雨がふります it rains	パンを食べます eat bread
月が出ます the moon is out	コーヒーを飲みます drink coffee
花がさきます flowers bloom	本を読みます read a book

20-1

2

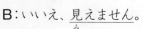　が見えます

　が聞こえます

When describing things that naturally come into sight or earshot, 〜が見えます or 〜が
聞こえます is used.

Conjunctive Form

noun	が	見えます
		聞こえます

Ex.1

（ホテルで）

A：私の部屋からふじ山が見えます。
Bさんの部屋からふじ山が見えますか。

B：いいえ、見えません。

Ex.2

A：子どものこえが聞こえますね。

B：ええ。外で子どもがあそんでいます。

Ex.1

(At a hotel)

A: I can see Mt. Fuji from my room.
B-san, can you see Mt. Fuji from
your room?

B: No, I can't.

Ex.2

A: I can hear children's voices.

B: Yes. Children are playing outside.

3

　のが

　のを

　のは

In sentences like テニスがすきです, テレビを見ます and 日本のまんがはおもしろいです,
nouns are used before が, を or は. When using verbs in place of nouns, 【plain form
verb】＋の is used.

漢字		が	むずかしい
漢字を書く	の		
テニス		が	すきです
テニスをする	の		
日本のまんが		は	おもしろいです
ゲームをする	の		

テレビ		を	見ます
ひこうきがとぶ	の		
山田さんの電話番号		を	知っています
山田さんがけっこんした	の		

Ex.1

私はおかしを作るのがすきです。

Ex.2

今朝トムさんが青木先生と話しているのを見ました。

Ex.3

A：一人でひっこしをするのはたいへんです。手つだいましょう。

B：ありがとうございます。

Ex.4

一人でご飯を食べるのはさびしいです。だれかといっしょに食べたいです。

Ex.1

I like making sweets.

Ex.2

This morning, I saw Tom-san talking with Aoki-sensei.

Ex.3

A: It's hard moving on your own. I'll help.

B: Thank you.

Ex.4

It's lonely eating alone. I want to eat with someone.

Vocabulary and Expression

ふじ山 Mt. Fuji ／見えます be able to see ／つもります pile up ／ん？ Huh?
聞こえます hear ／あっち over there

月 moon ／（月が）出ます (the moon) comes out ／ほし star ／鳥 bird ／なみ wave
けむり smoke ／しょうぼう車 firetruck ／サイレン siren ／くもります be cloudy
そうこ warehouse ／～たち：子どもたち plural suffix for people: children
よろこびます be happy ／めずらしい rare ／ご主人 your husband 〈honorific〉
めんどう（な）bothersome ／てんぼう台 observation deck ／やけい night view

20
-
1

〈Going for a walk〉

Ati: Oh, look. The cherry blossoms are in bloom.

Lee: Ah, you're right. It's spring already. Ah, over there. You can see Mt. Fuji.

Ati: There's snow on it. It's beautiful!

Lee: ...huh? I can hear music.

Ati: Yes. I can hear people singing.

Lee: It's coming from over there. Why don't we go check it out?

Ati: Yes, let's go.

Can-do Check ✔

☐ You can tell someone when something is falling.

Grammar Notes ✏

1 ▢▢▢▢▢▢ **ようになります**

When talking about a change like now being able to do something you weren't able to do before, **〜ようになります** is used.

Conjunctive Form

verb potential form ⟨-eru⟩	ようになります

Ex.1

前は料理ができませんでした。料理の学校へ行きましたから、今はかんたんな料理が<u>作れるようになりました</u>。

Ex.1

Before, I couldn't cook. After going to a cooking school, I'm now able to make simple recipes.

Ex.2

前は漢字が読めませんでした。今は、少し勉強しましたから、50字ぐらい<u>読めるようになりました</u>。

Ex.2

I wasn't able to read kanji before. But now, after studying a little, I can read about 50 kanji.

Ex.3

前はひこうきの中でインターネットが使えませんでしたが、今は<u>使えるようになりました</u>。

Ex.3

Before, you couldn't use the Internet on airplanes, but now you can.

2 ▢▢▢▢▢ **が** ▢▢▢▢▢

When you want to tell someone that something is about to fall or topple over, **〜が 【intransitive verb】** is used (☞ Lesson 20-1). Verbs used to describe an action that happens naturally are called intransitive verbs (**自動詞**).

Conjunctive Form

noun	が	intransitive verb

20 - 2

221

Ex.1

（ホテルの部屋<ruby>で<rt>へや</rt></ruby>）

ホテルの人：カードをドアのここにあててください。
ドアが<ruby>開<rt>あ</rt></ruby>きます。

A：はい。ドアが<ruby>開<rt>あ</rt></ruby>きました。

ホテルの人：このカードをここに入れてください。

A：はい。あ、<ruby>電気<rt>でんき</rt></ruby>がつきました。

ホテルの人：カードをとってください。

A：はい。あ、<ruby>電気<rt>でんき</rt></ruby>がきえました。

Ex.2

（レストランで）

A：あ、スプーンがおちたよ。

B：あ、ズボンがよごれちゃった。

Ex.3

（<ruby>会社<rt>かいしゃ</rt></ruby>で）

A：ミーティングが<ruby>始<rt>はじ</rt></ruby>まりますよ。

B：はい。<ruby>今行<rt>いまい</rt></ruby>きます。

Ex.1

(At a hotel room)

Hotel staff: Please touch here with your card. The door will open.

A: Okay. The door opened.

Hotel staff: Put this card here.

A: Okay. Ah, the lights turned on.

Hotel staff: Please take the card out.

A: Okay. Ah, the lights went out.

Ex.2

(At a restaurant)

A: Ah, your spoon fell.

B: Ah, my pants got dirty.

Ex.3

(At a company)

A: The meeting is about to start.

B: Okay. I'm going now.

Vocabulary and Expression 😀

たおれます fall over ／<ruby>強<rt>つよ</rt></ruby>い have a high tolerance for (alcohol) ／よごれます get dirty

われます split

マニュアル manual ／ジョギング jogging

〜キロ・キロメートル：15キロ 〜 kilometer(s): fifteen kilometers ／もくひょう goal

<ruby>閉<rt>し</rt></ruby>まります close ／つきます turn on ／ひも string ／<ruby>切<rt>き</rt></ruby>れます break, snap ／ふくろ bag

やぶれます tear ／むし bug, insect ／くつひも shoestrings ／<ruby>母親<rt>ははおや</rt></ruby> mother, mom

お<ruby>母<rt>かあ</rt></ruby>さん mother, mom ／あ〜あ Ah!

⟨At a restaurant⟩

Lee: Ati-san, do you have a high tolerance to alcohol?

Ati: I couldn't really drink before, but lately, I've been able to drink more.

Lee: Ah, it's going to fall (over)!

Ati: Ah!

Lee: Aw, it got all over me.

Ati: I'm sorry!

Lee: Aah, it's going to fall (down)!

Ati: Aah, it broke. I'm sorry! Lee-san, are you okay?

Lee: Yes. Excuse me.

20-2

3 たくさんお金が入ってる
かね

☐ You can talk about what to do when finding a lost item.

☐ You can describe where a lost item was found when bringing it to the police station.

Grammar Notes 🖋

1　　　　　て います

When you want to talk about something you can see like the look or condition of a room, 〜【intransitive verb】ています is used. When talking with friends, family or people that are close to you, 〜てる is used.

Conjunctive Form

verb て form	〈〜て〉	います
	〈〜で〉	る

Ex.1

A：ごみがおちています。そうじしましょう。

B：そうですね。テーブルもよごれています。ふきましょう。

Ex.2

A：さむいねえ。

B：うん。あ、まどが開いてる。閉めよう。
　　　　　　　　　　あ　　　　　し

Ex.1

A: There's trash (fallen) on the floor. Let's clean.

B: Yes. The table is dirty, too. Let's wipe it.

Ex.2

A: It's cold.

B: Yeah. Ah, the window is open. Let's close it.

2　　　　　　　　　　なくちゃ

When you want to talk about something that you must do, **〜なくてはいけません** is used. When talking with friends, family and people that are close to you, **〜なくちゃ** is used (☞ Lesson 19-2).

Conjunctive Form

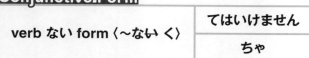

verb ない form 〈〜ない く〉	てはいけません
	ちゃ

Ex.1

A：もう5時だ。アルバイトに行かなくちゃ。

Ex.2

A：明日早いから、もうねなくちゃ。

B：うん。おやすみ。

Ex.1

A: It's already 5:00. I have to get to my part-time job.

Ex.2

A: I have to be up early tomorrow, so I'm going to bed now.

B: Okay. Good night.

Vocabulary and Expression 😊

交番 police box ／ひろいます pick up ／けいさつかん police officer ／ふんすい fountain
そば next to

なんだ Oh, that's it? ／とどけます deliver ／かくにんします confirm ／以下 less than
ていきけん commuter pass ／おおぜい many people ／今度 next time

Conversation Scenario 💬

〈Finding a wallet in the park〉

Kim: Ah, there's something (that has fallen) on the ground.

Tang: Huh? What is it?

Kim: Ah, it's a wallet. There's a lot of money in it.

Tang: You're right. We have to take it to the police box.

Kim: Yeah.

Kim: Excuse me, we found a wallet, but...

Police officer: Where did you find it?

Tang: At the park. It was on the ground next to a fountain.

1 どうなさいましたか

Can-do Check ✔

☐You can give a simple description of symptoms at the hospital and
arrange to see a doctor.

Grammar Notes 🖋

1 どうなさいましたか ― [_____]んです

When receptionists or nurses ask visitors to the hospital about their condition, or
when station employees talk to commuters in trouble, **どうなさいましたか。** is used. **どう
なさいましたか** is a polite version of **どうしましたか**. When answering this, **〜んです** is
used. The plain form is used before **んです** (☞ Lesson 12 - 4).

Conjunctive Form

verb plain form	かいだんからおちた	
い adjective plain form	あつい	**んです**
な adjective plain form 〈〜だ な〉	たいへんな	
noun plain form 〈〜だ な〉	休_{やす}みな	

Ex.1
病院_{びょういん}の受付_{うけつけ}の人_{ひと}：どうなさいましたか。
A：熱_{ねつ}があるんです。

Ex.2
駅員_{えきいん}：どうなさいましたか。
A：おなかが痛_{いた}いんです。

Ex.3
店員_{てんいん}：どうなさいましたか。
A：私_{わたし}のかさがないんです。

Ex.1
Hospital receptionist: What's the
matter?
A: I have a fever.

Ex.2
Station employee: What can I help
you with?
A: My stomach hurts.

Ex.3
Store clerk: What's the matter?
A: My umbrella is gone.

2　＿＿＿＿＿ので、＿＿＿＿＿おねがいします

When giving instructions to someone who is ill at a hospital or a customer at a store,
〜ので、〜おねがいします is used. **〜ので** is used to designate the reason for something.

「こちらへおねがいします。」＝こちらへ来てください。 Please come here/this way.

「お名前をおねがいします。」＝名前を言ってください。 Please tell me your name. ／名前を書いてく
ださい。 Please write your name.

Conjunctive Form

～ので、	noun that expresses instructions	おねがいします	
		verb て form 〈～て〉〈～で〉	ください

Ex.1

（病院で）

看護師：検査をしますので、こちらへおねがいします。
A：はい。

Ex.2

（店で）

店員：山田さま。カードをお作りしましたので、こちらに
　　　サイン（を）おねがいします。

Ex.1

(At a hospital)

Nurse: We're going to do some tests, so please come this way.

A: Okay.

Ex.2

(At a store)

Store clerk: Yamada-sama. Your card has been made, so please sign here.

Vocabulary and Expression 🐛

頭 head ／診察券 patient ID card ／保険証 insurance card
（熱を）はかります take (temperature) ／じゅんばん sequential order

のど throat ／せき cough ／くしゃみ sneeze ／気持ちが悪い feel sick ／しょくよく appetite
さむけがします feel a chill ／はきけがします be nauseous ／指 finger, thumb, toe
けがします be injured ／やけどします be burned ／（頭を）打ちます hit (one's head)
足 leg, foot ／はれます get swollen, swell ／整形外科 orthopedics ／レントゲン X-ray
体重 weight ／（体重を）はかります weigh ／血圧 blood pressure ／採血 drawing blood
検査室 examination room

Conversation Scenario 💬

⟨At the hospital⟩

Tang: Excuse me. It's my first time here.

Receptionist: Okay. What's the matter?

Tang: I've had a fever since yesterday, and my head hurts.

Receptionist: I see. We will make you a patient ID card, so may I see your insurance card?

Tang: Okay.

Receptionist: Please fill this out. Take your temperature, too.

Tang: Okay... I filled it out.

Receptionist: Okay then, your number will be called in order.

Tang: How long will it be until I'm called on?

Receptionist: I think it should be about 10 to 15 minutes.

Lesson 21   **2** かぜでしょう

☐You can explain your symptoms to the doctor and take a medical examination.

☐You can listen to the doctor's instructions and ask the doctor questions.

Grammar Notes 🖊

1  でしょう

When being examined by a doctor, and they are telling you the name of your illness or how long it will take to recover, **～でしょう** is used.

Conjunctive Form

verb plain form	でしょう
noun	

Ex.

医者：かぜでしょう。

A：そうですか。

医者：よくねてください。 すぐよくなるでしょう。

Ex.

Doctor: You likely have a cold.

A: I see.

Doctor: Please get plenty of sleep. You should get better right away.

2 **X　ないで　　　Y**

When explaining that you will not do 【action X】, but will do 【action Y】, **～ないで～** is used.

Conjunctive Form

verb ない form 〈～ない〉	で	～

Ex.1

（病院で）

医者：外に出かけないで、家にいてください。

A：はい。

Ex.1

(At a hospital)

Doctor: Stay at home and don't go out.

A: Okay.

Ex.2

いもうとは勉強しないで、ゲームをしています。

Ex.2

My younger sister plays games instead of studying.

3   X たら、 Y てもいいですか

When asking if you can do 【action Y】 after doing 【action X】, ～たら、～てもいいですか is used. When telling someone that they can do 【action Y】 after doing 【action X】, ～たら、～てもいいです is used.

Conjunctive Form

verb た form 〈～た〉〈～だ〉	ら、	verb て form 〈～て〉〈～で〉	も	いいですか
				いいです

Ex.1

A：げんきになったら、薬を飲まなくてもいいですか。

医者：いいえ。１週間ぐらいはつづけて飲んでください。

Ex.2

A：先生、テストが終わったら、帰ってもいいですか。

先生：はい、いいですよ。

Ex.3

この大学は、JLPTのN２にごうかくしたら、
日本語の試験を受けなくてもいいです。

Ex.1

A: Once I get better, can I stop taking the medicine?

Doctor: No. Please continue to take your medicine for about a week.

Ex.2

A: Sensei, once we've finished the test, may we go home?

Teacher: Yes, you may.

Ex.3

At this university, if you have passed the N2 level JLPT, you do not have to take the Japanese language test.

Vocabulary and Expression 😀

医者 doctor ／（のどを）みます examine (one's throat)

～分：３日分 prescription amount: medicine for three days

（薬を）出します prescribe, give (medicine) ／外出します go out ／下がります go down

無理をします overdo it, try too hard

- -

食べすぎ eat too much ／楽になります become comfortable

入院します be admitted into the hospital, stay in hospital ／リハビリ rehabilitation

ずっと for a long time ／運動 exercise ／右手 right hand ／しばらく a while ／左手 left hand

食後 after eating ／診察 examination ／（診察を）受けます get an examination

検査 examination, check up ／ひざ knee(s) ／退院します leave[be released from] the hospital

かゆい itchy ／ぬります apply ／具合 condition ／胃 stomach

胃カメラ検査 stomach examination with a camera

Conversation Scenario 💬

⟨In the doctor's office⟩

Doctor: What's the matter?

Tang: My head has been hurting since yesterday morning.

Doctor: You also have a fever.

Tang: Yes. And I've been coughing.

Doctor: Then, let me take a look at your throat. Please open your mouth. Ah, it's red. You likely have a cold.

Tang: Really?

Doctor: I'll give you three days' worth of medicine. Don't go out today, and get plenty of rest instead.

Tang: Okay. Can I go out once my fever goes down?

Doctor: Yes. But don't overdo it.

Tang: Okay.

Can-do Check ✔

☐ You can listen to and confirm instructions for taking medicine at a pharmacy.

Grammar Notes 🖊

1 _____ に _____

When talking about how many times someone should do something in a given time, like the dosage or frequency of medicine to be taken, **【given time】+ に +【frequency, amount】** is used. The particle **に** is often omitted.

Conjunctive Form

given time	（に）	frequency, amount

Ex.1

薬局の人：この薬は1日に3回飲んでください。
やっきょく ひと　　　くすり　　にち　　かい　の

A：はい。

薬局の人：1回2錠です。
やっきょく ひと　　かい　じょう

A：わかりました。1日に3回、1回2錠ですね。
　　　　　　　　　　にち　　かい　　かい　じょう

Ex.2

（スポーツジムで）

トレーナー：この体そうは1週間に3回以上やってくださ
　　　　　　　　たい　　　　しゅうかん　　かい いじょう
い。1回10分でいいです。
　　かい　ぶん

A：はい。

Ex.3

（学校で）
がっこう

先生：3か月に1回、レベルチェックのテストをします。
せんせい　　げつ　　かい

A：はい。

Ex.1

Pharmacy staff: Take this medicine three times a day.

A: Okay.

Pharmacy staff: Take two pills each time.

A: Okay. Three times a day, two pills each time.

Ex.2

(At a sports gym)

Trainer: Please do this exercise at least three times a week. Do it for 10 minutes each time.

A: Okay.

Ex.3

(At school)

Teacher: Once every three months, we have a level check test.

A: Okay.

2 　　いとき、

When you want to talk about what you are going to do at the time of a certain situation or circumstance, **～とき、 ～** is used.

Conjunctive Form

い adjective 〈～い〉	とき、	～
verb ない form 〈～ない〉		

Ex.1

（病院で）

医者：熱が高いときは、おふろに入らないでください。

A：はい。

Ex.1

(At a hospital)

Doctor: Don't take baths if you have a high fever.

A: Okay.

Ex.2

（病院で）

医者：おなかが痛くないとき、この薬は飲まなくてもいいです。

A：はい。

Ex.2

(At a hospital)

Doctor: You don't have to take this medicine when your stomach doesn't hurt.

A: Okay.

3 -1 　　ようにしてください

When you want to warn someone not to do something, **～ないようにしてください** is used.

Conjunctive Form

verb ない form 〈～ない〉	ようにしてください

Ex.1

医者：おさけをあまり飲まないようにしてください。

A：はい。

Ex.1

Doctor: Please try not to drink too much alcohol.

A: Okay.

Ex.2

薬局の人：ねる前に薬を飲んでください。忘れないようにしてください。

A：はい。

Ex.2

Pharmacy clerk: Please take this before going to sleep. Please be sure not to forget.

A: Okay.

Ex.3

先生：もうすぐ入学試験です。かぜをひかないようにしてください。

A：はい。

Ex.3

Teacher: The entrance exam is coming up. Please be careful not to catch a cold.

A: Okay.

◆ When you want to encourage someone to try their best to do something, **～ようにしてください** is used after the dictionary form of the verb.

Conjunctive Form

verb dictionary form	ようにしてください

Ex.1

医者：毎日きまった時間に食事をするようにしてください。
　　　 いしゃ　まいにち　　　　　　 じかん　　しょくじ

A：はい。

医者：早くねて、早くおきるようにしてください。
　　　 いしゃ　はや　　　　　はや

A：はい、わかりました。

Ex.2

先生：じゅぎょう中は日本語で話すようにしてください。
　　　 せんせい　　　　 ちゅう　にほんご　はな

A：はい。

Ex.1

Doctor: Please try to eat meals at a set time each day.

A: Okay.

Doctor: Please try to go to bed early and wake up early, too.

A: Okay, I understand.

Ex.2

Teacher: Please try to speak Japanese during class.

A: Okay.

③-2　　　　　　　ようにします

When talking about something that you yourself try not to do, **～ないようにします** is used. Similarly, when talking about something you will try to do, **ようにします** is used after the dictionary form of the verb.

Conjunctive Form

verb ない form 〈～ない〉	ようにします
verb dictionary form	

Ex.1

医者：運動をしたほうがいいですよ。
　　　 いしゃ　うんどう

A：はい。毎朝ジョギングをするようにします。
　　　　　 まいあさ

Ex.2

先生：ちこくしないようにしてください。
　　　 せんせい

A：はい。早くねて、早くおきるようにします。
　　　　　 はや　　　　　はや
夜ゲームをしないようにします。
よる

Ex.1

Doctor: You should get some exercise.

A: Okay. I'll try to go jogging every morning.

Ex.2

Teacher: Please try not to be late.

A: Okay. I'll try to go to bed early and wake up early, too. I'll try not to play games at night.

Vocabulary and Expression

以内 within
いない

退院 leaving [being released from] the hospital ／〜か月：3か月 counter for months: three months
たいいん   げつ   げつ

錠剤 tablet, pill ／かた shoulder(s) ／しっぷ cold patch ／はります apply (to the back) ／体 body
じょうざい   からだ

量 amount, portion(s) ／足ります be enough ／ふえます increase
りょう   た

できるだけ if possible, as 〜 as possible ／こな薬 powdered medicine ／カプセル capsule
くすり

かぜ薬 cold medicine ／はな水 runny nose
くすり   みず

Conversation Scenario

〈At the pharmacy〉

Pharmacist: This is your medicine.

Tang: Okay.

Pharmacist: Take the white one three times a day. Please take it after eating a meal.
Take this red one when you have a high fever.

Tang: Okay, I got it. Take the red one when I have a high fever and take the white
one after I eat.

Pharmacist: That's right. Please take the white one within 30 minutes of finishing
your meal. Please try not to forget.

Tang: Okay.

Pharmacist: Please take care.

Tang: Thank you.

Can-do Check ✓

☐ You can describe the situation and give your impression.

☐ You can say what is happening in a situation while looking at pictures.

Grammar Notes 🖊

1 ＿＿＿＿そうです

When making a conjecture based on something you have seen, **～そうです** is used.

Conjunctive Form

い adjective 〈～い〉	そうです
な adjective 〈～な〉	

Ex.1

（クラスメートを見て）

A：Bさん、うれしそうですね。何かいいことがあったんですか。
　　　　　　　　　　　　　　なに

B：はい。大学にごうかくしたんです。
　　　　だいがく

A：そうですか。よかったですね。おめでとうございます。

Ex.1

(After seeing a classmate)

A: You look happy, B-san. Did something good happen?

B: Yes. I got accepted to university.

A: I see. That's great. Congratulations.

Ex.2

（ひさしぶりに会った人を見て）
　　　　　あ　　ひと　み

A：Bさん、おげんきそうですね。

B：はい。おかげさまで。

Ex.2

(After seeing someone for the first time in a long time)

A: B-san, you look good.

B: Yes, thank you.

Ex.3

（どうりょうが一人で仕事をしているようすを見て）
　　　　　　　ひとり　しごと　　　　　　　　み

A：田中さん、たいへんそうですね。
　　たなか

B：ええ。少し手つだいましょう。
　　　　すこ　て

Ex.3

(After seeing a coworker working alone)

A: Tanaka-san looks really busy.

B: Yes. Let's help a little.

2 -1   verb dictionary form   ところです

When talking about something that you are about to do, 〜ところです is used.

Conjunctive Form

verb dictionary form	ところです

Ex.1

（電話で）

A：もしもし、Bさん、食事に行きませんか。

B：今料理ができて、これから食べるところなんです。

A：そうですか。じゃあ、また今度。

Ex.2

（ミーティングで）

A：すみません。おそくなりました。

B：あ、だいじょうぶですよ。ちょうど今から始めるところですよ。

Ex.1

(On the phone)

A: Hello, B-san? Why don't we go get something to eat?

B: I just cooked something and I'm about to eat now.

A: I see. Then, next time.

Ex.2

(At a meeting)

A: Excuse me. I'm sorry I'm late.

B: Ah, it's okay. We were just about to start.

2 -2   〜ている   ところです

When talking about something you are currently in the middle of doing, 〜ているところです is used.

Conjunctive Form

verb て form 〈〜て〉 〈〜で〉	いるところです

Ex.

（電話で）

A：もしもし。Bさんですか。

B：すみません。今バスにのっているところです。おりたら、電話します。

Ex.

(On the phone)

A: Hello? Is this B-san?

B: Sorry. I'm on the bus right now. I'll call you once I get off.

2-3　　verb た form　ところです

When talking about an action you have just finished, **〜たところです** is used.

Conjunctive Form

verb た form	〈〜た〉	ところです
	〈〜だ〉	

Ex.

（会社で）
かいしゃ

A：田中さん、いますか。
　　た なか

B：今帰ったところです。まだ近くにい
　　いま かえ　　　　　　　　　ちか
　　ると思います。
　　　おも

Ex.

(At work)

A: Is Tanaka-san there?

B: He just went home. I think he
　 should be nearby.

Vocabulary and Expression

しあわせ（な）happy, happiness

ごうかくします pass ／おばけやしき haunted house ／こわい scary

プレゼン・プレゼンテーション presentation ／ちょうど just

スポーツ大会 sport event ／たいそう warm-up exercise ／なわとび jump rope ／なわ rope
　　　　たいかい

ひょうしょう式 award ceremony ／ゆうしょうカップ trophy
　　　　　　しき

そつぎょう式 graduation ceremony ／ちがいます be different ／そつぎょう証書 diploma
　　　　　しき　　　　　　　　　　　　　　　　　　　　　　　　　　　　しょうしょ

Conversation Scenario

〈Showing wedding photos〉

Ati: Inoue-san, congratulations!

Shin: Congratulations!

Ogawa: How was Inoue-san's wedding?

Shin: Inoue-san looked so happy. I have some pictures.

Ogawa: Please show me.

Shin: This is after entering the venue. This is when they were cutting the cake.

Ogawa: They look happy.

Shin: This is when they were about to give their parents flowers.

Ogawa: Their parents look happy, too.

2 準備、できましたか
じゅん び

Can-do Check ✓

☐You can say what you are thinking after looking at a particular situation.

☐You can describe work progress in a simple way.

Grammar Notes ✏

1   ようです

When making a conjecture based on something you saw, heard or read, **～ようです** is used.

Conjunctive Form

verb plain form	
い adjective plain form	
な adjective plain form 〈～だ な〉	**ようです**
noun plain form 〈～だ の〉	

Ex.1

（いぬがなくこえを聞いて）
き

A：だれか<u>来た</u>ようですね。
き

B：そうですね。げんかんを見てきます。
み

Ex.2

（試験会場から出てくる人を見て）
し けんかいじょう　　で　　　ひと　み

A：試験、<u>むずかしかった</u>ようですね。
し けん

B：ええ。

みんな<u>つかれている</u>ようですね。

Ex.3

A：Cさん、あそこでまんがを読んで
よ

　　いますよ。<u>ひまな</u>ようですね。

B：ええ。Cさんに手つだってもらいま
て

　　しょう。

Ex.1

(After hearing a dog barking)

A: It seems that someone has come.

B: Yes. I'll take a look at the entranceway.

Ex.2

(After seeing people leaving an examination area)

A: It seems the test was pretty hard.

B: Yes. Everyone looks tired.

Ex.3

A: C-san is reading manga over there. He looks free.

B: Yes. Let's have C-san help us.

2　　　　　た ばかりです

When talking about an action that has just been finished and hardly any time has elapsed since then, **〜たばかりです** is used.

Conjunctive Form

verb た form 〈〜た〉〈〜だ〉	ばかりです

Ex.1

A：Bさん、日本の生活はいかがですか。

B：今年の10月に日本に<u>来たばかり</u>ですから、わからないことがたくさんあります。

Ex.2

A：お母さん、何か食べる物、ある？

B：え、さっきご飯を<u>食べたばかり</u>でしょう？

Ex.1

A: B-san, how is life in Japan?

B: I just came to Japan in October of this year, so there are a lot of things I don't know.

Ex.2

A: Mom, is there any food?

B: What? Didn't you just eat a minute ago?

Vocabulary and Expression 😀

準備 preparation ／コピー copy ／調子 condition ／修理します repair

- -

集まります gather ／救急車 ambulance ／じこ accident ／ペンキ paint

まだまだです I still have much to learn. ／あ〜っ Ah! ／パンフレット pamphlet, brochure

とどきます arrive ／注文します order ／プログラム program ／プリンター printer

Conversation Scenario 💬

〈Preparing for a meeting〉

Sarah: I did it!

- -

Yamamoto: Are the meeting room preparations complete?

Sarah: Yes, they are. All that's left is to copy the materials, and we're finished.

Yamamoto: When will the materials be finished?

Sarah: Lee-san is copying them right now, but the printer is acting up.

Yamamoto: Even though it was fixed just last week. That's a problem.

Yamamoto: Lee-san, how is it going?

Lee: Just a little more. Once they're finished, I'll take them straight to the meeting room.

Yamamoto: Please do.

Lee: Okay.

1 かばんをとられたんです

Can-do Check ✓

☐You can cry out against a thief that you notice.

☐You can file a damage report and explain what happened.

Grammar Notes 🖊

1 命令形 Imperative Form
めいれいけい

When forcefully telling someone to do something or giving a command, the imperative form of verbs is used. The [-e] form of the verb, such as 待て and かえせ, is called the imperative form (命令形).
めいれいけい

Ex.1

（火事がおきたとき）
か じ

火事だ！ にげろ！
か じ

Ex.1

(A fire has broken out)

Fire! Run!

Ex.2

（自転車の人に）
じ てんしゃ

おい、あぶない。気をつけろ！
き

Ex.2

(To someone riding a bicycle)

Hey, watch out. Be careful!

Ex.3

（サッカーの練習でコーチがせんしゅに）
れんしゅう

コーチ：はやく走れ。
はし

Ex.3

(Soccer team coach to players during practice)

Coach: Run faster.

1 -1 Imperative form of Group I Verbs

The imperative form is made by changing the syllable that comes before **ます** to one that ends in [e].

┌──────────────┐
│ ～い → ～え │
└──────────────┘

The imperative form of **～います** is **～え**.

いいます say → いえ

かいます buy → かえ

~き → ~け ／ ~ぎ → ~げ

The imperative forms of **~きます** and **~ぎます** are **~け** and **~げ**, respectively.

ききます listen → きけ

いそぎます hurry → いそげ

~し → ~せ

The imperative form of **~します** is **~せ**.

はなします talk → はなせ

~ち→~て

The imperative form of **~ちます** is **~て**.

まちます wait → まて

~に→~ね

The imperative form of **~にます** is **~ね**.

しにます die → しね

~び→~べ

The imperative form of **~びます** is **~べ**.

よびます call → よべ

~み→~め

The imperative form of **~みます** is **~め**.

よみます read → よめ

~り→~れ

The imperative form of **~ります** is **~れ**.

とります take → とれ

1-2 Imperative form of Group II Verbs

ます becomes **ろ**.

たべます eat → たべろ

みます see, watch → みろ

あけます open → あけろ

❶-3　Imperative form of Group Ⅲ Verbs

します becomes しろ, and きます becomes こい.

べんきょうします *study* → べんきょうしろ

せつめいします *explain* → せつめいしろ

もってきます *bring* → もってこい

❶-4　　　　　　　　な

When prohibiting someone from doing an action, **〜な** is used.

Conjunctive Form

verb dictionary form	な

Ex.1

（サッカーの練習でコーチがせんしゅに）
れんしゅう

コーチ：こら、止まるな。
　　　　　　と

Ex.2

（工場で工場長がおしゃべりをしている工員に）
こうじょう　こうじょうちょう　　　　　　　　　　こういん

工場長：しゃべるな。
こうじょうちょう

Ex.3

（工場のきんえんのマークのところで）
こうじょう

工場長：こら、ここでたばこをすうな。
こうじょうちょう

Ex.4

（しんにゅうきんしのマークを見て）
　　　　　　　　　　　　　み

A：これは、この部屋に入るなといういい
　　　　　　　　　へ　や　　はい

　　みです。

Ex.1

(Soccer team coach to players during practice)

Coach: Hey, don't stop.

Ex.2

(Factory manager to a worker chatting with someone)

Manager: Stop chatting.

Ex.3

(By a no-smoking sign at a factory)

Manager: Hey, no smoking here.

Ex.4

(By a do not enter sign)

A: This means do not go in this room.

2　　X　たら、　Y　た

When something unexpected happens or is discovered after a first action, 【action X】, ～たら、～た is used.

Conjunctive Form

verb た form 〈～た〉 〈～だ〉	ら、	verb た form 〈～た〉 〈～だ〉
		～ました

Ex.1

（病気で休んだ人に）

A：Bさん、もうかぜはだいじょうぶですか。

B：はい。よくねたら、元気になりました。

Ex.2

朝おきて、まどを開けたら、雪が降っていた。

Ex.3

A：今朝駅に行ったら、電車が止まっていました。

B：そうですか。たいへんでしたね。

Ex.1

(To someone who was absent due to illness)

A: B-san, is your cold all better?

B: I got better after getting some rest.

Ex.2

I woke up in the morning, and when I opened the window, it was snowing.

Ex.3

A: This morning when I went to the station, the trains had stopped.

B: Really? That's too bad.

3　　　　　　は　　　　　　　に　passive form

When someone has been the victim of some annoyance or harm, ～は～に 【passive form】 is used. However, when the subject of the sentence where someone has been annoyed or harmed is 私, 私は is sometimes omitted.

Conjunctive Form

person who was bothered	は	person who was being a nuisance	に	verb passive form

Ex.1

A：Bさん、どうしたんですか。

B：<u>先生<ruby>せんせい</ruby>にしかられた</u>んです。

Ex.1

A: B-san, what's wrong?

B: I was scolded by my teacher.

Ex.2

A：足<ruby>あし</ruby>、どうしたんですか。

B：電車<ruby>でんしゃ</ruby>の中<ruby>なか</ruby>でとなりにいた人<ruby>ひと</ruby>に<u>ふまれました</u>。

Ex.2

A: What happened to your foot?

B: It was stepped on by the person next to me on the train.

＊The passive form can also be used for instances when something is not a nuisance such as **先生<ruby>せんせい</ruby>にほめられました** or **先生<ruby>せんせい</ruby>に名前<ruby>なまえ</ruby>を呼<ruby>よ</ruby>ばれました** (☞ Lesson 19‑3).

Vocabulary and Expression

とります steal ／にげます run away ／ベンチ bench ／男<ruby>おとこ</ruby> man

コーチ coach ／けが injury ／ひっくりかえります flip over ／わ Whoa! ／ふみます step on
しかります scold ／わらいます laugh

Conversation Scenario

〈Going to a police station〉

Tang: Aah! Wait! Don't run away! Give me back my bag!

Tang: Excuse me. My bag has been taken.

Police officer: Where did this happen?

Tang: In Midori Park. I was talking to my friend on bench and a man took my bag and ran.

Police officer: I see. Please tell me the details over here.

Tang: Okay.

2 エアコンがつかないんです

Can-do Check ✔

☐When trouble happens, you can explain the situation to the person in charge and request for support.

Grammar Notes 🖊

1 ＿＿＿＿＿＿が＿＿＿＿＿＿んです

When explaining information and conveying a situation, **〜んです** is used.

Conjunctive Form

verb plain form	
い adjective plain form	**んです**
な adjective plain form〈〜だ な〉	
noun plain form〈〜だ な〉	

Ex.1

A：どうしたんですか。

B：おなかが痛いんです。

Ex.2

（ホテルの電話で）

A：もしもし。トイレの電気がつかないんですが。

ホテルの人：もうしわけありません。すぐ行きます。

Ex.3

（レストランで）

A：あのう、このコップ、

よごれているんですが。

店員：もうしわけありません。おとりかえします。

Ex.1

A: What's wrong?

B: My stomach hurts.

Ex.2

(On a hotel phone)

A: Hello. The light in the bathroom won't turn on.

Hotel staff: I'm sorry. I'll go there right away.

Ex.3

(At a restaurant)

A: Umm, this cup is dirty.

Store clerk: I'm sorry. I'll get you another one.

23 - 2

2 ＿＿＿＿＿＿かもしれません

When you are imagining or conjecturing about something that is not likely to happen but there is still a chance that it may, **〜かもしれません** is used.

Conjunctive Form

verb plain form	
い adjective plain form	
な adjective plain form 〈〜だ〉	かもしれません
noun plain form 〈〜だ〉	

Ex.1

（そらを見て）

A：ああ、今日は雨が降るかもしれませんね。

B：そうですね。かさを持って行きましょう。

Ex.1

(While looking at the sky)

A: Ah, it might rain today.

B: Yes. Let's take umbrellas.

Ex.2

（待ち合わせをしている。田中さんがまだ来ない。）

A：田中さん、おそいですね。電話しましたが、出ません。

B：私も今電話しましたが、出ません。来ないかもしれませんね。

Ex.2

(Waiting for Tanaka-san, who still hasn't come)

A: Tanaka-san is late. I called him, but he didn't answer.

B: I called him now, too, but he didn't answer. Maybe he's not coming.

3 ＿＿＿＿＿＿て も、＿＿＿＿＿＿

When talking about the results of an action not being as expected, **〜ても、〜** is used.

Conjunctive Form

verb て form	〈〜て〉 〈〜で〉	も、	〜

Ex.1

（学校で）

A：勉強しても、日本語が上手になりません。どうしたらいいですか。

先生：勉強したことを使って、話したり書いたりしてください。

Ex.1

(At school)

A: Even though I study, I'm not getting any better at Japanese.

Teacher: Please use what you've studied and practice talking and writing.

Ex.2

A：<u>運動をしても</u>、やせません。

B：甘いものを食べないほうがいいと思いますよ。

Ex.2

A: Even though I exercise, I just can't lose weight.

B: I think you shouldn't eat sweet things.

Vocabulary and Expression

リモコン remote control ／電池 battery

開きます open ／キャップ cap ／保険 insurance ／博物館 museum

サービスセンター service center ／あやまります apologize ／ゆるします forgive, accept

おこります get angry ／さがします look for ／見つかります be found ／はあ sigh

せんめん所 washroom ／でんきゅう light bulb ／スイッチ switch

23
-
2

Conversation Scenario

〈Speaking to the landlord〉

Tang: Huh?

Nishikawa: Yes? This is Nishikawa.

Tang: Hello? Sorry. This is Tang in room 101.

Nishikawa: Ah, hello, Tang-san.

Tang: Hello. Umm, I can't turn on my room's air conditioner. It might be broken.

Nishikawa: What? Did you try changing the batteries in the remote?

Tang: Yes. Even after changing them, it won't work.

Nishikawa: I see. I'll go check it out now.

Tang: Sorry. Thank you.

3 電車が止まっています
でんしゃ　と

Can-do Check ✔

☐You can explain that you are late and talk about what you'll do
thereafter.

Grammar Notes ✎

1 ＿＿＿＿＿＿＿＿＿ でしょう

When making a prediction or conjecture based on something, **～でしょう** is used
(☞ Lesson 21-2).

Conjunctive Form

verb plain form	
い adjective plain form	でしょう
な adjective plain form 〈～だ〉	
noun plain form 〈～だ〉	

Ex.1

（テレビの天気よほうで）
てんき

アナウンサー：明日は午後、雨が降るでしょう。
あした　ご ご　あめ　ふ

Ex.2

A：熱が下がるまでどれぐらいかかりますか。
ねつ　さ

医者：そうですね。１日か２日でよくなるでしょう。
いしゃ　　　　　　にち　ふつか

Ex.1

(On the TV weather forecast)

Announcer: Tomorrow afternoon, it
will likely rain.

Ex.2

A: How long will it be until my fever
goes down?

Doctor: Well, you should be better in
one or two days.

～かもしれません is used when making a conjecture on something that is not
very likely to happen, but there is still a possibility (☞ Lesson 23-2).

Ex.

A：じしんはいつおこるかわかりません。今日おこる
きょう
かもしれません。

B：そうですね。準備をしておいたほうがいいですね。
じゅん び

Ex.

A: We don't know when earthquakes
will occur. One could happen
today.

B: Yes. We'd better make
preparations.

2　　X　て、　　Y

When explaining something where X is the reason for Y, ～て、～ or ～で、～ are used.

Conjunctive Form

verb て form	〈～て〉、 〈～で〉、	
い adjective 〈～い く〉	て、	～
な adjective 〈～な〉	で、	
noun		

Ex.1

たくさん食べて、おなかが痛くなりました。

Ex.2

頭が痛くて、仕事ができません。

Ex.3

部屋が明るくて、ねられません。

Ex.4

アリさんはやさしくて、親切で、とてもいい人です。

Ex.5

たいふうで、電車がおくれました。

Ex.1

I ate so much that my stomach started hurting.

Ex.2

My head hurts so much that I can't do my work.

Ex.3

The room is so bright that I can't sleep.

Ex.4

Ali-san is gentle, kind and a really good person.

Ex.5

The trains were late because of the typhoon.

23
-
3

Vocabulary and Expression

アナウンサー announcer

晴れます be sunny, clear up ／ゴールデンウィーク golden week ／晴れ sunny ／むすこ son
いえ No. ／打ち合わせ business meeting ／だから therefore ／きめます decide
アイドル pop idol ／つたえます tell

⟨At the station⟩

Announcer: It will likely snow this afternoon.

Lama: Hello? Excuse me, manager. It's Lama.

Manager: Hello. Hello? Lama-san? It's so loud there I can't hear you!

Lama: I'm sorry. The trains have stopped due to the snow. I'm going to go by bus.

Manager: I see.

Lama: I think I'm going to be about 30 minutes late.

Manager: Okay. The bus is probably pretty rough, too. Please be careful.

Lama: Okay. Sorry.

1 おみやげ、ありがとうございます

Can-do Check ✓

☐You can say thanks after receiving a souvenir or present from a superior or coworker.

Grammar Notes 🏷

1 Passive Form Honorific Speech

When talking about someone of a higher status than you, you use honorific speech, but you can also use the passive forms of verbs. However, when using **〜てください**, the passive form should not be used. Instead, **お〜になってください** or the **て** form of the honorific form of the verb should be used as **〜てください**.

Ex.1

A：先生、この本、読まれましたか。

先生：いいえ、読んでいません。

A：おもしろいですよ。ぜひお読みになってください。

先生：そうですか。読んでみます。

Ex.2

（駅で）

A：あ、雨だ。どうしよう。

駅員：おきゃくさま、このかさを使われますか。

A：あ、ありがとうございます。

Ex.1

A: Sensei, have you read this book?

Teacher: No, I haven't.

A: It's interesting. Please read it.

Teacher: Really? Then I'll read it.

Ex.2

(At a station)

A: Ah, it's raining. What should I do?

Station employee: Would you like to use this umbrella, ma'am?

A: Oh, thank you.

2 　　　　　　そうです

When expressing your thoughts or feelings on something you have seen, **〜そうです** is used.

Conjunctive Form

い adjective 〈〜い〉	そうです
な adjective 〈〜な〉	

Ex.1

（ケーキの店でケーキを見て）

A：うわあ、おいしそうですね。

B：ええ。これにしましょう。

Ex.2

（まどの外を見て）

A：今日もあつそうですね。

B：そうですね。外へ出たくないですね。

Ex.3

（デパートで）

A：このなべ、べんりそうですね。

B：そうですね。でも、高いですね。

Ex.1

(At a cake store)

A: Wow, this looks delicious.

B: Yes. Let's get this one.

Ex.2

(Looking out of a window)

A: It looks hot today, too.

B: Yes. I don't want to go outside.

Ex.3

(At a department store)

A: This pot looks useful.

B: Yes. But it's expensive.

When making a conjecture about how someone else feels based on what you have seen, **〜そうです** is used (☞ Lesson 22 - 1).

Ex.1

（クラスメートを見て）

A：Bさん、うれしそうですね。何かいいことがあったんですか。

B：はい。大学に合格したんです。

A：そうですか。よかったですね。おめでとうございます。

Ex.1

(Looking at a classmate)

A: B-san, you look happy. Did something good happen?

B: Yes. I got into university.

A: Oh, really? That's great. Congratulations.

Ex.2

（どうりょうが歌を歌いながら仕事をしているようすを見て）

A：田中さん、楽しそうですね。

田中：ええ。今日はデートなんです。

Ex.2

(After seeing a coworker singing while working)

A: Tanaka-san, you look like you're having fun.

Tanaka: Yes. I have a date today.

3 -1 ＿＿＿が＿＿＿をくださいます

When talking about someone of a higher status is giving you a present, ～が～をくださいます is used. The verb くださいます is used instead of あげます.

Conjunctive Form

person of a higher status	が	thing	を	くださいます

Ex.1

（会社で）
かいしゃ

A：このおかし、課長がくださいました。
か ちょう

　　どうぞ。

B：ありがとうございます。

Ex.1

(At a company)

A: My section manager gave me these sweets. Have one.

B: Thank you.

Ex.2

（学校で）
がっこう

A：あ、おいしそうなおかしだね。

B：うん。先生がくださったんだよ。みんなで食べよう。
せんせい　　　　　　　　　　　　　　た

Ex.2

(At school)

A: Oh, those sweets look delicious.

B: Yeah. My teacher gave them to us. Let's all share them.

When talking about someone else receiving something from someone of a higher social status, **くださいます** is not used. Instead, **【person of a higher status】が【receiver】に【thing】をあげます** is used.

Ex.

課長が中村さんに北海道のおみやげをあげました。
か ちょう　なかむら　　ほっかいどう

Ex.

The section manager gave Nakamura-san a souvenir from Hokkaido.

3 -2 ＿＿＿が＿＿＿をくれます

When talking about being given a present by a friend, family member or someone of a lower status, ～が～をくれます is used. The verb くれます is used instead of あげます.

Conjunctive Form

person	が	thing	を	くれます

Ex.1

（会社で）
かいしゃ

A：きれいなハンカチですね。

B：いもうと**が**くれました。

Ex.2

（学校で）
がっこう

A：先生、これ、フィリピンのコインです。マリアンさん
せんせい

がくれました。

先生：へえ、いろいろなコインがありますね。
せんせい

Ex.1

(At a company)

A: That's a beautiful handkerchief.

B: My younger sister gave it to me.

Ex.2

(At school)

A: Sensei, these are some Philippine coins. Marian-san gave them to me.

Teacher: Wow, there are a lot of different coins.

Vocabulary and Expression 🍡

思ったより more than I thought
おも

そだてます raise ／用意 preparation ／ゆっくりします relax
ようい

おひさしぶりです It's been a while. ／おかげさまで thanks to you ／とまります stay over

父の日 Father's day ／むすめ daughter
ちち ひ

Conversation Scenario 💬

〈The manager has taken a trip〉

Yamamoto: These are for everybody. They're a souvenir from Hokkaido.

Sarah: Thank you. So, you went to Hokkaido?

Yamamoto: Yes.

Sarah: How was it?

Yamamoto: There was more snow than I thought there would be, and it was cold. But the food was delicious.

Sarah: I see.

Lee: Oh, this looks good.

Sarah: The section manager gave them to us.

Lee: Manager, thank you for the souvenirs. This is famous chocolate from Hokkaido, right? Thank you! Wow, they're delicious.

2 手伝ってくださって、ありがとうございました

Can-do Check ✓

□You can express your gratitude to someone who trained (helped) you at work.

Grammar Notes 🏷

1-1 ___ が ___ て くださいます

When graciously talking about something someone of a higher status has done for you, 〜が〜てくださいます is used.

Conjunctive Form

person of a higher status	が	verb て form 〈〜て〉〈〜で〉	くださいます

Ex.1

（会社で）

A：もう仕事が終わったんですか。早いですね。

B：課長が手伝ってくださいました。

A：そうですか。よかったですね。

Ex.2

（学校で）

A：あ、おいしい。Bさんが作ったの？

B：うん。先生が作り方を教えてくださったんだ。

Ex.1

(At a company)

A: Are you already done with your work? That was fast.

B: The section manager helped me.

A: I see. That's good.

Ex.2

(At school)

A: Oh, it's delicious. B-san, did you make it?

B: Yeah. My teacher taught me how to make.

1-2 ___ が ___ て くれます

When graciously talking about something someone of a lower status, or a friend or family member has done for you, 〜が〜てくれます is used.

Conjunctive Form

person of a lower status / person who is close to you	が	verb て form 〈〜て〉〈〜で〉	くれます

Ex.1

（学校で）

先生：ひっこし、もう終わったんですか。早いですね。

A：友だち**が**手伝ってくれました。

Ex.2

（学校で）

A：これ、Bさんだ。いい写真だね。

B：うん。日本に来るとき、弟**が**とってくれたんだ。

Ex.1

(At school)

Teacher: Are you already done with moving? That was fast.

A: My friend helped me.

Ex.2

(At school)

A: So this is you, B-san? It's a good picture.

B: Yeah. My brother took it for me before I came to Japan.

2 　　　　　て 来ます

When talking about leaving your current location to go do something and then come back later, 〜て来ます is used.

Conjunctive Form

verb て form	〈～て〉 〈～で〉	来ます

Ex.1

（会社を出たところで）

A：あ、かさを忘れた。すみません。取って来ます。
　　ちょっと待っていてください。

B：はい。

Ex.1

(After leaving a company)

A: Ah, I forgot my umbrella. Sorry. I'll go get it. Please wait a moment.

B: Okay.

Ex.2

（じゅぎょうの後、教室で）

先生A：あれ？　となりの部屋で音がしましたね。
　　　　だれかいるんでしょうか。

先生B：そうですね。見て来ます。

・・・・・

先生B：だれもいませんでしたよ。

先生A：え、気持ち悪いですね。

Ex.2

(In the classroom after class)

Teacher A: Huh? I heard a sound from the room next door. I wonder if someone is in there?

Teacher B: I'll go see.

・・・・・

Teacher B: There was nobody there.

Teacher A: What? How creepy.

Vocabulary and Expression 😊

うまくいきます It goes well. ／発音 pronunciation ／たすかります help out
はつおん

おれい something in return ／ごちそうします It's on me., Let me treat you.

奥さま your wife 〈honorific〉／最後 last ／支店長 branch manager
おく　　　　　　　　　　　　　　　　さいご　　　　　　　　　してんちょう

合格 pass ／つま my wife ／お兄さん older brother ／いります need, want ／ぶんぽう grammar
ごうかく　　　　　　　　　　　　　にい

Conversation Scenario 💬

〈Reporting on company training〉

Yamamoto: Antonio-san, your presentation today was really good.

Antonio: Really? Thank you.

Antonio: Nakamura-san, the presentation went well. The section manager praised me.

Nakamura: Really? That's good.

Antonio: Thank you for helping me.

Nakamura: No problem.

Antonio: I really appreciate you fixing my pronunciation. I'd like to buy you lunch as thanks, so would today be okay?

Nakamura: Uh, thank you.

Antonio: I'm going to go put this down. Please wait one moment.

Nakamura: Okay.

24
-
2

3 たいへんお世話になりました
せ わ

Can-do Check ✓

☐You can greet and express your thanks in front of everyone when you leave a workplace.

Grammar Notes 🖋

1 ［　　　　　］て いただきます

When talking about someone of a higher status helping you, 〜に〜ていただきます is used.

Conjunctive Form

person of a higher status	に	verb て form ⟨〜て⟩ ⟨〜で⟩	いただきます

Ex.1

先生：レポートの書き方はわかりますか。
せんせい　　　　　　　　か　かた

A：はい。先週青木先生に教えていただきました。
　　　せんしゅうあお き せんせい　　おし

Ex.2

（学校で）
がっこう

A：あ、きれいな写真集だね。Ｂさんの？
　　　　　　しゃしんしゅう

B：ううん。先生に貸していただいたの。
　　　　　せんせい　か

Ex.1

Teacher: Do you know how to write a report?

A: Yes. Aoki-sensei taught me last week.

Ex.2

(At school)

A: This is a beautiful photo album. Is it yours, B-san?

B: No. My teacher lent it to me.

2 ［　　　　　］て も、［　　　　　］

When talking about something that will not change no matter the circumstances, 〜ても、〜 is used.

Conjunctive Form

verb て form ⟨〜て⟩ ⟨〜で⟩	も、	～
い adjective ⟨〜い く⟩	ても、	
な adjective ⟨〜な⟩	でも、	
noun		

Ex.1

（会社で）
_{かいしゃ}

A：Bさん、毎日ジョギングをするんですか。
_{まいにち}

B：はい。雨が降っても、走ります。
_{あめ} _ふ _{はし}

Ex.2

A：今日はあついですね。私、あついのはすきじゃありま
_{きょう} _{わたし}
せん。

B：そうですか。私はあつくてもだいじょうぶです。
_{わたし}

Ex.3

（旅行会社で）
_{りょこうがいしゃ}

A：このツアー、いいね。

B：でも、高いからだれも行かないかもしれないよ。
_{たか} _い

A：ぼくは、一人でも行きたいな。
_{ひとり} _い

Ex.1

(At a company)

A: B-san, do you go jogging every day?

B: Yes. Even if it's raining, I go running.

Ex.2

A: It's hot today. I don't like hot weather.

B: Really? I'm okay with hot weather.

Ex.3

(At a travel agency)

A: This tour looks nice.

B: But it's expensive, so there may be none going on it.

A: I want to go, even if it's just me.

3　　　X　　た とき、　　　Y

When expressing that 【action Y】 will be done once 【action X】 is complete, **〜たとき、〜** is used.

Conjunctive Form

verb た form 〈〜た〉〈〜だ〉	とき、	〜

Ex.1

（学校で）
_{がっこう}

先生：大学のそつぎょう証書はありますか。
_{せんせい} _{だいがく} _{しょうしょ}

A：はい、家にあります。今度国へ帰ったとき、持って来
_{いえ} _{こんど} _{くに} _{かえ} _も _き
ます。

Ex.2

（店で）
_{みせ}

店員：いつもありがとうございます。今度来られたとき、
_{てんいん} _{こんど} _こ
このカードを見せてください。20%安くなります。
_み _{やす}

A：そうですか。ありがとうございます。

Ex.1

(At school)

Teacher: Do you have a university diploma?

A: Yes, it's at home. I'll bring it back the next time I go home to my country.

Ex.2

(At a store)

Store clerk: Thank you for continued patronage. Please use this card next time you come. You'll get a 20% discount.

A: I see. Thank you.

Ex.3

（学校で）
<ruby>学校<rt>がっこう</rt></ruby>

A：このボールペン、山田さんのじゃない？

B：さあ。<ruby>日曜日<rt>にちようび</rt></ruby>に<ruby>山田<rt>やまだ</rt></ruby>さんに<ruby>会<rt>あ</rt></ruby>うから、<u><ruby>会<rt>あ</rt></ruby>ったとき</u>
<ruby>聞<rt>き</rt></ruby>いてみるよ。

Ex.3

(At school)

A: Isn't this ball-point pen Yamada-san's?

B: I don't know. I'm going to see him this Sunday, so I'll ask him then.

Vocabulary and Expression 🐾

お<ruby>世話<rt>せ わ</rt></ruby>になりました Thank you for all your help. ／そうべつ<ruby>会<rt>かい</rt></ruby> farewell party

---

しめきり deadline ／ちょきんします save money ／<ruby>結婚記念日<rt>けっこん き ねん び</rt></ruby> wedding anniversary

スイーツ sweets ／<ruby>申し込<rt>もう こ</rt></ruby>みます apply ／ゼミ seminar ／ときどき sometimes

サービス service

Conversation Scenario 💬

〈Finishing training〉

Yamamoto: Please gather around, everyone. Go ahead, Antonio-san.

Antonio: Thank you for all your help. I'll be returning to my country the day after tomorrow. Thank you for teaching me so much over these three months.

Lee: Please come to Japan again sometime.

Antonio: I will.

Sarah: Lee-san, the farewell party starts at 7:00, but what will you do if you're not finished with work?

Lee: Hmm. I'll go even if I'm not finished!

Lee: Next time you come, let's go get some drinks again.

Antonio: Yes, I'm looking forward to it.

Sarah: Good luck in the future! Please do your best.

Antonio: I will.

1 ホテルをさがしておきます

Can-do Check ✔

☐You can decide on the things to prepare before a trip and who should be in charge of them.

Grammar Notes 🖊

1 ＿＿＿＿＿ て おきます

When talking about doing something in advance, **～ておきます** is used.

Conjunctive Form

verb て form	〈～て〉 〈～で〉	おきます

Ex.1

（会社で）

課長：会議は10時からです。それまでに会議室の準備をしておいてください。お茶の用意もおねがいします。

A：はい。わかりました。

Ex.2

（学校で）

先生：明日24課のテストをしますから、勉強しておいてください。

A：はい。

Ex.3

（家で）

子ども：お母さん、今日友だちがあそびに来るよ。

母：そう。じゃ、おいしいおかしを用意しとくね。あなたの部屋、そうじしといたほうがいいよ。

Ex.1

(At a company)

Section manager: The meeting is at 10:00. Please prepare the meeting room by then. Please have some tea ready, too.

A: Okay. I understand.

Ex.2

(At school)

Teacher: We're going to have a test on unit 24 tomorrow, so please study.

A: Okay.

Ex.3

(At home)

Child: Mom, my friends are coming over to play today.

Mother: Oh? Then I'll get some delicious sweets ready. You should clean up your room.

25-1

In conversation, **〜ておきます** or **〜ておく** are often shortened to **〜ときます** or **〜とく**.

Ex.1

（会社で）

A：会議が終わったら、電気、<u>けしといて</u>くださいね。

B：はい。

Ex.2

（友だちとしゅくだいをしている）

A：あ、どうしよう。 もうアルバイトの時間だ。

B：じゃあ、あとはぼくが<u>調べとく</u>よ。

A：ありがとう。

Ex.1

(At a company)

A: After the meeting is over, please turn out the lights.

B: Okay.

Ex.2

(When doing homework with a friend)

A: Oh, what should I do? It's already time for me to get to my part-time job.

B: Well then, I'll look up the rest.

A: Thanks.

2   はずです

When talking about something that you think is likely to or naturally going to occur, **〜はずです** is used.

Conjunctive Form

verb plain form	
い adjective plain form 〈〜い〉	**はずです**
な adjective plain form 〈〜だ な〉	
noun plain form 〈〜だ の〉	

Ex.1

（会社で）

A：今朝駅でCさんを見ましたよ。

B：え、Cさんは帰国しましたから、日本には<u>いないは</u>
<u>ずです</u>よ。

Ex.2

（学校で）

先生A：Cさんが、今日テストがあるのを知らなかった
と言っていましたよ。

先生B：え！昨日もおとといも言いましたから、<u>知って</u>
<u>いるはずです</u>。

Ex.1

(At a company)

A: I saw C-san at the station this morning.

B: What? C-san went back to his country, so I'm sure he's not in Japan.

Ex.2

(At school)

Teacher A: C-san said that she didn't know that we had a test today.

Teacher B: What? I'm sure she knew since I told everyone yesterday and the day before.

Ex.3

（バスていで）

A：バス、おそいですね。

B：もうすぐ来るはずですよ。このアプリに「あと２分」って書いてありますから。

Ex.3

(At a bus stop)

A: The bus is late.

B: I'm sure it'll be here soon. This app says just two more minutes.

Vocabulary and Expression 😎

安心（な）relieved, at ease ／まあ I guess. ／ガイドブック guidebook

今夜 tonight ／ひやします chill ／かざります decorate ／じしん earthquake

ほうほう method ／グループ group ／発表会 presentation ／校長先生 principle

〜行き：空港行き bound for 〜 : bound for the airport ／アラーム alarm

さっき just a moment ago ／タイマー timer ／起こします raise ／ほんやく translation

もう１回 one more time ／ふゆ休み winter break

Conversation Scenario 💬

〈Discussing travel〉

Ann (Inoue's wife): We should start getting ready for our trip to Okinawa this summer vacation soon.

Inoue: Uh, we still have some time, so we don't have to rush.

Ann: But wouldn't it be a relief if we made our reservations early?

Inoue: Well, I guess so. Okay.

Ann: Then I'll look for some plane tickets.

Inoue: Okay. I'll look for a hotel.

Ann: Where's the guidebook? It's not here.

Inoue: What? I put it there yesterday, so it must be there.

Ann: What? Where?

Inoue: There, by the TV.

Ann: Oh, there it is!

25-1

2 新婚旅行の場合は・・・
しんこんりょこう　ば あい

Can-do Check ✔

☐ You can research travel accommodations and discuss them with someone.

Grammar Notes ✎

1 　まだ　　　　　　ていません

When talking about something that you have planned to do but have not yet done, **まだ～ていません** is used. In conversation, **～ていません** is often shortened to **～てません**, and **～ていない** is often shortened to **～てない**.

Conjunctive Form

まだ	verb て form 〈～て〉〈～で〉	いません

Ex.1

（会社で）
かいしゃ

A：帰りましょう。2階の電気をけしましたか。
　　かえ　　　　　　かい　でんき

B：あ、まだけしていません。けして来ます。
　　　　　　　　　　　　　　　　　　き

Ex.1

(At a company)

A: Let's head home. Did you turn out the lights on the second floor?

B: Ah, not yet. I'll go turn them off.

Ex.2

（朝、学校で）
あさ　がっこう

A：おなかがすいた。

B：え？ まだ朝ご飯、食べてないの？
　　　　　　あさ　はん　た

A：ううん。もう食べた。
　　　　　　　　た

Ex.2

(At school in the morning)

A: I'm hungry.

B: Huh? You haven't eaten breakfast yet?

A: No, I have eaten.

Ex.3

（アルバイトの店で）
みせ

A：来月のシフトのきぼう、出してください。
　　らいげつ　　　　　　　　だ

B：すみません。まだ書いていません。すぐ書きます。
　　　　　　　　　　　か　　　　　　　　　　か

Ex.3

(At a part-time job)

A: Please submit your requests for next month's shifts.

B: Sorry, I haven't written it yet. I'll do it right away.

2 　場合（は）、

When talking about something decided or your own thoughts according to various circumstances, **〜場合は、〜** is used. **は** can be omitted.

Conjunctive Form

verb plain form		
い adjective plain form 〈〜い〉	場合（は）、	〜
な adjective plain form 〈〜だ な〉		
noun plain form 〈〜だ の〉		

Ex.1

（旅行で）

旅行会社の人：明日のお昼ご飯は、<u>天気がいい場合</u>は、公園でバーベキューをします。<u>雨の場合</u>は、公園の近くのレストランで食べます。

Ex.2

（コンビニで）

店員：しはらいは現金でも、銀行のカードでも、コンビニのカードでもできます。

A：ポイントがつきますか。

店員：はい。<u>コンビニのカードの場合</u>は、100円で1ポイントです。<u>銀行のカードの場合</u>は、200円で1ポイントです。

Ex.1

(On a trip)

Travel agent: For lunch tomorrow, if the weather is clear, we are going to barbeque in the park. If it rains, we will eat at a restaurant near the park.

Ex.2

(At a convenience store)

Store clerk: You can pay using cash, a bank card or a convenience store card.

A: Will I get points?

Store clerk: Yes. If you use a convenience store card, you will get one point for every 100 yen. If you use a bank card, you will get one point for every 200 yen.

25 -2

3 -1 　なきゃ

When talking with friends or family about something that you must do, **〜なきゃ** is used. **〜なきゃ** means the same thing as **〜なければなりません**.

Conjunctive Form

verb ない form 〈〜ない〉	きゃ

Ex.1

（学校で）
_{がっこう}

A：テストどうだった？

B：あまりよくなかった。<u>勉強しなきゃ</u>。
_{べんきょう}

Ex.2

（家で）
_{いえ}

兄：今日は早く<u>ねなきゃ</u>。
_{あに} _{きょう} _{はや}

いもうと：どうして？

兄：明日は出張で、７時のひこうきなんだよ。
_{あに} _{あした} _{しゅっちょう} _じ

Ex.1

(At school)

A: How was the test?

B: It wasn't so great. I need to study.

Ex.2

(At home)

Brother: I need to go to sleep early today.

Sister: Why?

Brother: My business trip is tomorrow, and my flight is at 7:00.

3-2　なければ なりません

When talking about something you are obligated to do, **〜なければなりません** is used.

Conjunctive Form

verb ない form 〈〜ない〉	ければなりません

Ex.1

お年よりは大切に<u>しなければなりません</u>。
_{とし} _{たいせつ}

Ex.2

（学校で）
_{がっこう}

A：どうしても漢字を<u>勉強しなければなりません</u>か。
_{かん じ} _{べんきょう}

先生：はい。しょうらい日本語の先生になりたいなら、
_{せんせい} _{に ほん ご} _{せんせい}
　　　しっかり漢字を勉強してください。
　　　_{かん じ} _{べんきょう}

Ex.3

（会社で）
_{かいしゃ}

A：社員旅行、あまり行きたくないんですが、
_{しゃいんりょこう} _い
　　<u>行かなければなりません</u>か。
　　_い

B：ぜったいではありませんが、ふだんいっしょに仕事を
　　　　　　　　　　　　　　　　　　　　　　　_{し ごと}
　　しない人と知り合うチャンスですから、行ったほうが
　　_{ひと} _{し あ} _い
　　いいと思いますよ。
　　_{おも}

Ex.1

We must take care of the elderly.

Ex.2

(At school)

A: Do I have to study kanji no matter what?

Teacher: Yes. Please study kanji hard if you want to be a Japanese teacher in the future.

Ex.3

(At a company)

A: I don't really want to go on the company outing. Do we have to go?

B: You don't absolutely have to, but I think you should because it's a good chance to get to know the people you don't usually see at work.

Vocabulary and Expression

全室 all rooms, every room ／オーシャンビュー ocean view ／しかも moreover
ぜんしつ

特別（な）special ／シャンパン champagne ／記念写真 commemorative photo ／やった〜 Alright!
とくべつ   き ねんしゃしん

〜室：3室 counter for rooms: three rooms
しつ　　　しつ

たぶん probably ／お子さま your child〈honorific〉／料金 fee ／半額 half off
　　　　　　　　　こ　　　　　　　　　　　　　　　　　　りょうきん　　　　　　はんがく

受け取ります receive ／ひつよう（な）necessary ／ページ page ／いんさつします print
う　と

警報 warning ／ヨーグルト yogurt ／しょうみきげん best before date
けいほう

（電話が）かかります get (a phone call) ／お先に I'm going now. ／じょせい female
でん わ　　　　　　　　　　　　　　　　　　　　　　さき

ふりこみます transfer money to a bank account

Conversation Scenario

〈Booking a hotel〉

Ann (Inoue's wife): Hey, did you find a hotel?

Inoue: Ah, sorry. Not yet.

Ann: Then, how about here? All of the rooms have an ocean view!

Inoue: Wow.

Ann: And what's more, they have champagne and commemorative photos just for
newlyweds.

Inoue: That's great. Oh, there're some rooms available.

Ann: Alright! We have to hurry up and reserve it. There are only three left.

Inoue: Yeah, let's reserve it.

**25
-
2**

3 もう買ってあります
か

Can-do Check ✓

☐You can ask and talk about how the travel preparations are progressing.

Grammar Notes 🖊

1 ＿＿＿＿ て 来ます
き

When saying that you will come to where someone is after doing a certain action or that you will be doing a certain action as you come to where someone is, **〜て来ます** is
き
used.

Conjunctive Form

verb て form	〈〜て〉 〈〜で〉	来ます き

◆Here, **て来ます** is used to express doing something before or while coming to where
き
someone is.

Ex.1	**Ex.1**
（電話で） でんわ A：もしもし。これから帰るよ。 かえ B：わかった。あ、とちゅうのコンビニで飲み物を買って の もの か 来て。 き	(On the phone) A: Hello? I'm coming home now. B: Okay. Oh, on your way here, buy something to drink at a convenience store.
Ex.2	**Ex.2**
（電話で） でんわ A：もしもし、今会議が終わりました。そちらにもどります。 いま かいぎ お B：はい。すみませんが、会議室のまどを閉めて、電気を かいぎしつ し でんき けして来てください。 き A：はい。わかりました。	(On the phone) A: Hello? The meeting is over. I'm coming back there. B: Okay. Sorry, but please close the windows and turn off the lights in the meeting room and come back. A: Okay. I got it.

◆Here, **て来_きます** is used to express coming to where someone is after having done a certain action.

Ex.

（旅行の説明で）
りょこう　せつめい

旅行会社の人：このツアーはたくさん歩きますから、歩
りょこうがいしゃ　ひと　　　　　　　　　　　　　　　　ある
きやすいくつを<u>はいて来て</u>ください。雨が降ったとき
　　　　　　　　　　　き　　　　　　　あめ　ふ
の用意<u>もして来て</u>ください。出発の時間は早いです
よう　い　　　き　　　　　　　　しゅっぱつ　じ　かん　はや
が、朝ご飯を<u>食べて来て</u>ください。
　　あさ　はん　　た　　　き

Ex.

(Giving an explanation about a trip)

Travel agent: We are going to do a lot of walking on this tour, so please come wearing shoes that are easy to walk in. Please be ready for rain, as well. Our departure time is early, but please eat breakfast beforehand.

When talking about doing a certain action before coming back to where you are, **〜て来_きます** is used (☞ Lesson 24 - 2).

Ex.1

（会社で）
かいしゃ
A：山田さんは？
　　やま　だ
B：あ、今<u>呼んで来ます</u>。
　　　いま　よ　　　き

Ex.1

(At a company)
A: Where's Yamada-san?
B: I'll go get him.

Ex.2

（コンビニの前を通ったときに）
　　　　　　まえ　とお
つま：あ、コンビニでぎゅうにゅうを<u>買って来る</u>。
　　　　　　　　　　　　　　　　　　か　　く
　　　ちょっと待ってて。
　　　　　　　ま
おっと：わかった。

Ex.2

(When passing by a convenience store)
Wife: Ah, I'm going to go get some milk at the convenience store. Wait a minute.
Husband: Okay.

2　　　　　**て 行_いきます**

When talking about going somewhere after doing an action or going somewhere while doing an action, **〜て行_いきます** is used. When not doing an action while going somewhere, **〜ないで行_いきます** is used.

Conjunctive Form

verb て form 〈〜て〉 〈〜で〉		行きます い
verb ない form 〈〜ない〉	で	

Ex.1

A：では、X社へ行きます。

B：今日は雨が降るかもしれないので、かさを持って行ったほうがいいですよ。

A：ええ、そうします。

Ex.2

母：今日は寒いから、コートを着て行ったほうがいいよ。

子ども：はい。

Ex.3

おっと：いってきます。

つま：あ、コーヒー飲んで行かないの？

おっと：うん。コンビニによって、コーヒーを買って行くから、いいよ。

Ex.4

（会社で）

A：あ、もう1時です。時間がないから、お昼を食べないで行きましょう。

B：そうですね。しかたがないですね。

Ex.1

A: Okay, I'm going to X Company.

B: It might rain today, so you should take an umbrella.

A: Okay, I will.

Ex.2

Mother: It's cold today, so you should wear a coat.

Child: Okay.

Ex.3

Husband: I'm going now.

Wife: Ah, why don't you have some coffee before you go?

Husband: I'm going to stop by a convenience store and get some coffee, so that's okay.

Ex.4

(At a company)

A: Oh, it's already 1:00. We don't have much time, so let's skip lunch and go.

B: Yes. It can't be helped.

3　て あります

When talking about confirming that preparations were made, **～てあります** is used.

Conjunctive Form

verb て form 〈～て〉〈～で〉	あります

Ex.1

（学校で）

先生：みなさん、教科書に名前が書いてありますか。

A：はい、書いてあります。

Ex.1

(At school)

Teacher: Have you all written your names on your textbooks?

A: Yes, I have.

Ex.2

（ホテルで）

A：パーティーの準備はどうですか。

B：テーブルといすは<u>ならべてあります</u>。エアコンも<u>つけ
てあります</u>。

A：料理と飲み物は？

B：<u>用意してあります</u>。

Ex.3

（家を出るとき）

A：あ、電気とガス、もう一度チェックしなくちゃ。

B：<u>けしてあるよ</u>。

A：まどは？

B：<u>閉めてある</u>。かぎも<u>かけてあるよ</u>。

Ex.2

(At a hotel)

A: How are the preparations for the party?

B: The tables and chairs are all lined up. The air conditioner is turned on, too.

A: How about the food and drinks?

B: They're ready.

Ex.3

(When leaving the house)

A: Ah, I need to check on the lights and gas one more time.

B: They're off.

A: And the windows?

B: They're closed. The door is locked, too.

Vocabulary and Expression

シャンプー shampoo ／だいたい almost

レインコート raincoat ／厚い thick ／待ち合わせします meet ／おみまい pay a hospital visit
～部：1部 ～ packet(s) (of paper): a packet ／ああ～ Oh, so that's why. ／ならべます line up
プロジェクター projector ／（かぎを）かけます lock ／（でんげんを）切ります turn off
カイロ hot pack

Conversation Scenario

〈Preparing for a trip〉

Inoue: Hello? I'm going home now.

Ann (Inoue's wife): Okay. Ah, buy some shampoo for the trip on your way home.

Inoue: Okay. What about medicine? We should bring some stomach and fever medicine, too.

Ann: Oh, I already bought some.

Inoue: Thanks.

25
-
3

Inoue: I'm home.

Ann: Welcome back.

Inoue: How is packing going?

Ann: I'm mostly done. Ah, I haven't packed the camera.

Inoue: Oh, let's put that in my bag.

1 大使館へ行くそうです
たい し かん　い

Can-do Check ✓

☐You can take a message and relay it to others.

Grammar Notes 🖊

1 ＿＿＿＿ そうです

When telling someone something that you heard from someone else or read, **～そうです** is used. When talking about who you heard something from, **～に聞いたんですが／聞いたんだけど** or **～の話によると** are used. When talking about where you got some information from, **～によると**, **～で聞いたんですが／聞いたんだけど**, **～で見たんですが／見たんだけど** or **～で読んだんですが／読んだんだけど** is used.

Conjunctive Form

people	に聞いたんですが	verb plain form	
	の話によると	い adjective plain form	
source of information	によると	な adjective plain form 〈～だ〉	そうです
	で聞いたんですが		
	で見たんですが で読んだんですが	noun plain form 〈～だ〉	

Ex.1

（待ち合わせで）

A：もしもし。すみません。ちょっとおくれます。

B：わかりました。

・・・・・

B：Aさんは少しおくれるそうです。

C：そうですか。

Ex.2

（会社で）

A：今朝テレビのニュースで見たんですが、来年から休日がふえるそうですね。

B：それはうれしいですね。

Ex.1

(When waiting for someone)

A: Hello? Sorry. I'm going to be a little late.

B: Okay.

・・・・・

B: A-san is going to be a little late.

C: I see.

Ex.2

(At a company)

A: I saw on the news this morning that there are going to be more holidays next year.

B: I'm glad to hear that.

26-1

Ex.3

(学校で)
<ruby>学校<rt>がっこう</rt></ruby>

A: <ruby>山田<rt>やまだ</rt></ruby><ruby>先生<rt>せんせい</rt></ruby>に<ruby>聞<rt>き</rt></ruby>いたんだけど、<ruby>来月<rt>らいげつ</rt></ruby>からこのクラスに<ruby>新<rt>あたら</rt></ruby>しい<ruby>先生<rt>せんせい</rt></ruby>が<ruby>来<rt>く</rt></ruby>るそうだよ。

B: へえ。どんな<ruby>先生<rt>せんせい</rt></ruby>かな。

A: <ruby>男<rt>おとこ</rt></ruby>の<ruby>先生<rt>せんせい</rt></ruby>だそうだよ。

Ex.3

(At school)

A: I heard from Yamada-sensei that there's going to be a new teacher starting next month.

B: Wow. What kind of teacher are they?

A: I heard it's a male teacher.

When you are talking about a conjecture about how someone feels based on something you saw about someone else, **～い そうです** or **～な そうです** are used (☞ Lesson 22-1).

Ex.1

A: トムさん、うれしそうですね。

B: <ruby>何<rt>なに</rt></ruby>かいいことがあったんでしょう。

Ex.1

A: Tom-san sure looks happy.

B: Something good probably happened to him.

Ex.2

(会社で)
<ruby>会社<rt>かいしゃ</rt></ruby>

A: <ruby>木田<rt>きだ</rt></ruby>さん、たいへんそうですね。

B: ええ。トラブルがあったそうですよ。

Ex.2

(At a company)

A: Kida-san looks like he's having a rough time.

B: Yes. I heard something happened to him.

When you are talking about your feelings or thoughts based on something you saw, **～い そうです** or **～な そうです** are used (☞ Lesson 24-1).

Ex.1

A: このケーキ、おいしそうですね。3つください。

<ruby>店員<rt>てんいん</rt></ruby>: ありがとうございます。

Ex.1

A: This cake looks delicious. Three, please.

Store clerk: Thank you.

Ex.2

A: この<ruby>仕事<rt>しごと</rt></ruby>、だれかに<ruby>手伝<rt>てつだ</rt></ruby>ってもらいたいですね。

B: <ruby>山田<rt>やまだ</rt></ruby>さんは? ひまそうですよ。

A: そうですね。じゃ、<ruby>山田<rt>やまだ</rt></ruby>さんにたのみましょう。

Ex.2

A: I wish someone would help me with this job.

B: How about Yamada-san? He seems free.

A: Yes. I'll ask Yamada-san then.

2 ＿＿＿＿＿＿と言っていました

When talking about something someone else has said, **～が～と言っていました** is used.

Conjunctive Form

person	が	verb plain form	と言っていました
		い adjective plain form	
		な adjective plain form 〈～だ〉	
		noun plain form 〈～だ〉	

Ex.1

（駅で）

A：みどり公園まで何で行きましょうか。

B：駅員が、ここからみどり公園まではバスで30分かかると言っていましたよ。

A：30分ですか。遠いんですね。

Ex.2

（会社で）

A：田中さんが、駅前にできたハンバーガーの店はちょっと高いけどおいしいと言っていましたよ。

B：へえ。じゃあ、今日はそこに行ってみましょう。

Ex.1

(At the station)

A: How shall we get to Midori Park?

B: The station employee said it'll take 30 minutes to get to Midori Park by bus from here.

A: Thirty minutes, huh? That's pretty far.

Ex.2

(At a company)

A: Tanaka-san said the hamburger store is a little expensive but really good.

B: Really? Then, let's go there today.

3 ＿＿＿＿＿＿ように（と）伝えてください
＿＿＿＿＿＿ように（と）言ってください

When telling a person to tell someone else something to do, **～ように（と）伝えてください** or **～ように（と）言ってください** are used. When saying who that someone else is, **【person】に～ように（と）伝えてください／言ってください** is used.

Conjunctive Form

| person | に | verb dictionary form | ように（と） | 伝えてください |
| | | verb ない form 〈～ない〉 | | 言ってください |

Ex.1

（学校で）

先生：Aさん、マリーさんに発表の準備をするように伝えてください。

A：はい、わかりました。

Ex.1

(At school)

Teacher: A-san, please tell Marie-san to get her presentation ready.

A: Okay, I will.

Ex.2

（会社で）
<ruby>会社<rt>かいしゃ</rt></ruby>

<ruby>課長<rt>かちょう</rt></ruby>：みんなに<ruby>水曜日<rt>すいようび</rt></ruby>は６<ruby>時<rt>じ</rt></ruby>に<ruby>帰<rt>かえ</rt></ruby>るように<ruby>伝<rt>つた</rt></ruby>えてください。

Ａ：はい。

Ex.3

（駅で）
<ruby>駅<rt>えき</rt></ruby>

<ruby>駅員<rt>えきいん</rt></ruby>Ａ：おきゃくさんにむりに<ruby>電車<rt>でんしゃ</rt></ruby>にのらないように<ruby>言<rt>い</rt></ruby>って
ください。

<ruby>駅員<rt>えきいん</rt></ruby>Ｂ：はい。

Ex.2

(At a company)

Section manager: Please tell everyone to go home at 6:00 on Wednesdays.

A: Okay.

Ex.3

(At a station)

Station employee A: Please tell the comuters not to rush onto the train.

Station employee B: Okay.

Vocabulary and Expression

<ruby>大使館<rt>たいしかん</rt></ruby> embassy ／じつは actually ／えっ Wait, what? ／それで and then

<ruby>天気予報<rt>てんきよほう</rt></ruby> weather report ／とちゅう in the middle of ／<ruby>画家<rt>がか</rt></ruby> painter ／<ruby>出席者<rt>しゅっせきしゃ</rt></ruby> attendee
まどガラス window glass

Conversation Scenario

〈Getting a call from a friend〉

Kim: Hello?

Tang: Hello, Kim-san. I have a favor to ask you.

Kim: Huh? What is it?

Tang: Can you tell the teacher that I'm going to take today off?

Kim: What's wrong?

Tang: Actually, I lost my passport.

Kim: What? That's terrible.

Tang: Yeah. So I'm going to go to the embassy.

Kim: I see. I'll tell the teacher.

Kim: Sensei, I just heard from Tang-san that he lost his passport, so he's going to the embassy today.

Aoki: What? His passport?

Kim: Yes. So, he said he's going to be absent from school today.

Aoki: I see. Please tell him to contact the school.

Kim: Okay.

2 ないちゃったんだって

Can-do Check ✓

☐ You can talk about things to people based on information that you heard from others.

Grammar Notes ✎

1 ＿＿＿＿＿＿＿＿＿って。

When talking to friends, family or people close to you about something you heard from someone else or something you heard or read yourself, **～って。** is used. **～って** means the same thing as **～と言っていました** (☞ Lesson 26 - 1).

Conjunctive Form

verb plain form	
い adjective plain form	
な adjective plain form 〈～だ〉	って。
noun plain form 〈～だ〉	

Ex.1

（天気予報を見て）
子ども：お母さん、台風が来てるって。
母：え、そうなの。日曜日のバーベキュー、だいじょう
　　ぶかな。

Ex.2

（学校で）
A：台風が来たら、学校、休みだって。
B：え、ほんと？
A：うん。山本先生が言ってたよ。

Ex.1

(While looking at the weather forecast)

Child: Mom, I heard that there's a typhoon coming.

Mother: What? Really? I wonder if we'll still have the barbeque on Sunday.

Ex.2

(At school)

A: I heard that school will be cancelled when the typhoon comes.

B: What? Really?

A: Yeah. Yamamoto-sensei said so.

2 ＿＿＿＿＿＿＿＿＿ことにします

When talking about something that you have decided yourself, **～ことにします** is used.

Conjunctive Form

verb dictionary form	ことにします
verb ない form 〈〜ない〉	

Ex.1

A: 今年の夏休みは帰国しないことにしました。

B: そうですか。何をするんですか。

A: アルバイトをして、日本で旅行します。

Ex.2

（会社で）

A: 私、来年の3月に結婚をすることにしました。

B: え、それはおめでとうございます。

Ex.1

A: I've decided not to go back to my country this summer vacation.

B: I see. What are you going to do?

A: I'm going to work at my part-time job, then travel around Japan.

Ex.2

(At a company)

A: I've decided to get married next March.

B: Oh, congratulations.

Vocabulary and Expression

ラブストーリー love story ／子犬 puppy ／ストーリー story

食事会 dinner party ／ねえねえ hey ／行き先 destination ／オーロラ aurora

サプライズパーティー surprise party ／おすすめ recommendation

さくらもち rice cake with bean paste wrapped in a preserved cherry leaf

Conversation Scenario

〈Asking the teacher about a movie〉

Kim: Sensei, what did you do last weekend?

Aoki: I went to see a movie. It was *Kaze ga Fuku*.

Kim: Wow. What kind of movie is it?

Aoki: It's a love story ...

Kim: Hey, why don't we see *Kaze ga Fuku* this weekend?

Marie: Huh? *Kaze ga Fuku*?

Kim: Yeah. It's a love story about a sick girl and a college student.

Marie: I see. I wanted to see *Koinu no Ruuku*.

Kim: I see. But Aoki-sensei said that *Kaze ga Fuku's* story was really good.

Marie: Really?

Kim: She said she cried.

Marie: Oh, really? Then let's go see it!

3 転勤するらしいです
てんきん

Can-do Check ✓

□You can speak with other people about inaccurate information.

Grammar Notes ✏

1　　　　　　　らしいです

When talking about something another person said or you heard or read somewhere but you think is uncertain, **～らしいです** is used. When talking with friends or family, **～らしい** is used.

Conjunctive Form

verb plain form	
い adjective plain form	
な adjective plain form 〈～だ〉	らしいです
noun plain form 〈～だ〉	

Ex.1

（会社で）
かいしゃ

A：X社が新しいスマホを出すらしいですよ。
　　しゃ　あたら　　　　　　　だ

B：え、どんなのですか。

A：カメラがよくなっているらしいです。

B：へえ。早く見たいですね。
　　　　はや　み

Ex.2

（テレビの番組を見て）
　　　　　ばんぐみ　み

A：じょゆうのリカがりこんするらしいよ。

B：え、もう？　去年結婚したばかりなのに。
　　　　　　きょねんけっこん

Ex.3

（学校で）
がっこう

A：台風が来たら、学校、休みになるらしいよ。
　たいふう　き　　　がっこう　やす

B：え、ほんと？

A：うん。Cさんが言ってたよ。
　　　　　　　　い

B：ふうん。先生に聞いてみよう。
　　　　　せんせい　き

Ex.1

(At a company)

A: I heard X Company is going to release a new smart phone.

B: Huh? What kind?

A: It seems that the camera has gotten better.

B: Wow. I can't wait to see it.

Ex.2

(Watching a TV show)

A: I heard the actress Rika is going to get divorced.

B: What? Already? And she only just got married last year.

Ex.3

(At school)

A: I heard that school is going to be cancelled when the typhoon comes.

B: What? Really?

A: Yeah. C-san said so.

B: Really? Let's ask the teacher.

26
－
3

281

2 そんな [____]

When talking about something that is the same as something another person has mentioned, **そんな〜／そのような〜** is used. In conversation, **そんな〜** is often used.

Conjunctive Form

そんな	noun

Ex.1

（学校で）

A：テストがない学校へ行きたいな。

B：そんな学校、ないよ。

Ex.1

(At school)

A: I want to go to a school that has no tests.

B: Such a school doesn't exist.

Ex.2

（道で）

A：すみません。赤いぼうしをかぶって赤いシャツを着た人がここを通りませんでしたか。

B：さあ、そんな人、見ませんでしたよ。

Ex.2

(On the road)

A: Excuse me. Has a person wearing a red hat and a red shirt passed by here?

B: Hmm, I haven't seen anyone like that.

3 [____] に します
   [____] く します

When talking about how to change something, **〜にします** is used with **な** adjectives, and **〜くします** is used with **い** adjectives.

Conjunctive Form

な adjective 〈〜な に〉	します
い adjective 〈〜い く〉	

Ex.1

（会議室で）

A：明るくて、発表のスライドがよく見えませんね。

B：部屋の電気を少しくらくしましょう。

Ex.1

(In a meeting room)

A: It's so bright that I can't see the presentation slide.

B: Let's turn the room's lights down a little.

Ex.2

（学校で）

先生：今となりのクラスでテストをしていますから、しずかにしてください。

A：あ、すみません。

Ex.2

(At school)

Teacher: They are taking a test in the class next door right now, so please be quiet.

A: Oh, sorry.

Ex.3

（びよういんで）

びようし：今日はどうなさいますか。
きょう

A：あつくなってきたので、みじかくしたいんです。

Ex.3

(At a hair salon)

Hairdresser: What would you like today?

A: It's gotten hot, so I'd like to make it a little shorter.

Vocabulary and Expression 🧑‍🤝‍🧑

転勤します be transferred ／営業 sales ／ショック shock
てんきん　　　　　　　　　　えいぎょう

〜中：仕事中 during, in the middle of 〜 : during work
ちゅう　しごとちゅう

ぜったい（に）absolutely ／ピンク pink ／学費 tuition ／上がります increase
がくひ　　　　あ

ホームレス homeless ／味 taste, flavor ／マンション condominium, apartment
あじ

Conversation Scenario 💬

〈Hearing coworkers talking〉

Nakamura: Yamaguchi-san, when are you going to Fukuoka?

Yamaguchi: I'm moving on the first of next month.

Sarah: Hey, I heard Yamaguchi-san from the sales department is being transferred.

Ati: What? Is that true? What a surprise! Where to?

Sarah: The Fukuoka branch office. They said he's going to move on the first of next month.

Ati: Huh. Who did you hear that from?

Sarah: Yamaguchi-san and Nakamura-san were talking about it just now.

Ati: I see.

Shin: Excuse me. Please be quiet during work hours.

Sarah and Ati: Ah, sorry.

**26
-
3**

1 ニュースで見たんですが

Can-do Check ✓

☐You can communicate the news or weather forecasts that you found out
about.

☐You can speak with others about social problems while using simple
words and phrases.

Grammar Notes 🖊

1 　　　　　　そうです

When talking about something that you assume will continue to occur based on what
you have seen, **〜そうです** is used.

Conjunctive Form

verb ます form 〈〜ます〉	そうです

Ex.1

（空を見て）
そら　み

A：雨が降り<u>そうです</u>ね。
あめ　ふ

B：ええ。かさを持って行ったほうがい
も　い

いですね。

Ex.1

(Looking at the sky)

A: It looks like it's going to rain.

B: Yes. We should take umbrellas.

Ex.2

（駅で）
えき

A：あぶない。あの人、かいだんから
ひと

<u>落ちそうです</u>よ。
お

B：ほんとだ。よっているようですね。

Ex.2

(At a station)

A: Careful! That person looks like he's
going to fall down the stairs.

B: You're right. He looks drunk.

When making a conjecture about how someone else feels based on what you see, **〜い そうです** or **〜な そうです** are used (☞ Lesson 22 - 1).

Ex.

A：あ、おまつりですね。

B：ええ。みんな楽_{たの}しそうですね。

Ex.

A: Oh, it's a festival.

B: Yes. Everyone looks like they're having fun.

When talking about something you think or feel based on what you see, **〜い そうです** or **〜な そうです** are used (☞ Lesson 24 - 1).

Ex.

A：山田_{やまだ}さん、元気_{げんき}そうですね。

B：ええ。病気_{びょうき}がなおって、よかったですね。

Ex.

A: Yamada-san looks healthy.

B: Yes. I'm glad his illness has gone away.

When telling someone information that someone else said or you heard or read somewhere, **〜そうです** is used. **そうです** is used after the plain form (☞ Lesson 26 - 1).

Ex.

A：今朝_{けさ}テレビのニュースで見_みたんですが、大_{おお}きい台風_{たいふう}が来_きているそうですね。

B：そうですか。来週_{らいしゅう}の旅行_{りょこう}、心配_{しんぱい}ですね。

Ex.

A: I saw on the news this morning that there's a big typhoon coming.

B: Really? Now I'm worried about next week's trip.

2　　　　　　　**た まま、**

When talking about the current condition of something remaining unchanged, **〜たまま、〜** is used.

Conjunctive Form

verb た form	〈〜た〉〈〜だ〉	まま、	〜

Ex.1

（町で）

A：あの人、雨がやんだのに、かさを
　　さしたまま、歩いていますよ。

B：日がさかもしれませんよ。

Ex.2

（ホテルで）

A：あ、部屋の電気、つけたままだ。

B：だいじょうぶ。すぐきえるから。

Ex.3

（会社で）

A：ミーティングが終わったので、まどを閉めますね。

B：あ、ここ、このあと使いますから、開けたままにして
　　おいてください。

A：わかりました。

Ex.1

(In town)

A: That person is walking with her umbrella still open even though it has stopped raining.

B: It might be a parasol.

Ex.2

(At a hotel)

A: Oh, the light in the room is still on.

B: That's okay. It'll go off soon.

Ex.3

(At a company)

A: The meeting is over, so I'll close the windows.

B: Oh, we're going to use this room after this so please leave them open.

A: Okay.

Vocabulary and Expression

温暖化 global warming ／関係 relation ／原因 cause ／ CO_2 carbon dioxide
へらします reduce

取れます take off ／ふうせん balloon ／なくなります run out ／充電器 charger
（バスが）出ます depart ／（事故が）起きます occur ／不便（な）inconvenient
ポケット pocket ／あいさつします greet
ヒートアイランドげんしょう heat island phenomenon ／こもります be heated ／屋上 roof
ベランダ veranda

Conversation Scenario

〈Speaking during the break〉

Lee: It looks like it's going to rain.

Ati: Yes, it does. Ah, I left the meeting room windows open when I left the room. I'll go close them.

Lee: I saw on the news this morning that there's a big typhoon coming.

Ati: Oh, really? There have been a lot of big typhoons this year.

Lee: It may be related to global warming.

Ati: Global warming, huh? The cause of global warming is increasing CO_2 levels. So, if we decrease CO_2 levels, there may be fewer big typhoons.

Lee: That's it. Let's research that.

27
-
1

Can-do Check ✓

☐You can ask questions and listen to explanations when talking about the
cultures and customs of each other's country.

Grammar Notes 🖋

1-1 ＿＿＿＿＿ というのは、＿＿＿＿＿ のことです

When explaining what kind of thing something is, ～というのは、～のことです is used.

Conjunctive Form

noun	というのは、	verb plain form	noun	のことです
		い adjective plain form		
		な adjective plain form 〈～だ な〉		
		noun ＋ の		

Ex.1

A:「しょくにん」というのは何<small>なん</small>ですか。

B:「しょくにん」というのは、手<small>て</small>で物<small>もの</small>を作<small>つく</small>る仕事<small>しごと</small>をする
　　人<small>ひと</small>のことです。

Ex.1

A: What is a *shokunin*?

B: A *shokunin* is someone who makes
things by hand for a living.

Ex.2

A:「パティオ」というのは何<small>なん</small>ですか。

B: たてものの中<small>なか</small>のにわのことです。

Ex.2

A: What is a *patio*?

B: It's a garden inside of a building.

1-2 ＿＿＿＿＿ というのは、＿＿＿＿＿ ことです

When explaining what a certain word means, ～というのは、～ことです is used.

Conjunctive Form

～	というのは、	verb plain form	ことです
		い adjective plain form	
		な adjective plain form 〈～だ な〉	

Ex.1

（図書館で）

A：「へんきゃく」というのは何ですか。

図書館の人：借りた本やＣＤなどを返すことです。

Ex.2

（駅で）

A：「こしょう中」というのはどういう意味ですか。

B：今こわれていて使うことができないという意味です。

◆ When asking what something means, **〜というのは何ですか** is used. When talking with friends or family members, **〜って、何?** is used.

Ex.

A：「そうべつかい」って、何？

B：会社をやめる人とか国へ帰る人といっしょに食事をする会のことだよ。

Ex.1

(At a library)

A: What is *henkyaku*?

Librarian: It means returning books or CDs that you borrowed.

Ex.2

(At a station)

A: What does *koshouchuu* mean?

B: It means that something is currently broken and cannot be used.

Ex.

A: What's a *soubetsukai*?

B: It's a party where people eat together with people who are quitting their company or leaving the country.

2 　　　　　　と、　　　　　

When talking about a condition that happens naturally under a certain condition, **〜と、〜** is used.

Conjunctive Form

verb — **dictionary form** / **ない form 〈〜ない〉**	と、	〜
い adjective 〈〜い〉 〈〜くない〉		
な adjective 〈〜だ〉 〈〜じゃない〉		
noun 〈〜だ〉 〈〜じゃない〉		

27-2

Ex.1

日本では、春になると、さくらがさきます。

Ex.1

In Japan, when spring comes, the cherry blossoms bloom.

Ex.2

A：朝早く起きると、気持ちが
いいですね。

B：そうですね。

A：天気がいいと、海が青く見えますね。

B：そうですね。

Ex.2

A: Waking up early in the morning feels good.

B: Yes, it does.

A: If the weather is clear, the ocean looks blue.

A: Yes, it does.

Ex.3

A：駅の近くはいつも人が多いですね。

B：そうですね。でも、日曜日だと人が少ないのでしず
かですよ。

Ex.3

A: There are always so many people near the station.

B: Yes. But, there are fewer people on Sundays, so it's quiet.

3 　　　X　て、　　　Y

When talking about how you will use 【method X】 to do 【action Y】, ~て、~ is used.

Conjunctive Form

verb て form	〈～て〉、 〈～で〉、	～

Ex.1

じしょを使って、ことばの意味を調べます。

Ex.1

I'm going to use a dictionary to look up the meaning of the word.

Ex.2

自転車にのって、学校へ行きます。

Ex.2

I'm going to ride my bike and go to school.

Ex.3

A：この料理、おいしいですね。
どうやって作りましたか。

B：「クックノート」というアプリを見て、
作りました。

Ex.3

A: This food is delicious. How did you make it?

B: I looked at an app called *Cook Note* and made it.

Vocabulary and Expression

年賀状 New Year's postcard ／年末 end of the year ／新年 New Year ／あいさつ greeting
はがき postcard ／明けましておめでとうございます Happy New Year!

レベル level ／チェックします check ／敷金 security deposit ／ご飯 a bowl of rice
おかわり second helping ／わりかん splitting the cost ／このへん around this area
こうよう autumn leaves ／夏 summer ／ほたる firefly ／冬 winter ／図 map
ボクシング boxing ／気分転換 change of pace
せつぶん start of traditional Japanese spring, start of February ／まめ bean
まきます throw, scatter ／おに demon ／おい出します kick out ／モンスター monster

Conversation Scenario

〈Talking on the way back home〉

Sarah: Today was busy, too, wasn't it?

Ogawa: That's because it's the end of the year. Have you already written your *nengajo*?

Sarah: Huh? What is *nengajo*?

Ogawa: *Nengajo* are greeting cards for the New Year. In Japan, at the end of the year, we write *nengajo*.

Sarah: Wow.

Ogawa: We write things like "Happy New Year" or "congratulations on the New Year" to greet people.

Sarah: I see. I'll try writing some.

27 - 2

3 じゅくに行かせようかな

Can-do Check ✓

☐You can talk about children's education in an uncomplicated manner.

Grammar Notes ✎

1 [   ] なさい

When commanding children to do something, **〜なさい** is used.

Conjunctive Form

verb ます form 〈〜ます〉	なさい

Ex.1

（小学校で）
しょうがっこう
先生：5時ですよ。もう帰りなさい。
せんせい じ　　　　　　　　　　かえ
子ども：はい。
こ

Ex.2

（家で）
いえ
母：早くご飯を食べなさい。
はは はや　　はん　た
子ども：うん。
こ
母：ゲーム、やめなさい。
はは
子ども：うん。
こ

Ex.1

(At an elementary school)

Teacher: It's 5:00. Go home already.

Child: Okay.

Ex.2

(At home)

Mother: Hurry up and eat your food.

Child: Okay.

Mother: Stop playing games.

Child: Okay.

2 [   ] を [causative form   ]

When talking about instructing or forcing someone else to do something, **〜を**

【**causative form**】 is used.

Conjunctive Form

person	を	verb causative form

Ex.1

（動物病院で）

犬のかい主：最近元気がないんです。

医者：もっと運動させたほうがいいですね。毎日外で走らせてください。

Ex.2

A：Bさん、夏休みにふじ山で小学生のキャンプがありますよ。子どもたちを行かせませんか。

B：いいですね。行かせましょう。

Ex.3

（会社で）

A：Bさん、Cさんからお電話です。

B：はい。

・・・・・

B：お待たせしました。Bです。

Ex.1

(At a veterinarian's office)

Dog owner: She hasn't been too energetic lately.

Doctor: You should have her exercise more. Please let her run outside every day.

Ex.2

A: B-san, there's a summer camp for elementary school students at Mt. Fuji. Why don't we send our kids?

B: That sounds nice. Let's send them.

Ex.3

(At a company)

A: B-san, there's a call from C-san for you.

B: Okay.

・・・・・

B: Sorry to keep you waiting. It's B.

The verb form used in 待たせます or 行かせます is called the causative form (使役形).
The form [-seru], as in 待たせる or 行かせる, can also be used.

2-1 Causative Form of Group I Verbs

The causative form of verbs is made by changing the syllable that comes before ます to one that ends in [a], then adding せます.

～い → ～わ

The causative form of ～います is ～わせます.

いいます say → いわせます

～き → ～か ／ ～ぎ → ～が

The causative forms of ～きます and ～ぎます are ～かせます and ～がせます, respectively.

ききます listen → きかせます

いそぎます hurry → いそがせます

| ~し → ~さ |

The causative form of **~します** is **~させます**.

はなします talk → はなさせます

| ~ち → ~た |

The causative form of **~ちます** is **~たせます**.

まちます wait → またせます

| ~に → ~な |

The causative form of **~にます** is **~なせます**.

しにます die → しなせます

| ~び → ~ば |

The causative form of **~びます** is **~ばせます**.

よびます call → よばせます

あそびます play → あそばせます

| ~み → ~ま |

The causative form of **~みます** is **~ませます**.

よみます read → よませます

| ~り → ~ら |

The causative form of **~ります** is **~らせます**.

とります take → とらせます

2-2　Causative Form of Group II Verbs

ます becomes **させます**.

たべます eat → たべさせます

みます see, watch → みさせます

あけます open → あけさせます

2 -3 Causative Form of Group Ⅲ Verbs

します becomes **させます**, and **きます** becomes **こさせます**. 【noun】 **＋ します** becomes 【noun】 **＋ させます**.

あんないします guide ➜ あんないさせます

せつめいします explain ➜ せつめいさせます

Vocabulary and Expression 😀

じゅく cram school ／子 child ／ばかり only ／お子さん your child 〈honorific〉

小学～年生：小学４年生 primary school student: fourth grade ／やっぱり just as I thought

こら Hey! ／外国 foreign country ／インフルエンザ influenza ／じゃあね See you later.

Conversation Scenario 💬

〈Speaking about children's education ①〉

Ogawa: Hello. I'm coming home now. What are you doing now?

Ogawa's son: Playing video games.

Ogawa: Video games again? Do your homework.

Ogawa's son: Okay.

Ogawa: All my kid does is play video games, and I don't know what to do about it.

Sarah: How old is your child?

Ogawa: He's 10. He's in fourth grade.

Sarah: Kids around the world love playing video games.

Ogawa: True. It's so hard getting them to study. I guess I should send him to cram school.

Sarah: What? You're going to send an elementary school student to cram school?

Ogawa: His friends are going, too.

27 -3

4 子どもに好きなことをさせたいです

Can-do Check ✓

☐You can talk about the situation of children's education in your own
country and say your opinion on it.

Grammar Notes ✐

1-1 ＿＿＿＿＿のため（に）、＿＿＿＿

When stating your objective of doing something, **〜ために** is used, but when 〜 is a
noun, **〜のために** is used. The **に** in **ために** can be omitted.

Conjunctive Form

noun + の	ため（に）、	〜

Ex.1

（大学で）

A：日本語の研究のため、１年間ブラジルの大学へ行く
ことにしました。

B：そうですか。ブラジルですか。

Ex.2

（学校で）

A：入学試験の準備のため、アルバイトをやめました。

B：そうですか。がんばってください。

Ex.3

（市役所で）

市民：子どもたちの安全のために、どうろにしんごうを
つけてください。

市長：わかりました。

Ex.1

(At university)

A: In order to research Japanese, I've
decided to go to a university in Brail
for one year.

B: Oh, really? Brazil?

Ex.2

(At school)

A: In order to prepare for the school
entrance exam, I've quit my part-
time job.

B: I see. Good luck.

Ex.3

(At a city hall)

Citizen: Please install a traffic light on
the road for the safety of our
children.

Mayor: Okay.

1-2　　　　　　　ため（に）、

When the objective is a verb, **～ため** is used. **に** can be omitted.

Conjunctive Form

verb dictionary form	ため（に）、	～

Ex.1

（学校で）

A：アルバイト、始めたの？

B：うん。バイクを買うために、ちょきんしたいから。

Ex.2

（会社で）

A：Cさん、結婚するために、家をさがしてるらしいよ。

B：へえ。いいなあ。

Ex.3

（学校で）

A：レポートを書くために、日本の小説を読もうと思ってるんだ。

B：すごいね。がんばって。

Ex.1

(At school)

A: Have you started your part-time job?

B: Yeah. I'm saving up to buy a motor bike.

Ex.2

(At a company)

A: C-san is looking for a house so he can get married.

B: Wow. That's great.

Ex.3

(At school)

A: In order to write my report, I think I'm going to read more Japanese novels.

B: That's amazing. Good luck.

2　　　　　　に　　　　　を　　causative form

When using the causative form of verbs in the form 【noun】＋を＋【verb】, as in 本を読みます, 漢字を書きます and 映画を見ます, ～に～を 【causative form】 is used.

Conjunctive Form

person doing the action	に	noun	を	verb causative form

Ex.1

（学校で）

先生A：B先生は、いつも学生に漢字を何回書かせますか。

先生B：私は10回書かせています。

Ex.1

(At school)

Teacher A: B-sensei, how many times do you usually have your students write kanji?

Teacher B: I make them write them 10 times.

Ex.2

（会社で）

課長：山田くんに出張のほうこくをさせますが、来週の
月曜日でいいでしょうか。

部長：いいですよ。

Ex.2

(At a company)

Section manager: I'm going to have
Yamada-kun give a report about his
business trip, so is next Monday
okay?

Department manager: That's fine.

＊When using verbs that do not use 【noun】＋を, 【person doing the action】 を 【verb
causative form】 is used (☞ Lesson 27 - 3).

Vocabulary and Expression 🌚

進学 continuing one's education ／親 parent ／英会話 English conversation ／しょうらい future
（子どもが）できます have (a baby)

研究 research ／けんこう health ／安全（な）safe ／シートベルト seatbelt
しゅうしょくします get a job ／今まで until now ／いっしょうけんめい with all one's effort
後かたづけ straighten up after ／おしゃべり chat

Conversation Scenario 💬

〈Speaking about children's education ②〉

Sarah: Cram schools are places where you can study in order to continue their
education, right?

Ogawa: Yes. In Japan, many parents make their children attend cram schools.

Sarah: Oh, really?

Ogawa: How is it in your country?

Sarah: Well... In my country, many parents make their children learn English or
sports.

Ogawa: I see. If you have kids in the future, what would you have them do?

Sarah: I would want them to do whatever they wanted to do.

Ogawa: Me, too. But studying is important, too.

Sarah: That's true.

1 おじゃまします

Can-do Check ✓

☐You can visit a Japanese person's home and greet them.

Grammar Notes 🖊

1-1　お ＿＿＿＿＿ ください

When asking a favor of or giving instructions to someone you do not know or someone of a higher social status, **お～ください** is used instead of **～てください**.

Conjunctive Form

お	verb ます form 〈～ます〉	ください

Ex.1

（銀行で）

銀行の人：おきゃくさま、こちらで番号のカードを<u>お取り</u>
　　　　<u>ください</u>。<u>お取り</u>になったら、あちらで<u>お待ちください</u>。

A：はい。

Ex.2

（店で）

A：これ、家に送ってください。

店員：はい。では、こちらにお名前とご住所を<u>お書きく</u>
　　　<u>ださい</u>。

Ex.1

(At a bank)

Bank teller: Please take a number card here, ma'am. Once you've taken a card, please wait over there.

A: Okay.

Ex.2

(At a store)

A: Please send this to my house.

Store clerk: Okay. Then, please write your name and address here.

1-2　ご ＿＿＿＿＿ ください

When using verbs in the form 【noun】＋する, as in 説明する and 連絡する, ご～ください is used.

Conjunctive Form

ご	noun	ください

Ex.1

（パーティーで）

A：Bさん、あちらの方を<u>ご紹介ください</u>ませんか。

B：はい。ご紹介しましょう。

Ex.1

(At a party)

A: B-san, could you introduce me to that person?

B: Okay. I'll introduce you.

Ex.2

（ミーティングで）

A：次は、Ｂさん、調査のけっかをごほうこくください。

B：はい。では、ほうこくします。

Ex.2
(At a meeting)
A: Next, B-san, please report the results of the examination.
B: Okay. Here is my report.

2 _____ ようになります

When talking about something you did not do before but do now, **〜ようになります** is used.

Conjunctive Form

verb dictionary form	ようになります

Ex.1

（会社で）

A：Ｂさん、最近早く帰るようになりましたね。

B：ええ。仕事の後でえいごを習っているそうです。

Ex.2

（学校で）

A：みんな休み時間も日本語で話すようになったね。

B：うん。日本語で話せるようになったからね。

Ex.1

(At a company)

A: B-san has started going home early lately.

B: Yes. I hear she's learning English after work.

Ex.2

(At school)

A: Everyone has started speaking in Japanese even during their free time.

B: Yeah. That's because we're now able to speak Japanese.

When talking about something that you used to do but do not do now, **〜なくなります** is used.

Ex.1

A：最近手紙を書かなくなりました。

B：そうですね。メールで連絡するようになりましたからね。

Ex.2

A：子どもたちがテレビを見なくなったそうですね。

B：ええ。ゲームをする子どもがふえているそうです。

Ex.1

A: People don't write letters these days.

B: Yes. Because we can now communicate using e-mail.

Ex.2

A: It seems like children are watching less TV.

B: Yes. It seems that there are also more children that play video games.

Ex.3
A：工事のため、エレベータがしばらく<u>使えなくなります</u>。

B：え、それは困りますね。

Ex.3
A: Due to construction, we won't be able to use the elevator for a while.

B: What? That's a problem.

When talking about something you were not able to do before but are able to do now, 【**potential form verb**】＋**ようになります** is used (☞ Lesson 20 - 2).

Ex.

A：日本語の勉強はどうですか。

B：漢字が<u>読めるようになりました</u>。

Ex.

A: How is studying Japanese going?

B: I can read kanji now.

Vocabulary and Expression 🐾

おじゃまします May I come in? Sorry to disturb you. ／赤ちゃん baby ／主人 husband

こちらこそ Thank you, too. ／家事 housework

かけます sit ／持ち帰ります take home ／利用します use

うちの〜：うちの会社 my 〜：my company ／ヨーロッパ旅行 trip to Europe

ごらんください Please take a look. ／休み時間 break time ／（お）米 rice

Conversation Scenario 💬

〈Visiting a senior coworker's home〉

Sarah and Lee: Hello.

Yamashita: Hello. Please come in.

Sarah and Lee: Sorry for disturbing you.

Sarah: Yamashita-san, this is for your baby.

Yamashita: Thank you. Ah, this is my husband. This is Sarah-san and Lee-san.

Yamashita's husband: Nice to meet you. Thank you for always helping my wife.

Lee: No, she's the one always helping us.

Yamashita's husband: Please have some tea.

Sarah: Ah, sorry. Thank you.

Lee: So, your husband does housework.

Yamashita: Yes, he has started doing some recently.

Sarah: That's so kind of him.

2 最近、仕事はどうですか
さいきん　しごと

Can-do Check ✓

☐ You can ask and speak about the recent situation at work.

Grammar Notes ✎

1 ［　　　　　］て、［　　　　　］

When talking about how much time has passed since doing an action, **～て、【how much time has passed】** is used.

Conjunctive Form

verb て form	〈～て〉、 〈～で〉、	how much time has passed

Ex.1
A：私は日本に来て、1年になります。Bさんは、どれぐ
　　わたし　にほん　き　　ねん
　らいですか。

B：私は日本に来て、明日でちょうど2年です。
　　わたし　にほん　き　　あした　　　　　ねん

Ex.2
日本語の勉強を始めて、5か月になります。
にほんご　べんきょう　はじ　　　げつ

Ex.1
A: It's been one year since I came to Japan. B-san, how long has it been for you?

B: It'll be two years tomorrow since I came to Japan.

Ex.2
It's been five months since I started studying Japanese.

2 ［　　　　　］ように、［　　　　　］

When talking about something you are doing to complete a goal or something you are being careful of, **～ように、～** is used. However, when using verbs that express possibility, such as **見える**, **聞こえる**, **わかる** and **なる**, the dictionary form is used.
　　　　　み　　　　き

Conjunctive Form

verb potential form		
verb ない form 〈～ない〉	ように、	～
verb dictionary form		

Ex.1

いつでもご飯を作って食べられるように、ざいりょうを
買っておきます。

Ex.1

I buy ingredients so I can make food and eat any time.

Ex.2

A：すみません。コンビニで赤のボールペン2本とマスク
とティッシュを買ってきてください。

B：あ、はい。ちょっと待ってください。忘れないように、
メモします。

Ex.2

A: Excuse me. Please buy two red ball-point pens, a face mask and tissues at the convenience store.

B: Oh, okay. Please wait one moment. I'll write it down so I don't forget it.

Ex.3

（パーティーで）

A：自分の紙コップがどれかわかるように、名前を書いて
おきましょう。

B：それはいいですね。

Ex.3

(At a party)

A: Let's write our names on our paper cups so we don't forget whose is whose.

B: That sounds good.

Vocabulary and Expression

プロジェクト project ／ざんぎょう overtime ／体をこわします become sick

うまく well ／ビジネス日本語 business Japanese ／エプロン apron ／通勤 commute
まあまあ So-so., Alright.

Conversation Scenario

〈Talking about things at work〉

Yamashita's husband: How long has it been since you came to Japan?

Sarah: One year.

Lee: Same for me.

Yamashita's husband: I see. You're good at Japanese.

Sarah: Thank you. But I still have a lot to learn.

Yamashita: How is work going these days?

Sarah: We started a new project, so we're busy.

Yamashita: I see. That's tough. Are you working overtime?

Lee: Yes, sometimes. But I'm trying to go home at 6：00.

Yamashita: Please take care not to wear yourself out.

Sarah and Lee: I will. Thank you.

28
-
2

3 たいへんそうですね

Can-do Check ✔

☐You can listen to another person's recent work situation and give your thoughts on it.

☐You can say goodbye at the end of a visit.

Grammar Notes 🖊

1 　　　　　　　　**みたいです**

When telling someone that something is similar to something else, **〜みたいです** is used.

Conjunctive Form

noun	みたいです

Ex.1

A：寒いですね。
　　さむ

B：ええ。まだ10月ですが、冬みたいですね。
　　　　　　がつ　　　　ふゆ

Ex.2

A：うわあ、公園、今日は人が多いですね。
　　　　こうえん　きょう　ひと　おお

B：おまつりみたいですね。

Ex.1

A: It's cold, isn't it?

B: Yes. It's only October, but it feels like winter.

Ex.2

A: Whoa! There are so many people at the park today.

B: It's like a festival.

◆ 【noun X】 **＋ みたいな ＋** 【noun Y】 can also be used.

Conjunctive Form

noun	みたいな	noun

Ex.

A：Cさん、日本語が上手ですね。
　　　　にほんご　じょうず

B：ええ、日本人みたいな話し方ですね。
　　　　にほんじん　　　はな　かた

Ex.

A: C-san is good at Japanese.

B: Yes, she speaks like a Japanese person.

◆【noun】＋みたいに＋【verb/adjective】 can also be used.

Conjunctive Form

noun	みたいに	verb
		い adjective
		な adjective

Ex.

A：あの子、かわいい！

B：ええ。人形みたいにかわいいですね。

Ex.

A: That kid is cute!

B: Yes. She's as cute as a doll.

2　　　　　とき、

When talking about when you regularly do an activity, **〜とき、〜** is used.

Conjunctive Form

verb plain form	とき、	〜
い adjective plain form		
な adjective plain form 〈〜だ な〉		
noun plain form 〈〜だ の〉		

Ex.1

A：Bさんは、買い物するとき、インターネットを使いますか。

B：ええ、よく使います。店に行かなくてもいいので、便利です。

Ex.1

A: B-san, when you shop, do you use the Internet?

B: Yes, I use it often. It's convenient since I don't have to go to the store.

Ex.2

A：コーヒーが好きですか。

B：はい。リラックスしたいとき、いつもコーヒーを飲みます。

Ex.2

A: Do you like coffee?

B: Yes. I always drink coffee when I want to relax.

Ex.3

A：仕事がたいへんなとき、いつも手伝ってくださって、ありがとうございます。

B：いいえ。困ったときは、いつでも言ってください。

Ex.3

A: Thank you for always helping me when I'm having trouble with work.

B: No problem. Let me know anytime you're having trouble.

28
-
3

305

Ex.4

A: 休みのとき、何をしていますか。

B: 友だちと買い物に行ったり、テニスをしたりしています。

Ex.4

A: What do you do on your days off?

B: I do things like go shopping with my friends or play tennis.

3 -1 ＿＿＿＿＿＿＿＿か、＿＿＿＿＿

When talking about something, someone or some time that is unknown,

【interrogative word】 ～か、～ is used.

Conjunctive Form

	verb plain form	か、	～
interrogative	い adjective plain form		
	な adjective plain form ⟨～だ⟩		
	noun plain form ⟨～だ⟩		

Ex.1

A: げんかんのベルがなりましたね。

B: ええ。だれが来たか、見て来ましょう。

Ex.1

A: The entranceway doorbell rang.

B: Yes. I'll go see if someone is here.

Ex.2

A: あれ？ Cさんは？

B: さあ。どこへ行ったか、わかりません。

Ex.2

A: Huh? Where's C-san?

B: Who knows? I don't know where he went.

Ex.3

A: 金曜日のミーティング、何時からか知っていますか。

B: 3時からですよ。

Ex.3

A: Do you know what time Friday's meeting is going to start?

B: It starts from 3:00.

3 -2 ＿＿＿＿＿＿＿＿かどうか、＿＿＿＿

When not using interrogative words, ～かどうか、～ is used.

Conjunctive Form

verb plain form	かどうか、	～
い adjective plain form		
な adjective plain form ⟨～だ⟩		
noun plain form ⟨～だ⟩		

Ex.1

A：このカメラ、よさそうですね。高いでしょうか。

B：<u>高いかどうか</u>、調べてみましょう。

Ex.2

A：夏休み、帰国しますか。

B：<u>帰国するかどうか</u>、まだ決めていません。

Ex.1

A: This camera looks good, doesn't it? I wonder if it's expensive.

B: Let's look it up and see if it's expensive or not.

Ex.2

A: Are you going back to your country during summer vacation?

B: I haven't decided whether I'm going to go back or not.

Vocabulary and Expression 😃

天使 angel ／なき出します begin to cry ／子そだて child-rearing

風 wind ／モデル model ／わっ Ah! ／こおり ice ／アルバイトします do a part-time job

プロ pro; professional ／通います attend

Conversation Scenario 😃

〈Listening about raising children〉

Sarah: Wow, she's so cute. She looks like an angel.

Yamashita's husband: Yes, but I never know when she might start crying.

Sarah: Really? That sounds tough.

Yamashita: Yes, it is. I don't have any time for myself.

Lee: I see.

Yamashita: Ah, but when the baby is asleep, I do things like read books and drink tea. My husband also often helps me.

Lee: Huh. I don't know if I'd be able to raise a child myself.

Lee: Thank you for today, and thank you for the meal.

Yamashita: Don't mention it. Tell everyone I said hi.

Sarah: I will. Sorry to have bothered you. Good bye.

Yamashita's husband: Come again some time.

28 - 3

Lesson 29 ▶ **1** 30分も待たされたんです
ぷん　　ま

Can-do Check ✓

☐ You can talk about things you think are unsatisfying or unpleasant to others.

Grammar Notes ✐

1-1　　　　X　　　のため（に）、　　　Y

When talking about the cause and effect of something, 〜のため（に）、〜 is used. に is sometimes omitted. Here, X is the cause and Y is the effect or result.

Conjunctive Form

noun	のため（に）、	〜

Ex.1

（駅のアナウンス）
えき

駅員：ただ今、事故のために、電車が遅れています。
えきいん　　　　いま　　じ こ　　　　　でんしゃ　おく
　　　申しわけありません。
　　　もう

Ex.2

（会社で）
かいしゃ

A：課長、申しわけありません。かぜのため、熱がありま
　　かちょう　もう　　　　　　　　　　　　　　　　　ねつ
　　す。病院へ行かせていただきたいのですが。
　　　びょういん　い

課長：わかりました。お大事に。
かちょう　　　　　　　　　だいじ

Ex.1

(Station announcement)

Station employee: The train is currently running late due to an accident. We apologize.

Ex.2

(At a company)

A: Excuse me, manager. I have a fever because of my cold. I'd like to be allowed to go to the hospital.

Section manager: Okay. Please take care.

1-2　　　　X　　　ため（に）、　　　Y

When the X is not a noun, 〜ため（に）、〜 is used. に is sometimes omitted.

Conjunctive Form

verb plain form		
い adjective plain form	ため（に）、	〜
な adjective plain form 〈〜だ な〉		
noun plain form 〈〜だ の〉		

Ex.1

（アルバイトで）

A：すみません。今日は<u>時間がないため</u>、ここまでしかできませんでした。

店長：わかりました。では、明日つづきをおねがいします。

Ex.2

（会社で）

A：今朝は電車が<u>遅れたため</u>、会議に間に合いませんでした。

B：たいへんでしたね。

Ex.1

(At a part-time job)

A: Sorry. I don't have much time today, so I was only able to get this much done.

Store manager: Okay. Then, please do the rest tomorrow.

Ex.2

(At a company)

A: Because the trains were late this morning, I didn't make it to the meeting in time.

B: That must have been tough.

---

2 ⬜⬜⬜⬜ しか ⬜⬜ ません

When talking about there not being enough or adequate amount or degree of something, **〜しか〜ません** is used.

Conjunctive Form

noun	しか	〜ません
		verb ない form 〈〜ない〉

Ex.1

A：ジュース、買いませんか。

B：あ、私は今、<u>100円しかありません</u>。

Ex.2

A：元気がありませんね。

B：ええ。今朝は時間がなくて、<u>コーヒーしか飲んでいない</u>んです。

Ex.1

A: Why don't we buy some juice?

B: Ah, all I have right now is 100 yen.

Ex.2

A: You look down.

B: Yes. I didn't have much time this morning, so all I had was coffee.

3 　　　　　　　　　に　causative passive form

When talking about having to do something that you did not want to do or being forced to do something by someone else, **〜に【causative passive form】** is used.

Conjunctive Form

person	に	verb causative passive form

Ex.1

（会社で）

A：おはようございます。お疲れのようですね。

B：ええ。昨日の夜、友だち**に**飲**ま**されてしまって。

Ex.2

（会社で）

A：たばこ、やめたんですか。

B：はい。つま**に**やめ**さ**せられました。

Ex.3

A：子どものとき、毎日ピアノの練習を**させられ**ました。

B：私は英語を習いに行か**され**ました。

Ex.1

(At a company)

A: Good morning. You look tired.

B: Yes. My friend made me drink last night.

Ex.2

(At a company)

A: Did you quit smoking?

B: Yes. My wife made me quit.

Ex.3

A: When I was child, I was made to practice the piano every day.

B: I was made to go learn English.

When the causative form is changed from **〜せます** to **〜せられます**, it is called the causative passive form (**使役受身形**).

For Group I verbs, their causative passive forms are **〜せられます** and **〜されます**.

Group I verbs	Causative form	Causative passive form [〜せられます]	Causative passive form [〜されます]
待ちます	待たせます	**待たせられます**	**待たされます**
読みます	読ませます	**読ませられます**	**読まされます**

〜せられる and **〜される** forms can also be used, as in 待たせられる, 待たされる and 読ませられる, 読まされる.

3-1　Causative-Passive Form of Group I Verbs

The causative form is made by changing the syllable before **ます** to one that ends in [a], then adding **せられます** or **されます**.

～い → ～わ

The causative passive form of **～います** is **～わせられます** or **～わされます**.

いいます say ➡ いわせられます／いわされます

かいます buy ➡ かわせられます／かわされます

～き → ～か ／ ～ぎ → ～が

The causative passive form of **～きます** is **～かせられます** or **～かされます**.

The causative passive form of **～ぎます** is **～がせられます** or **～がされます**.

ききます listen ➡ きかせられます／きかされます

いそぎます hurry ➡ いそがせられます／いそがされます

～し → ～さ

The causative passive form of **～します** is **～させられます**. **～さされます** cannot be used.

はなします talk ➡ はなさせられます

～ち → ～た

The causative passive form of **～ちます** is **～たせられます** or **～たされます**.

まちます wait ➡ またせられます／またされます

～に → ～な

The causative passive form of **～にます** is **～なせられます** or **～なされます**.

しにます die ➡ しなせられます／しなされます

～び → ～ば

The causative passive form of **～びます** is **～ばせられます** or **～ばされます**.

よびます call ➡ よばせられます／よばされます

あそびます play ➡ あそばせられます／あそばされます

～み → ～ま

The causative passive form of **～みます** is **～ませられます** or **～まされます**.

よみます read ➡ よませられます／よまされます

～り → ～ら

The causative passive form of **～ります** is **～らせられます** or **～らされます**.

とります take ➡ とらせられます／とらされます

3 -2 Causative-Passive Form of Group II Verbs

ます becomes させられます.

たべます eat → たべさせられます

みます see, watch → みさせられます

あけます open → あけさせられます

3 -3 Causative-Passive Form of Group III Verbs

します becomes させられます, and きます becomes こさせられます. 【noun】+ します becomes 【noun】+ させられます.

あんないします guide → あんないさせられます

せつめいします explain → せつめいさせられます

Vocabulary and Expression

アナウンス announcement ／ただ今 right now ／信号機 traffic light ／故障 broken
見合わせます be suspended

- -

専門家 specialist ／水不足 water shortage ／夕べ evening ／うで arm ／かのじょ girlfriend
いっぱい a lot ／残業します do overwork ／強風 strong wind ／ていしゃします stop

Conversation Scenario

〈Waiting for the train〉

Station announcement: Train operation is currently suspended due to a traffic light
malfunction.

Shin: Ah, she said the traffic light is malfunctioning.

Sarah: There's nothing we can do. Let's wait a bit.

- -

Shin: I wonder how much longer it's going to take.

Sarah: Ah, we only have 15 minutes left. I'll call Ati-san.

- -

Shin: Ati-san, sorry to keep you waiting.

Sarah: We were waiting on the platform for 30 minutes. My legs hurt.

Ati: That must've been tough.

Can-do Check ✓

☐ You can communicate to others about things that made your upset, such as getting warned or ordered by someone.

☐ You can give advice on what to do after hearing someone's troubled situation.

Grammar Notes ✏

1-1　　　　　な　と

When telling someone that you or someone else said not to do something, **〜なと〜** is used (☞ Lesson 23 - 1).

Conjunctive Form

verb dictionary form	な	と	〜

Ex.1

（パーティーで）

A：あれ、おさけは飲まないですんか。
　　　　　　　　　　の

B：はい。医者に飲むなと言われているんです。
　　　　いしゃ　の　　　　　い

Ex.1

(At a party)

A: Huh? Do you not drink alcohol?

B: Yes (I don't drink alcohol). My doctor tells me not to drink.

Ex.2

（会社で）
かいしゃ

A: 子どものころ、父に食べながら話すなと言われました。
　　こ　　　　ちち　た　　　　はな　　　　い

B：そうですか。

Ex.2

(At a company)

A: When I was a kid, my father told me not to talk while eating.

B: Really?

1-2　　　　　　　　と

When telling someone that you or someone else said to do something, **〜と〜** is used (☞ Lesson 23 - 1).

Conjunctive Form

verb imperative form	と	〜

Ex.

（会社で）

A：子どものころ、父に家の中であそぶな、外であそべと
言<ruby>言<rt>い</rt></ruby>われましたよ。

B：私<ruby>私<rt>わたし</rt></ruby>もです。

Ex.

(At a company)

A: When I was a kid, my father told me
not to play in the house and to play
outside.

B: Mine did, too.

2 （さ）せて いただけませんか

When politely asking for permission to do something, **〜ていただけませんか** is used.
This is a much more polite expression than **〜てもいいですか**.

Conjunctive Form

て form of causative form〈〜（さ）せて〉	いただけませんか

Ex.1

（アルバイトで）

A：店長<ruby>店長<rt>てんちょう</rt></ruby>、すみません。来週<ruby>来週<rt>らいしゅう</rt></ruby>の水曜日<ruby>水曜日<rt>すいようび</rt></ruby>、試験<ruby>試験<rt>しけん</rt></ruby>があるので、
アルバイトを休<ruby>休<rt>やす</rt></ruby>ませていただけませんか。

店長<ruby>店長<rt>てんちょう</rt></ruby>：わかりました。がんばってください。

Ex.1

(At a part-time job)

A: Manager, I'm sorry. I have a test next
Wednesday, so would it be okay if I
take that day off?

Store manager: Okay. Good luck.

Ex.2

（店<ruby>店<rt>みせ</rt></ruby>で）

店員<ruby>店員<rt>てんいん</rt></ruby>：お客<ruby>客<rt>きゃく</rt></ruby>さま。こちらのまどを閉<ruby>閉<rt>し</rt></ruby>めさせていただけま
せんか。

A：あ、はい。どうぞ。

Ex.2

(At a store)

Store clerk: Ma'am, may I close this
window?

A: Ah, yes. Go right ahead.

Vocabulary and Expression

痛<ruby>痛<rt>いた</rt></ruby>っ Ouch! ／お客<ruby>客<rt>きゃく</rt></ruby>さん customer, client, guest, patron〈honorific〉 ／うわ〜 Yikes! ／急<ruby>急<rt>きゅう</rt></ruby>に suddenly

向<ruby>向<rt>む</rt></ruby>こう opposite side ／報告<ruby>報告<rt>ほうこく</rt></ruby> report ／体調<ruby>体調<rt>たいちょう</rt></ruby> body condition ／早退<ruby>早退<rt>そうたい</rt></ruby>します leave work early
受験<ruby>受験<rt>じゅけん</rt></ruby>します take an exam ／見学<ruby>見学<rt>けんがく</rt></ruby>します observe ／（シャツを）かえます change (a shirt)

⟨After a leg injury⟩

Tang: Ouch!

Lama: What's wrong?

Tang: Yesterday, a customer at work stepped on my foot.

Lama: Yikes! That looks painful.

Tang: And they didn't even apologize after I said, "ouch."

Lama: What? That's terrible. Shouldn't you go to a hospital?

Tang: I have to work at my part-time job today. The manager told me not to just suddenly take time off, so I can't.

Lama: Why don't you call him?

Tang: Hmm...

Tang: Hello, it's Tang. I'm sorry, but I want to go to the hospital because my foot hurts. May I take today off?

3 消したんじゃなくて、消えたんです
け　　　　　　　　　き

Can-do Check ✓

☐You can give reasons(excuses) in an uncomplicated manner.

☐You can say your thoughts after hearing someone's failures or worries.

Grammar Notes ✎

1-1　　X　　ない　で　　　　Y

When talking about doing action Y without having done action X, **～ないで～** is used.

Conjunctive Form

verb ない form〈～ない〉	で	～

Ex.1

（学校で）
がっこう

先生：はじめは、じしょを見ないで読んでください。じ
せんせい　　　　　　　　　　　　み　　　　　よ
しょを見ないで読んでわかったことを、友だちと話し
　　　　み　　　　よ　　　　　　　　　とも　　　　はな
合ってください。
あ

A：わかりました。

Ex.1

(At a school)

Teacher: First, please read this without looking at a dictionary. Talk to your friends about what you learned by reading without looking at a dictionary.

A: Okay.

Ex.2

（駅で）
えき

A：このカード、便利ですよ。お金を使わないで、電車に
　　　　　　　べんり　　　　　　おかね　つか　　　　　でんしゃ
もバスにものることができますし、買い物もできます。
　　　　　　　　　　　　　　　　　　か　もの

B：いいですね。

Ex.2

(At a station)

A: This card is useful. You can use it to ride the train or the bus or even go shopping without using any money.

B: That's great.

1-2　　X　　て　　　Y

When talking about doing action Y while in the condition of having done action X, **～て～** is used (☞ Lesson 25-3).

Conjunctive Form

verb て form 〈～て〉〈～で〉	～

Ex.1

（びじゅつかんで）

びじゅつかん員：かばんやお荷物をロッカーに入れて、
中にお入りください。

Ex.2

（アルバイトで）

A：店長、申しわけありません。今日は予定がありますの
で、残りの仕事はBさんにたのんで、帰ってもいいで
しょうか。

店長：わかりました。そうしてください。

Ex.1

(At an art museum)

Art museum staff: Please put your bags
and belongings in a locker before
entering.

Ex.2

(At a part-time job)

A: Manager, I'm sorry, but I have plans
today, so can I ask B-san to handle
the rest of my work so can I go
home?

Store manager: Okay. Go ahead.

2 -1　　　X　　んじゃなくて、　　Y

When saying "I won't do X, I will do Y" or "not X, Y", **〜んじゃなくて、〜** is used.

Conjunctive Form

verb plain form		
い adjective plain form	**んじゃなくて、**	**〜**
な adjective plain form 〈〜だ な〉		

Ex.1

（パーティーで）

A：これ、おいしいですね。どうやって作ったんですか。

B：それは作ったんじゃなくて、買ったんです。

A：そうですか。

Ex.2

（パーティーで）

A：ピザ、食べないの？　きらいなの？

B：きらいなんじゃなくて、ダイエットしてるの。

Ex.1

(At a party)

A: This is delicious. How did you make
it?

B: I didn't make it; I bought it.

A: I see.

Ex.2

(At a party)

A: Do you not eat pizza? Do you hate
it?

B: I don't hate it; I'm on a diet.

29 - 3

2-2　　　　X　　じゃなくて、　　Y

When X is a noun, **~じゃなくて、~** is used.

Conjunctive Form

noun	じゃなくて、	～

Ex.1

A：アップルジュースを買ってくるんですね。

B：いいえ。アップルジュースじゃなくて、パイナップル
　　ジュースです。

A：あ、わかりました。

Ex.1

A: So I'm going to go buy apple juice, right?

B: No. Not apple juice; pineapple juice.

A: Ah, okay.

Ex.2

A：ミーティングは3時からですね。

B：いいえ。3時じゃなくて、3時30分です。

A：そうでしたか。ありがとうございます。

Ex.2

A: The meeting is from 3:00, right?

B: No. Not 3:00, 3:30.

A: I see. Thank you.

3-1　　　verb　　すぎます

When talking about doing something too much or to too great a degree, **~すぎます** is used.

Conjunctive Form

verb ます form 〈～ます〉	すぎます

Ex.1

A：どうしたんですか。

B：食べすぎて、おなかが痛いんです。

Ex.1

A: What's wrong?

B: I ate too much and my stomach hurts.

Ex.2

（会社で）

A：Cさん、働きすぎて、病気になったそうですよ。

B：え、それはよくないですね。

Ex.2

(At a company)

A: It seems that C-san worked too hard and fell ill.

B: What? That's no good.

3-2　　adjective　すぎます

When something is at too great a degree, **~すぎます** is used. The dictionary form of **すぎます** is **すぎる**.

Conjunctive Form

い adjective 〈～い〉	すぎます
な adjective 〈～な〉	

Ex.1

（ふどうさん屋で）

店員：この部屋はいかがですか。新しいし、広いですよ。

A：でも、高すぎます。

Ex.2

A：水がきれいすぎると、魚が住めないそうです。

B：そうですか。

Ex.1

(At a realtor)

Store clerk: How about this room? It's new and spacious.

A: But it's too expensive.

Ex.2

A: I hear if water is too clean, fish won't be able to live in it.

B: Oh, really?

Vocabulary and Expression

アンケート調査 survey ／結果 result ／集計します add up ／保存します save
デスクトップ desktop ／ファイル file ／整理します organize

説明書 instruction manual ／おっと Oops! ／アレルギー allergy ／食堂 dining hall
下ります go down ／バドミントン badminton ／スカッシュ squash ／答え answer
ぜんぜん not ～ at all

Conversation Scenario

〈Inputting data〉

Lee: Huh? The data disappeared.

Nakamura: What? What data?

Lee: The results of the survey.

Nakamura: What?! After we all did our best and gathered all of the data, you deleted it without saving it?

Lee: I saved it! I didn't delete it; it disappeared.

Nakamura: Then, it may be somewhere on your computer.

Lee: Really?

Nakamura: Hey, Lee-san, you have too many files on your desktop. You should organize it.

Lee: Okay.

1 いいアイデアですね

Can-do Check ✓

☐You can explain and give your opinion about recent popular topics in an uncomplicated manner.

Grammar Notes 🖊

1 _____ がします

When talking about experiencing a smell, sound or taste, **〜がします** is used.

Conjunctive Form

smell sound taste	がします

Ex.1

A：いいにおいがしますね。何のにおいでしょうか。

B：これです。この花のにおいです。

Ex.2

（会社で）

A：となりの部屋で音がしましたね。
　　だれかいるんでしょうか。

B：今日は休みですから、だれもいないはずですが。

Ex.3

（レストランで）

A：これ、なつかしい味です。

B：そうですね。私たちの国の料理の味がしますね。

Ex.1

A: Something smells good. What's this smell?

B: It's this. It's the smell of this flower.

Ex.2

(At a company)

A: I heard a noise from the room next door. I wonder if there's someone there.

B: They're closed today, so there shouldn't be anyone there.

Ex.3

(At a restaurant)

A: This flavor is a nostalgic one.

B: Yes, it tastes like the food in our country.

② 受身形　Passive Form

The passive form (受身形) can be used for things other than people, such as in **建物が建てられた**, **英語が使われている** and **本が読まれている** (☞ Lesson 19-3, 23-1).

Conjunctive Form

noun	が	verb passive form

Ex.1

A：イギリスで毎年有名なテニスの試合が行われていますが、見たことがありますか。

B：はい。テレビで放送されますから、毎年見ています。

Ex.1

A: Every year in England, a famous tennis championship is held. Have you ever seen it?

B: Yes. It's broadcasted on TV, so I watch it every year.

Ex.2

A：私の国、フィリピンでは、英語とタガログ語と自分の生まれたしまのことばが使われています。

B：そうですか。たくさんのことばが使われているんですね。

Ex.2

A: In my country, the Philippines, English, Tagalog and our own language on the island where I was born are spoken.

B: Oh, really? A lot of languages are spoken.

③-1　て いきます

When talking about a change that will continue into the future, **～ていきます** is used.

Conjunctive Form

verb て form 〈～て〉 〈～で〉	いきます

Ex.1

A：インターネットが広く使われるようになりましたね。

B：ええ。今後もインターネットを使う人はふえていくでしょうね。

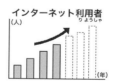

インターネット利用者
(人)
(年)

Ex.1

A: The Internet is now being used far and wide.

B: Yes. More people will likely come to use the Internet in the future.

Ex.2

（会社で）

A：たばこを吸う人がへりましたね。

B：ええ。はいがんなどの病気もへっていくといいですね。

Ex.2

(At a company)

A: The number of people who smoke has decreased.

B: Yes. I hope the number of people with lung cancer decreases, too.

30-1

3 -2 　　　　て きます

When talking about a change that has continued up until now, **〜てきます** is used.

Conjunctive Form

verb て form	〈〜て〉 〈〜で〉	きます

Ex.1

A：おはようございます。寒くなってきましたね。

B：そうですね。もうすぐ12月ですからね。

Ex.2

A：新しい駅ができて、このあたりもにぎやかになってきましたね。

B：ええ。カフェもふえてきましたね。

Ex.1

A: Good morning. It's gotten cold, hasn't it?

B: Yes, since it's almost December.

Ex.2

A: Since they made that new station, this area has gotten livelier.

B: Yes. The number of cafes has increased, too.

Vocabulary and Expression 😃

アイデア idea ／〜年前：100年前 〜 year(s) ago: a hundred years ago ／建てます build
落ち着きます calm down ／再利用します reuse ／空き家 empty house ／どんどん gradually

ふしぎ（な）mysterious ／竹 bamboo ／世界中 in the world, around the world ／言語 language
ほんやくします translate ／オリンピック Olympics ／この前 last time ／行います hold (an event)
少しずつ little by little ／けいざい economics ／今後 from now on ／きんちょうします be nervous
自信 confidence ／においぶくろ sachet ／古民家 old Japanese-style house

Conversation Scenario 💬

〈In front of a cafe〉

Ati: Huh? It smells good, like coffee.

Shin: It's this. It's a cafe.

Ati: Huh. It looks like it's a house that was build 100 years ago.

Shin: A hundred years. It's old.

Ati: Let's go inside.

Ati: Oh, it's nice. It's so calming.

Shin: Fixing and renovating old houses is a great idea, since it seems the number of old abandoned houses is rising.

Ati: That's true. Using them in this way is probably going to become more and more necessary.

30-1

2 **働きやすい環境をつくるべきです**

_{はたら} _{かんきょう}

Can-do Check ✓

☐You can share your opinion about social topics.

Grammar Notes ✏

1 _____ **んじゃないでしょうか**

When using **〜と思う** or **〜だろうと思う** to downplay your thoughts or ideas, **〜んじゃな**

_{おも} _{おも}
いでしょうか is used.

Conjunctive Form

verb plain form	
い adjective plain form	
な adjective plain form 〈〜だ な〉	んじゃないでしょうか
noun plain form 〈〜だ な〉	

Ex.1

A：寒いですね。雪が降るんじゃないでしょうか。

_{さむ} _{ゆき} _ふ

B：え、雪ですか。見てみたいです。

_{ゆき} _み

Ex.2

（会社で）

_{かいしゃ}

A：会議の時間をみじかくするために、会議で話すことを

_{かいぎ} _{じかん} _{かいぎ} _{はな}
先に出席する人に伝えておいたらいいんじゃないで

_{さき} _{しゅっせき} _{ひと} _{つた}
しょうか。

B：そうですね。話すことを考えておけば、会議をはやく

_{はな} _{かんが} _{かいぎ}
進められますね。

_{すす}

Ex.1

A: It's cold, isn't it? I wonder if it won't snow.

B: What? Snow? I want to see that.

Ex.2

(At a company)

A: In order to shorten the time of the meeting, shouldn't we tell the people who are going to attend the meeting what we are going to talk about at the meeting ahead of time?

B: Yes. If we think about what we are going to say ahead of time, we'll be able to proceed with the meeting more quickly.

2 _____ **べきです**

When strongly expressing your own opinion that something must be done, **〜べきです**
is used. When strongly expressing your own opinion that something must not be
done, **〜べきじゃありません** is used. When expressing that this is your own opinion, **〜べ**
きだと思います or **〜べきじゃないと思います** is used.

_{おも} _{おも}

Conjunctive Form

verb dictionary form	べきです
	べきじゃありません

Ex.1

A：あの二人、なかがよくないですね。いっしょに仕事を
するのに、困ります。

B：おたがいに相手の考えをよく聞くべきです。

C：そうですね。話し方にも注意するべきだと思います。

Ex.2

A：おまつりで朝までさわいでいる人がいたそうです。

B：楽しかったのでしょうが、ほかの人にめいわくになる
ことをするべきじゃありませんね。

A：そうですね。

Ex.1

A: Those two don't get along. Since they have to work together, it's a problem.

B: They should listen to one another.

C: Yes. I think they also need to be careful of how they speak to each other.

Ex.2

A: It seems there were people partying at the festival until morning.

B: I'm sure it was fun for them, but they shouldn't do things that could be a nuisance to others.

A: That's right.

Vocabulary and Expression

約束を守ります keep a promise ／文化 culture ／習慣 custom ／理解します understand

敬語 honorific language ／以上 more than, over ／大事（な）important
ノー残業デー a workday with no overtime ／売り上げ sales ／のびます extend
リフレッシュします refresh

Conversation Scenario

〈Speaking in class〉

Lama: I saw on TV that the number of foreigners working in Japan is increasing.

Kim: Ah, I saw that, too.

Aoki: Are you all thinking about working in Japan in the future?

Kim: Yes. I want to work at a Japanese company.

Lama: But working with Japanese is probably difficult. You have to be on time and keep your promises.

Kim: Isn't that true in any country, though?

Lama: Yes, but it's hard to work the same way Japanese people do.

**30
-
2**

Tang: I think so, too. I think both Japanese and foreigners should understand each other's culture and traditions more.

Aoki: That's right. Japanese companies should create environments that are easy for foreigner employees to work in.

文型さくいん　Grammar Index
ぶんけい

〈著　者〉 **ヒューマンアカデミー日本語学校**　http://hajl.athuman.com/

ヒューマンアカデミー日本語学校は1987年に大阪校、1991年東京校、2015年には日本初の産学官連携の日本語教育機関となる佐賀校を開校した。
日本語教育プログラムを国内、およびアジアやヨーロッパを中心に海外でも提供する。
グループ親会社のヒューマンホールディングスは2004年JASDAQ上場。
全日制、社会人、児童向けロボット教室、カルチャースクール、日本語、海外留学など、
多種多様な教育事業を全国主要都市のほか、海外でも展開している。

〈執筆者〉 **辻 和子**　ヒューマンアカデミー日本語学校東京校校長
　　　　　 小座間 亜依　ヒューマンアカデミー日本語学校東京校専任講師

つなぐにほんご　初級　文法解説書　英語版

2019年12月20日　初版第1刷発行

著者	ヒューマンアカデミー日本語学校
翻訳	Malcolm Hendricks
イラスト	福場さおり
装丁	岡崎裕樹
編集・DTP	朝日メディアインターナショナル株式会社
発行人	天谷修身
発行	株式会社アスク出版

〒162-8558 東京都新宿区下宮比町2-6
TEL 03-3267-6864　FAX 03-3267-6867
https://www.ask-books.com/

印刷・製本　　大日本印刷株式会社